GIRLFIGHTING

Betrayal and Rejection among Girls

LYN MIKEL BROWN

GIRLFIGHTING

Betrayal and Rejection among Girls

New York University Press • *New York and London*

NEW YORK UNIVERSITY PRESS
New York and London
www.nyupress.org

First published in paperback in 2005

Library of Congress Cataloging-in-Publication Data
Brown, Lyn Mikel, 1956–
Girlfighting : betrayal and rejection among girls / Lyn Mikel Brown.
p. cm.
Includes bibliographical references and index.
ISBN 0–8147–9915–9 (cloth : alk. paper)
ISBN 0–8147–9951–5 (pbk. : alk. paper)
1. Teenage girls—Psychology.   2. Interpersonal conflict in adolescence.
3. Anger in adolescence.   4. Aggressiveness in adolescence.
5. Girls—Psychology.   6. Interpersonal conflict in children.
7. Anger in children.   8. Aggressiveness in children.
9. Women—Socialization.   10. Female friendship.   I. Title.
HQ798.B723   2003
305.235—dc21   2003011179

New York University Press books are printed on acid-free paper,
and their binding materials are chosen for strength and durability.

Manufactured in the United States of America

c 10 9 8 7 6 5 4 3 2
p 10 9 8 7 6 5 4 3

To my friend, Connie DiCenzo Coleman,
and to our daughters,
Maya, Elizabeth, Alexandra, and Caroline

Contents

Acknowledgments

In the early stages of this project, in 1999, Sharon Barker, the Director of the Women's Resource Center at the University of Maine, phoned me out of the blue one afternoon to see if I might want to collaborate with her on a proposal to the American Association of University Women Educational Foundation's University Scholar-in-Residence Award program. This was a leap of faith on her part, since we had met just twice before. But there were good vibes in those previous meetings and I jumped at the opportunity. Sharon and I began making plans, we wrote a proposal, and the AAUW Educational Foundation accepted the Girlfighting Project. For this I am truly grateful to AAUW, not only because it provided generous support for this work, but also because it made possible a collaboration with an amazing woman who has enriched my life. I want to thank the University of Maine and the Women's Resource Center, especially Jenn Ladd, for all the varied ways they welcomed me to campus. I also wish to thank my home institution, Colby College, particularly dean of faculty Ed Yeterian, and Bets Brown and Linda Goldstein of College Relations for the many ways they helped to make this collaboration possible.

This book is but one piece of the larger project Sharon and I envisioned. Just as important was the outreach we accomplished in the two years we collaborated. Sharon worked tirelessly to ensure that what we proposed had real significance for girls and for those working with girls across the state. We talked about the implications of girlfighting with UM faculty and graduate students, brought together teachers and school administrators to think about schooling practices, and worked with an advisory group of high school girls. We reported our findings, via teleconference, to a range of organizations and nonprofits around the state of Maine, and we tied it all together in the fall of 2002 with a conference that brought nearly four hundred people—parents, teachers, health care providers, program developers—together with nationally known scholars to consider the relationships between girlfighting, sexuality, and body image. Finally, in collaboration with the Maine Women's Health Campaign, we gathered leaders of girls' organizations and programs across the state to consider what this research suggests about our work with Maine girls. It's been quite a journey.

I've had so much help collecting and analyzing the data on which this book rests. Thanks to Jill Taylor who shared her copies of the Cambridge School Study with me and to Elizabeth Debold who shared her copies of interviews from the Tobin and Atrium Studies. Thanks to Patti Feuereisen—a source of constant support—who connected me with Brooklyn Friends School and with high school girls in New York City, and to Sandy Grande for interviewing girls in Cleveland and for teaming up with me on our "Chick Flicks" discussions. I also want to thank Carrie Johnston for all she did to organize and facilitate our girls' advisory group. And I absolutely could not have done this without the expert research assistance and good humor of Corie Washow and Jennie Todd. Corie patiently learned the Listening Guide method, analyzed interview data, and made trips with me to Cambridge to help sift through, read, and copy interviews; Jennie offered all kinds of administrative support at UM, read interviews and developed themes to pursue in my writing; both transcribed interviews, did content analyses, read and commented on sections of this book. I'm grateful to Jennie O'-Donnell, who helped with an extensive literature search and gave so much good energy to the project in its early stages.

This research is also supported by funds given by Colby's Interdisciplinary Studies Division and the W. T. Grant Foundation to the Murray Research Center at the Radcliffe Institute for Advanced Study, Harvard University. A special thanks to the staff at the Murray Research Center who helped me locate and piece together data sets that had just been delivered in boxes and were not yet organized.

It took me a while to find the right home for this book, and I'm so glad to have found my editor, Jennifer Hammer, at NYU Press. Her enthusiasm and support was just what I needed to stay focused and finish writing and her excellent advice has improved the book significantly.

I'm especially grateful to all the girls from all the studies who told their personal truths with such clarity and confidence. I've learned an incredible amount from them. I've also learned a great deal from some amazing women who took the time to think hard with me about girl-fighting. In addition to Sharon Barker, I want to thank Mary Madden, Aileen Fortune, and Dot Foote for all they have done to ground this project in reality. Thanks to Aileen and Dot for taking the time to read and make suggestions on the last chapter. I want to express my deepest gratitude to my colleagues Janie Ward and Sharon Lamb, both of whom read the entire first draft of the book and offered extensive comments and suggestions. I have a wonderful memory of sitting in a Mexican restaurant with Sharon Lamb and Mary Madden one evening talking about the last two chapters. I still have the scribbled notes I made on a salsa-stained paper napkin, to which I've referred many times and which I've placed in a journal for safekeeping.

In every research project I tackle, I struggle with the tension between the constraints of conducting research and the complicated realities of girls' lives. I've allayed this tension in recent years by developing service learning and social action projects in the courses I teach. While these projects are great for all involved, they are necessarily short-lived and I found myself longing for something I could stay with and develop over time. So it was not by chance that, as this project began to develop, I began a parallel collaboration with two remarkable women, Karen Heck and Lynn Cole. Together we created a nonprofit called Hardy Girls Healthy Women, the goal of which is to provide hardiness zones—places that offer control, challenge, and commitment—for girls in central Maine. Hardy Girls has become an exciting space for me to translate theory into practice, to offer ideas, receive sustenance, and to work with an ever-widening collective of girls and women I admire and respect. I'm so grateful for the ongoing encouragement and support.

Writing about girlfighting has brought me to a new clarity about the significance of female friendships in my life. Each summer I return to my hometown and fall into the rhythm of my oldest and dearest childhood friendship with Connie DiCenzo Coleman, to whom I dedicate this book. Our conversations provide me with daily reminders of what's most important in life. A very special thanks to Betty Sasaki, Deborah Tolman, and Sarah Willie for running with me, enduring my various neuroses, and providing heavy doses of loving reality when I need it most.

Finally, I want to thank my family. My husband, Mark Tappan, makes it possible for me to do this work. His endless generosity of spirit, boundless love, and support provide a homeplace where there is always space to enjoy the best parts of life. Our daughter Maya, all enthusiasm, inquisitiveness, and determination, reminds me to remain wide open to the world and grounds me in the everyday. I also want to thank my parents—my mother, Diane, who taught me to have faith in people, to see goodness in everyone, and my father, Lindy, who instilled in me a healthy irreverence and desire to question authority. I take these lessons, and the tensions inherent in them, to heart.

Introduction

Bad Girls, Bad Girls, Whatcha Gonna Do?

NO MORE SUGAR AND SPICE and everything nice. Suddenly the world is filled with mean and nasty girls. Recently there have been a slew of popular books that tell us "girls just want to be mean," and give advice about "how to tame them."[1] How could we not have seen it before? There were so many clues, after all. There was Amy Fisher, Tonya Harding, and Linda Tripp, all competitive and jealous and ready to take out their female rivals. All ripe for taming. The media agrees; in fact, it led on the story. Long before books on the subject emerged, talk shows, reality shows, soap operas, sitcoms, and feature films showcased women and girls who compete and fight over boys or status as the most popular girl. TV for the younger set is no exception. There are little Angelica of the *Rugrats* and Helga of *Hey Arnold!* regular cartoon Eddie Haskells, all sweet and innocent to adults and Wicked Witches of the West to other children.

The reason books and reports that depict girls as nasty, catty, and mean are so provocative is that they relay something both disturbing and familiar. It shouldn't be, but it is so true, we think. We women know this, don't we? We were victims or perpetrators once. We can identify. Men know it too—manipulation and duplicity have been part and parcel of the very definition of femininity. But this is exactly why such a caricature is so dangerous. Fundamentally, it's the same old same old. It's familiar because it conforms to all the old stereotypes we have of girls and women—as deceitful, complaining, and jealous. It's familiar because it's an old story about the essential nature of femininity—"girls will be girls," naturally and indirectly mean; it's a stage all girls go through and from which most never emerge. And it's familiar in its trivializing, simplistic notions of girls' anger and aggression. Girls fight about popularity and boys and clothes. The fighting is all so, well, "girlish." They cry, and as one author of a book on girls' social hierarchies explained, "I really do hate it when their faces get all splotchy, and everyone in gym class or whatever knows they've been crying."[2]

This shift from nice to mean and nasty girls is very interesting and worth wondering about—this either-or, girl as victim or girl as aggressor, good girl or bad girl. It strikes me as a false dichotomy simply because the world doesn't work that way; people are never so simple. Indeed, as Gregory Maguire, in his novel *Wicked* reminds us, the so-called Wicked Witches of the world have their own story to tell and it's by no means a simple tale.[3] Fundamentally, it's a political story about battling the surveillance and control of girls' bodies, minds, and spirits; a story that varies with social context, with race, class, and sexual orientation. It's a story about containment and dismissal that gets acted out by girls on other girls because this is the safest and easiest outlet for girls' outrage and frustration. It's a story about who gets taken seriously and listened to; a story about rage at the machine channeled through relationships and performed in the everyday spaces girls occupy. And it's a story about justified anger at a world that devalues girls and encourages them to distance and disinfect themselves from all things feminine.

This book is different from popular books on girls' meanness to other girls. First of all, it's based on research. I didn't write it to shock anyone or to make girls' treatment of other girls tantalizing or titillating or to underscore a "girls will be girls" message. I wrote it to provide some reality to those depictions. While my subject is girlfighting and I detail how and why girls fight with and betray other girls, I don't represent all girls as either nasty or mean or victims of nasty or mean girls. The research doesn't support that picture and I don't think the world works like that. As novelist Anne Lamott says, "It is so much easier to embrace absolutes than to suffer reality" and "reality is unforgivingly complex."[4] This book is about girls' complex and often contradictory realities, especially when it comes to their anger and aggression. It's a book that tells how, from a very young age and in uneven and varied ways, girls are introduced to a "Reality" that encourages them to distrust other girls and women and, in some cases, turns them against themselves and against one another.

In other words, I don't describe the nasty ways girls can undermine each other as proof that girls can be just as "bad" as boys—of course girls can express all range of human emotions and behaviors. But I hope to provide a developmental understanding and a theoretical explanation, lacking in recent conversations, for why they are more likely to choose certain pathways over others. This approach involves listening to girls, certainly, but always with an ear to the ways their language and understandings of themselves reflect something beyond the psychological to the ways our society influences behavior. It's a fine line to walk, to be sure, but if we don't attempt the balancing act we risk becoming hopelessly mired in the personal, writing new versions of old self-help books that put all the blame and responsibility for change on girls and remove the motivation to address media images or to consider what it would take to improve social contexts and institutions like schools. As social psychologist Carol Tavris argues, "The psychologizing of social problems is so much easier, because psychology directs us to look inward, to personal solutions rather than institutional changes."[5] As educational scholars Pam Bettis and Natalie Adams suggest, when trying to understand developing identities it's as important to ask "Where am I?" as it is to ask the proverbial "Who am I?"[6]

Some, of course, would argue with such a social and political explanation of girlfighting. Girlfighting is biological, they would say. Girls and women, like primates, are predisposed to gathering in groups, competing for alpha males, rejecting females who are positioned on the lower castes of the social system—oh, and to preening and grooming each other. In the eternal pendulum swing between nature and nurture, biology as an explanation for human behavior has made a comeback.

But most biological arguments used by social scientists to explain human social behavior are overly simplistic. All organisms are affected by social and contextual factors—this is not an either-or proposition. We know that repeating social responses to infants can affect brain growth and functioning; that certain kinds of outside stimuli can influence brain structure and chemistry. And we know that changes in social patterns, tied to evolution, would take a great expanse of time to develop. Biology doesn't account for the rather sudden recent increase we have seen in girlfighting or the fact that female violent crime has escalated since the 1990s. And biology doesn't account for the very different ways girls in different social circumstances and cultural contexts choose to express their anger at other girls or the fact that some girls resist girlfighting altogether.

The biology argument reminds me of a paper I read some years ago by the philosopher Iris Marion Young. In "Throwing Like a Girl," Young takes on a rather glib argument made by a colleague that the differences between the ways boys and girls throw is a "biological, not an acquired, difference."[7] Her analysis interrogates the "rather ordinary ways" in which girls and women move differently from boys and men, and shows how deeply situated they are in our culture. How a girl learns to move reveals more about opportunities for early spatial development, practice, and a girl's very complicated relationship to power in patriarchal culture than it does about being essentially female. Today, with girls excelling in sports, we see plainly how "throwing like a girl" is more about practice than biology, but this was an eye-opening article in the 1980s. Indeed, it's good to recall history with some humility when referring to the nature of human behavior. It was as recently as in the 1970s that the "objective science" of psychiatry categorized homosexuality as a perversion, and in 1969 that Arthur Jenson scientifically "proved" the superiority of the white race, an argument reflected as recently as 1994 in a best-selling book, *The Bell Curve*.

Since the mid-1980s or so I've listened to hundreds of girls talk about their thoughts and feelings, and for this book alone I've relied on interviews with 421 girls of different economic, racial, and geographic backgrounds. I've tried to tell a complicated story of what it means for a girl to grow up in a social and political world that was not of her making or made with her health and well-being foremost in mind. I've learned a lot about how girls change and grow and make sense of the world and how girls who are located differently in the social world, whether because of class, race, ethnicity, or sexual orientation, experience this world and make sense of it in different ways. I've listened most intently to the ways girls of different ages draw attention to the quality of relationships between people and how deeply such concerns affect them and influence what they value and how they act in the world. And I've grown increasingly concerned that girls focus too much on the personal and psychological aspects of their lives and not enough on the social and political.

In all this work, two seemingly contradictory themes emerge over and over again. First, girls depend on close, intimate friendships to get them through life. The trust and support of these relationships provide girls with emotional and psychological safety nets; with their friends behind them, they can do and say things that are remarkably creative and brave and "out of character." With their friends at their back they will stand on principle, rebuke a school bully, report sexual harassment or abuse, develop a radically new idea, fight stereotypes. This theme saturates the psychological literature, which suggests that one of the primary differences between girls and boys is the way girls develop and maintain their intimate friendships. This is also the public story girls are more than willing to tell and endorse—a nice story of support and safety and pleasure.

Second, girls can be excruciatingly tough on other girls. They can talk behind each others' backs, tease and torture one another, police each others' clothing and body size, and fight over real or imagined relationships with boys. They can promote a strict conformity to the norms and rules of idealized femininity, threaten rejection and exclusion, and reinforce gender and racial stereotypes. In so doing they not only hurt other girls and get hurt, but in their search for power and visibility, they also unwittingly participate in and maintain our society's largely negative views of girls' and women's relationships as untrustworthy, deceitful, and manipulative.

This second theme is less likely to be documented by social scientists, even though it's overtaken the popular press. It is not the whole story but it is, as radio personality Paul Harvey says, "the rest of the story." It tends to emerge in private conversations with and among girls themselves or in their written stories and narrative accounts of their lives; it tends to be enacted out of the view or control of adults. It's often a secret story, a private accounting of anger, resistance, anxiety, and fear. As such it tends to surface, often in exaggerated form, in sites that girls frequent: magazines like *Seventeen* or *Girls' Life*, internet sites and chat rooms, ads targeted at girls, movies, TV sitcoms, and soap operas. This theme also reverberates in adult women's stories of hidden betrayals and deceit in the workplace and in other contexts where power is both desired and contested. This is what journalists and TV talk show hosts want to talk about because it's sometimes true, usually juicy, and always familiar and easy to lace with shame and blame.

I'm not attempting in this book to reconcile the seemingly irreconcilable differences between these two versions of girls' and women's reality, but to explain how both arise from a common source. We can't tell one story without the other; they are inextricably linked. Both exist because both reflect girls' desire for intimacy as well as their larger struggle for voice, power, safety, and legitimacy. Girls desperately need the support of their friends to remain emotionally, psychologically, and physically whole in a world that takes them less seriously, values their looks and their bodies above all else, and still requires that they please boys and men to succeed. But in a sexist climate, it is also simply easier and safer and ultimately more profitable for girls to take out their fears and anxieties and anger on other girls rather than on boys or on a culture that denigrates, idealizes, or eroticizes qualities associated with femininity. Girlfighting is not a biological necessity, a developmental stage, or rite of passage. It is a protective strategy and an avenue to power learned and nurtured in early childhood and perfected over time. Undermining other girls for attention or boys' favor is qualitatively no different from jealously protecting one's small piece of patriarchal pie from other women. The bigger question, too infrequently asked, is who cut the pie this way in the first place?

If these two contradictory stories of girls' friendship and girlfighting are, indeed, deeply entwined and rooted in the same soil, tracing one will inevitably lead to the other. Entering the world of girlfighting in its many forms does lead to girls' and ultimately to women's friendships, but in ways that are often surprising and unpredictable. Part of being an acceptable girl in a culture so deeply infused with white middle-class values, is to be, or at least appear to be, "nice." So girls who buy into prevailing views of femininity are likely to hide the "bad" or "shameful" parts of their relationships when they can. Girls who, because of race, ethnicity, sexual identity, or class define femininity differently or who experience being female as something more active and direct and physical are put in their place and soon learn about the advantages offered to those who assimilate or pass. Those who resist, who refuse to map onto any simple notion of girlhood, risk being labeled troublemakers, stupid, or worse.

Conversations with girls, especially when they feel safe enough to speak openly, offer more chance for girls' private and public struggles to be expressed and understood. Here girls speak about the sometimes open and often subterranean world of girlfighting and the pain of being excluded, picked on, or talked about that goes on just out of their parents' and teachers' view. Here they express the meaning of their open anger at other girls and their fears of being ostracized, teased, or beaten up. And here they begin to articulate the untenable situation, the impossible bind they find themselves in—between being seen as either all good or all bad. It's this dichotomy—the very split played out in the press between nice girls and nasty—that threatens to divide girls, to pull them away from the reality of their experiences and nuanced relationships with other girls and with boys. This split, and the girlfighting that arises from it, serves a cultural purpose.

Girls' voices and their struggles, both above and underground, drew me to this topic. I had heard so many stories about girlfighting in interviews with girls, usually when I didn't ask about them. Questions about morality, unfairness, or invisibility, about feeling good or bad about oneself or feeling angry or sad, questions about what society values in a girl and woman, often led in one way or another to girls' struggles with other girls. This pattern, coupled with growing evidence that fighting and troublemaking behavior are on the rise for girls, prompted me to look more closely. I wanted to hear and know more. What are girls fighting about and why? When does girlfighting begin, how does it develop and change over time, and what aspects of our culture encourage or discourage it? And why should we care—what effects does it have on girls and on society?

This book reports interviews with girls from first grade through high school, diverse with respect to race and social class. I reanalyzed interview data from six studies conducted between 1986 and 1995 at the Harvard Project on Women's Psychology and Girls' Development, now housed at the Henry A. Murray Research Center at Radcliffe.[8] Together these studies provide rich interview material from groups of girls in rural, suburban, and urban areas of the Northeast as well as the suburban and urban Midwest; they are white girls and girls of color; from poor, working-class, middle-class, and wealthy families; in both private and public schools. In addition to these studies I also reanalyzed interviews and focus group material from three of my own studies on working-class girls in Maine and I collected new data from four additional contexts: one in suburban Maine, two in New York, and one in Cleveland, Ohio.[9]

Facing such a voluminous amount of data, I needed a plan that would allow me to tune into the complexity of girls' voices *and* to write about them sometime before the next century. Most of the Harvard Project studies were analyzed using the Listener's Guide, an interpretive method that allows one to follow different voices in an interview text.[10] As a result, I was able to review detailed worksheets generated by the Listening Guide method and focus on a selection of interviews that addressed girls' conflicts and struggles with other girls. With the help of research assistants Corie Washow and Jennie Todd, I used these interviews to develop a list of categories or content areas. We then read the remainder of the interviews for girls' experiences with such issues as popularity, cliques, media messages and expectations, sexuality, perfection, competition, and gossip. We also read for stories of loyalty or resistance to girlfighting and of genuine or close friendship with other girls. We distinguished direct and physical fighting from indirect or more relational forms of aggression. We collected these narratives and separated them by age groups. In addition, I used the girls' stories to develop a new interview protocol and in subsequent group and individual conversations I was able to pursue these various content areas more directly.

As a result of this analysis I was able to track some things and not others and conclude some things and not others. First, girls talk as much as or more about their closeness with other girls and the things they need and want from their friends and peers as they do about the jealousies, fights, pressures, and anxieties they experience. Most often these experiences of closeness and anger are deeply connected. And yet, if they are asked about friendship, the importance of intimacy prevails; if they are asked about experiences of anger and conflict, examples of girlfighting prevail. No surprise here: to a certain degree you get what you ask for. Again, my concern in this book is not with which experience triumphs, but with how we understand the impact of culture on the nature of girls' relationships with other girls and the impact of girlfighting on the culture. I focus on girlfighting not because I think it's the only or even the primary thing girls experience with other girls, but because I think it has causes and damaging effects beyond the purely psychological.

Second, it's nearly impossible to extricate close friendships from the experience and pressure of peer relationships. This is a distinction made in the social science literature but it isn't a very useful one, especially when it comes to understanding girls. How close friendships are experienced and played out is inextricably connected to peer groupings. Moreover, in this media age, the notion of peer exceeds any specific group of peers. TV and movies project a "normal" range of acceptable girl behaviors against which media-savvy girls are pressed to compare or distance themselves. Girls' friendships and peer groups, influenced by the media, are entwined and laced with anxiety and expectations that may have little to do with their everyday experiences.

Given this reality, it seemed important to begin my exploration of girlfighting by examining cultural messages girls receive in the media. In the first chapter, then, I illustrate how our gender-saturated culture is a setup for girlfighting and how the messages and images we feed girls ultimately prepare the ground for what Phyllis Chesler terms "woman's inhumanity to woman."[11] It doesn't have to be so, but too often the various persecutions girls visit on other girls arise out of either their desire to meet unattainable feminine ideals—to get a boy, to be loved—or their resistance to such ideals and their denigration of femininity—to be one of the guys, to be taken seriously. Here again is the setup, the false dichotomy. Both paths lead to divisions, separations, and cruelties and ultimately ensure that the current social reality in which "female" is subordinate and "male" is dominant will continue uninterrupted. Both lead girls to compete with and judge other girls rather than to name and stand together against the double standards that support sexism and injustice.

Next I begin a developmental journey through girlhood. Drawing from the social science literature and girls' own accounts of their experiences, I address the often convoluted and opaque world of girlfighting and, because they are so intimately entwined, the world of close friendships that sustain, protect, and encourage girls' voices. Moving from childhood through adolescence, my goal is to show, chapter by chapter, how social and cultural messages meet up with psychological realities that then feed into and create culture. In the penultimate chapter I consider the implications of this research for women and for society, and in the last chapter I explore possibilities for intervention that I hope will be of interest to parents, teachers, therapists, and counselors.

Certainly it is my belief that the girls' voices in this book will move all of us to feel compassion for the difficulties and subtleties of growing up female, as well as to admire the joys, strengths, and the creative resistance strategies girls have developed. But mostly I want to encourage awareness of and critique of the larger socializing forces at work in children's lives. Girls fight for a reason; they choose their battles and they choose their means of fighting for a reason. This work is meant to undermine the persistent undercurrent of belief in girls' and women's "natural" pettiness, cattiness, and irrational meanness when it comes to their relationships and the notion that girlfighting is a "natural" developmental stage. Above all, it is an attempt to get closer to the truth as Adrienne Rich defines it; truth not as any one thing, but an increasing complexity.[12]

1

Reading the Culture of Girlfighting

SARA, A TWENTY-YEAR-OLD COLLEGE STUDENT, sits forward in her chair in a way that suggests earnestness. Her wavy dark hair is pulled back in a ponytail; her intense brown eyes hold my gaze whenever she comments or answers a question. She has an air of self-assurance. I think about this as I stand before this classroom full of students, mostly sophomores like Sara; a room full of adolescents here to learn about adolescence. I recall her paper; it's somewhere in the pile I'm handing back today, still speaking to me, pulling at me. The assignment was autobiographical, to explore a significant moment in early adolescence. Sara chose to reveal her painful, protracted search for popularity:

> It was in fourth grade that I discovered what popularity meant . . . friends, security, and the envy of my peers. . . . I started to associate myself with the popular girls. I worked my way in slowly, quietly, and took a back seat to the "leaders" of the group. I dressed like they did, walked like they did. . . . I remember using a valley girl voice for the second half of fourth grade, placing "like" in between almost every word. It was difficult and drove me and my parents crazy, but it was necessary in order to attain rank.
>
> By fifth grade I was there. I was popular. I made sacrifices along the way, losing touch with my best friend who didn't fit the "mold," using my allowance to supplement the clothes allowance my parents gave me in order to buy the designer clothes, spending my winter recesses freezing on the playground because wearing a hat wasn't cool, sleeping over at strangers' houses where I wasn't comfortable because the hostess had popular status, and putting down others in order to ensure my place at the top.
>
> Talking behind "friends'" backs became second nature, and I became an excellent liar to deal with the rare occasions when people confronted me about my inconsistencies. . . . They called us the "clan," even the teachers did, and I always thought of it as a fitting

and endearing title. It gave us an aura of being elite, exclusive, and that was exactly what we were. . . .

On the surface, I assumed everyone loved me by the time I reached sixth grade. I was no longer the quiet one, the follower; I had become the leader who was being mimicked by twelve insecure followers. The strange thing was, I loved my friends dearly. We had slumber parties where we stayed up all night talking. We went on bike rides together, shopped together, even studied together. The times I treasured most were those that I spent with these girls as individuals. As a group we were a magnificent force whose wrath was feared by our unpopular peers. . . . We cut down others because we didn't know how else to en-sure that we wouldn't be the ones teased relentlessly. We were selec-tive about who we hung out with so others would feel privileged if we accepted them. . . .

As the leader, I encouraged my friends to find fault in others. I did-n't see any other way for us to maintain an image of perfection unless others were imperfect. In this way I wanted to ensure that I would re-main the leader of our group. I'd seen others fall from the throne, fi-nally seen for their conniving and hurtful ways, and I worked over-time to be sure that didn't happen to me. I was a liar, able to deceive anyone, and lucky for me I was good at all of this. After two years of practice at being just the right amount of nasty, I had everyone con-vinced that my life was perfect.

Within the group, I picked one target to put down, seeing in her the goodness and the ability to reveal to the others the type of person I was. I made her days difficult, finding her sensitive areas and using them as ammunition against her. She was from a home where her mother had a mental illness and her father was an alcoholic, some-thing that I knew was abnormal and easy to justify as faulty. Despite the fact that such things were out of her control, the others followed my lead and teased her as often and as harshly as I did. I was success-ful; she finally left the group and didn't reappear until the eighth grade when she was ready to confront me.

Sara can reveal this not so pretty story of her girlhood, in part be-cause hers is a tale of redemption. At the end of sixth grade, a teacher falsely accused her of a misdeed, saying, "I know deep in my gut that you did this. You are the type of person who would do this." This floored Sara—the jig was up; unbeknownst to her, others had seen and judged. Slowly she began to awaken to the fact that "my peers despised me; they all wanted to be me, but they hated me. . . . Everyone treated me with respect, wanted to gain popularity by associating with me, but they were all talking about me behind my back."

When Sara pulled away, she "found that I was quickly replaced." And worse, she was now the target. The popular group she had once led

> came back for me with a vengeance. They were still a powerful force and were able to convince the entire school to hate me. There were notes on my desk when I got to class that read 'DIE BITCH!' and I couldn't get so much as a look from any guys. They ruined me, devastated me to the point of missing nineteen days of school in eighth grade and I felt I deserved every minute of it.

Until fairly recently, bullying and aggression have been seen as boys' issues. In the spring of 2001 I went to the foremost national conference on educational research and attended a number of panels on bullying, all so crowded that the audience flowed out the doors and stood in the hallways, straining to listen. Not one panelist addressed girlfighting or girl bullying, of the sort Sara describes, in any significant way. The clear assumption, among professionals at least, was that it was a boy problem. The same was true for the many articles in newspapers and magazines that followed the spate of school shootings. Identifying a bully really meant identifying the characteristics of a boy bully—and a white boy bully at that.[1] In fact, it's true that only one of the twenty-nine school shooters has been a girl, and the more visible signs of bullying such as fist fights, pushing, and harassing and threatening behavior, were more likely to involve boys.

When it came to fighting or bullying, girls were a different matter or perhaps no real matter at all. There have been books written on girl gangs and violent girl behavior, but because such depictions of girls have been racialized—stereotyped and marginalized by the popular press as a problem of urban girls of color—educators have tended to dismiss the larger realities of girls' anger and aggression these books address. Instead, the prevailing assumption has long been that girls are good at relationships; that their friendships and peer relationships, in particular, are responsive and healthy and, in spite of petty bickering and minor conflicts, devoid of really serious problems. Social science research on friendship has confirmed this for the most part. Intimacy is central to girls' friendships and girls rely heavily on their best friends for love and support. Adolescent girls spend more time with their friends than do boys,[2] have smaller groups of friends than boys,[3] expect and receive more kindness, loyalty, commitment, and empathic understanding from their best friends than do boys,[4] and are more likely than boys to have open, self-disclosing relationships with their female peers.[5]

But there has also been a prevailing view that complaining and bickering, deceit, and back-stabbing are normal aspects of growing up female and thus not worthy of serious scholarly attention. Girls are simply, by nature, catty and mean to one another but compared to, say, shooting their classmates, this is nothing. When it came to really serious bullying behavior, girls were the victims, not the perpetrators. This cultural misconception has enormous power. When Carol Gilligan and I wrote about girls' struggles to hold onto their thoughts and feelings at early adolescence, their loss of voice received all the attention. No one seemed particularly interested in the younger outspoken girls or the girls who fought back and resisted "the tyranny of nice and kind."[6] Popular books like *Reviving Ophelia* reinforced the image of a girl-victim crumbling under the weight of a girl-toxic culture.[7]

What a difference a few years make. First of all, no one likes to feel like a victim and in time girls began to write and edit their own books: *Girl Power, Ophelia Speaks, Listen Up!* and *Adios Barbie.*[8] It's not that simple or one-sided, the young authors explained—we speak, we fight back, we don't just consume, we create; no one story or experience defines us. These books joined the work of a growing collection of feminist psychologists and "Girl Studies" scholars who have been attending to the day-to-day realities of being a girl, writing about alternatives to the victim story, and exploring new versions of girlhood connected to social and cultural context, history, and the material conditions of girls' lives.[9] Taking their lead, writers of more popular books have attempted to reclaim pejorative terms directed at girls and women and to question their persistence in the culture. My shelves display a series of titles that would shock my mother: *Cunt, Bitch, Slut,* and the less provocative *Promiscuities* and *Fat Talk.*[10] Part of the process of reclamation is an appreciation of how these terms are used by girls and women to control and undermine other girls and women.

It's perhaps not surprising, given these developing views of girls as more active and complicated and culture as less monolithic and absolute, that new versions of girlhood have emerged—girls as smart, strong, athletic, brave, resistant. Out of these versions, a new popular ideal, some might say a counterideal, has developed: girl as fighter. In response to girl as victim, which fed off stereotypes of femininity as passive and vulnerable, girl as fighter is assertive, usually smart, psychologically tough, physically strong.[11] Again, there have always been girlfighters, but they have been easily dismissed as outsiders to ideal (white and middle-class) femininity: the delinquent, the violent gang girl, the tough streetwise girl. This dismissal, of course, was a way of defending the white ideal against the ever-encroaching reality that things were more complicated. This new version of girl as fighter places a desire for power and visibility firmly within the cultural definition of femininity. The girlfighter is now just as likely to be the girl who does well in school, who plays sports, the girl teachers like, the girl next door.

But there's something suspicious about this shift from victim to fighter. In the media there's been a pendulum swing—girlfighting was way out; now it's so in. TV offers us a range of smart fighters from *Alias* and *CSI* to *Buffy the Vampire Slayer*, *Charmed*, and *Birds of Prey*, while movies are filled with the likes of Lara Croft and Charlie's Angels. Like girl as victim, the girlfighter maps too easily onto familiar assumptions about femininity. She's more in than outlaw because her fighting is mediated by qualities that make her pleasing—and sexually appealing—to men. She redeems herself through her beauty, occasional vulnerability, and her romantic relationships. Indeed, if we consider the rise of the girlfighter in popular culture, I think we can see how she reinforces as much as she challenges long-standing assumptions about the "nature" of girls and women.

THE GOOD, THE BAD, AND THE UGLY

It's odd that just as girls began to assert their complicated realities and just as girlfighting, fraught as it is, emerged in the popular press, we became obsessed in this culture with the "mean" girl. Mean girls began to surface in the news media in the mid-1990s, as real concern for girls' anger and aggression collided with the titillating nature of girlfighting.

A young writer for *YO!* asked, "Are girls turning meaner?"[12] The *Boston Sunday Globe* announced, "Schools see rise in girls fighting."[13] An article entitled "Mean Streak" in the *Chicago Tribune* claimed "girls have a knack for cruelty."[14] *Girls' Life* asked, "Do mean girls finish first?" and advised readers to "beat a bully at her own game."[15] A *New York Times Magazine* special "How to" issue featured a nasty fight between two popular high school girls.[16] Newspaper articles reported that a Texas beauty queen was stripped of her crown for threatening cheerleaders' lives, while a Canadian beauty queen lost hers for assaulting another contestant. An article in *New Moon Magazine for Girls and Their Dreams* was entitled simply, "In Seventh Grade, All Girls Are Mean to All Other Girls."[17] At the same time, reports began to show that even if the total number of girls committing violent crimes is still small compared to boys, physical girlfighting and girl-initiated violence have increased exponentially since the mid-1980s or so.[18]

In response to such articles and reports, psychological research on relational forms of aggression or what some refer to as alternative aggressions, long buried under the "girl as victim" stereotype, started to garner public attention.[19] Relational aggression, more typical of and more stressful to girls than boys, is characterized by such behaviors as gossiping or spreading rumors about someone or threatening to exclude or reject them "for the purpose of controlling" their behavior.[20] Relational aggression is often indirect. In fact, as Sara and her friends illustrate, the goal is to hurt another person in such a way that it looks as though there has been no intention at all. It's a strategy used more often by those with less power because it protects one from retaliation or from punishment by those in control. It's a very useful strategy for girls because it provides a cover for unfeminine emotions like anger.

But *equating* girlfighting with relational aggression again pushed girls' violent behavior and physical fighting to the margins: now meanness was "normal" but physical fighting was still deviant, unredeemable, outside the realm of typical girl behavior. This new view of girlfighting as psychological and relational warfare has thus done little to challenge feminine stereotypes. Indeed, popular books on the issue seemed to undermine their own attempts to affirm the power of relational aggression to cause girls long-term emotional and psychological damage. Adding pejorative labels like "fruit cup girl" to the lengthy list of dismissive terms adolescent girls already have for one another, even with the best of intentions, only reaffirmed girlfighting as trivial.[21]

When rooting out girl meanness becomes a goal in and of itself, we risk losing the bigger picture. Let's catch, label, and fix "it" and then what? We'll have our girls back? And which girls are we talking about? Clearly the Barbie doll-like images and the advice about raising a "gamma girl" that prevailed recently in the flurry of magazine articles about girls' relational aggression indicate that the concern is really about middle-class white girls.[22] Moreover, neither the literature on relational aggression nor the popular accounts of the ways girls enact it on each other seem to address the larger issue of power. Little consideration has been given to the fact that a girl's social context, the options available to her, and the culture in which she lives will affect how she aggresses. No substantive consideration has been given to the fact that girlfighting might have something to do with the range of injustices and indignities girls experience in their daily lives.

The view of girlfighting as trivial is all too familiar. Girlfighting still gets our attention when it takes extreme forms, as it so often does in the media. Real-life conflicts such as those between Nancy Kerrigan and Tanya Harding, Amy Fisher and Mary Jo Buttafuoco, Monica and Linda made headlines and allowed us a voyeuristic look inside girlfighting. Because fighting among girls or their adult women counterparts is considered at once shocking, shameful, and funny, it's laced with eroticism and becomes the fodder of sitcoms, talk shows, and soap operas. This is the motivation behind women's prison movies, various forms of female wrestling, stories about cheerleaders or beauty queens who go awry, soap opera back-stabbing and Jerry Springer-type "bitch-slapping." As one high school girl explains, "guys see two girls fighting and think they're getting passionate and maybe the girls might start kissing and maybe the guys can get in on it." "Guys invented the concept of jello-wrestling," another young woman agrees, "so that they could watch girls fight."

It becomes hard to take the issue very seriously. The Canadian beauty queen who took out her competitor ended up on the cover of *Playboy* wearing only boxing gloves. In the 1980s women in the night-time soap, *Dynasty*, tore each others' clothes off in a public fountain to huge ratings. The ad for a more contemporary night-time soap, *Titans*, advertised the thinly veiled animosity between the two female leads: as the women walk by each other smirking and rolling their eyes, the voice-over announces, "If you can't say anything nice, pull up a chair." Peruse the channels and it seems that every man in prime time wants to watch a girlfight. When a physical fight breaks out between Rachel and her sister on the sitcom *Friends*, Phoebe shouts, "Oh my God, shouldn't we stop them?" Joey responds, "Are you out of your mind? Let's throw some Jello on them!" When the slapping and hair pulling finally ends, Chandler, after publicly shaming the women, leans over and whispers, "By the way, that fight was totally arousing." You don't even have to enjoy a girlfight to get the significance. As two female friends fight for his attention, Will, the gay leading man on the sitcom *Will and Grace*, commiserates with his gay friend Jack about the erotic subtext: "Too bad this is lost on us."

It's important to appreciate how the culture, from a very early age, sets girls up for girlfighting. When I ask fifteen-year-old Bahtya why there's so much infighting in her school, she says simply:

> It's the popular thing to do. TV, media, newspapers, it's like they teach girls you're supposed to fight. And if anybody had any common sense in their head, they'd know you don't have to fight with the girls in school.... Like I mean, you watch TV, you watch MTV, you watch anything, and there's always a fight going on between the popular girls at school. A lot of it is, I mean, you get into a fight and the whole school knows about it. Therefore your popularity goes up. You become more widely known. You're the girl that's in the fight with the other girl. It's like the attention, whether it's positive or negative. It's a constant competition or race for attention.

What strikes me about Bahtya's analysis is how closely entwined media messages and school behavior are for her—how she moves from one to the other without missing a beat. And yet she also doesn't quite believe the hype; she has "common sense in [her] head." Of course socialization is not that simple—girls meet these messages with a range of questions, responses, and viewpoints—but there's no doubt that the increase in images of girlfighting on TV and in movies contributes to the normalizing of both physical and relational aggression of girls toward other girls. It's not that girls are fighting more, but that it's not so hidden, not so pressured to go underground. The boxing legacies of Ali, Frazier, and Foreman, after all, have been handed down to daughters. Rarely is there a contemporary show for kids of any age with a girl, token or not, who doesn't physically fight or isn't verbally tough—that is, if she has any respect or power on the show. Consider the comment from a female lead in the TV show *Birds of Prey*: "Men. Can't live with 'em. Might as well beat the crap out of 'em." These girls fight over a lot of things, but they almost never fight for girls' rights or against the unfairnesses and injustice or cruelty lobbed at other girls.

In fact, fighting itself is not the problem. One can make a strong case for teaching girls how to box or do karate, not only to protect themselves, but so they can experience a full sense of power, physical and mental. Indeed, Simone de Beauvoir, writing in the 1950s, saw the benefits to fighting that transcended competitive sports "which means specialization and obedience to artificial rules." Such activity "is by no means the equivalent of a free and habitual resort to force," she argued. Sport "does not provide information on the world and the self as intimately as does a free fight."[23]

> for a man to feel in his fists his will to self-affirmation is enough to reassure him of his sovereignty. Against any insult, any attempt to reduce him to the status of object, the male has recourse to his fists, exposure of himself to blows: he does not let himself be transcended by others, he is himself at the heart of his subjectivity . . . anger or revolt that does not get into the muscles remains a figment of the imagination. . . . This lack of physical power [in girls] leads to a more general timidity: she has no faith in a force she has not experienced in her body.[24]

It's this sense of power, this refusal to be reduced to the status of object, this desire to be at the heart of her subjectivity, that so often lies behind both girls' growing participation in sports and an increase in physical fighting. The problem is that the girlfighting girls see in the media is often enacted in their female relationships and is usually about containment of other girls rather than about testing physical limits. It's likely to be motivated by desire for heterosexual romance, envy for male attention, or beauty competitions. Stories in which boys' desires and their realities are central—as they still are in much of the media aimed at children and adolescents—frame girls as competitors who need to please or to prove their desirability.

LIVING LA VIDA MICKEY

The much-touted transition to the third millennium is now behind us, there is talk about third-wave or even postfeminism, and still it is not uncommon to hear, above the general clamor of children's voices on any given playground, shouts of "girl stain," threats of "girl cooties," taunts like "go play with the girls" or "you throw like a girl." Girls are still seen by boys as pollutants, as contaminators, as carriers of a deadly strain of femininity. These seemingly innocent insults are given cultural weight by the media and socializing institutions like schools, and are engaged with and passed on by children themselves.[25] It is still considered an insult of great magnitude to call a boy a girl; the reverse, of course, is not true.

Television perpetuates such views and the messages come early and frequently. The world of prime-time TV is still largely a white male world—65 percent of the characters are male; 35 percent are female and 75 percent of the characters are white.[26] TV for young children is not much different. Although we have to account for animal characters, boy characters prevail with shows like *Clifford, Caillou, Franklin, Little Bill, Stanley, Arthur, Jimmy Neutron: Boy Genius, Dexter's Laboratory, Doug, Sponge Bob, Rupert, Hey Arnold!*—the list is seemingly endless. Even PBS, in their proud venture into original programming for preschoolers, missed the obvious. Five of their six "Bookworm Bunch" shows feature male characters.[27] The most striking female character in this sea of interesting and adventuresome boys is "Elizabeth the emotional pig" in *Marvin the Tap-Dancing Horse*. Elizabeth is a sniveling, self-blaming whiner who consistently annoys the other characters by worrying and crying all the time.

There are some cartoons with girl leads, certainly more than there used to be—*Dora the Explorer, The Proud Family, Kim Possible,* and *The Wild Thornberrys*, for example[28]—but mostly they are token girls in a medium still tightly controlled by the assumption that girls will watch boys, but boys will not watch girls.[29] These girl characters—whether yellow monsters, brave Pokémon trainers, clever wizards, or extreme skateboarders—live in a world monopolized by boys and their friendships and interests; and so girls and especially groups of girls or girlfriends are pretty much absent.

But it is not as simple as the percentage of male to female characters. Abundant in movies and television shows for the youngest children are messages about negotiating heterosexuality and romance in ways that subordinate, objectify, or denigrate girls and pit them against one another. Disney's remake of traditional fairy tales and folk stories is perhaps the most obvious offender—admittedly an easy target. But the strategic rerelease of these movies as videos makes them perpetually contemporary and ubiquitous. In *Cinderella*, *Snow White*, and *Sleeping Beauty* a girl escapes the cruel world of bitter women to the safety of romance. Chosen by a prince, she's saved from women's wrath, deceit, and jealousy. This is a common story that has at its heart the separation of girls from women. Girls are promised happy endings if they sacrifice female relationships. "Happily ever after" is a "fantasy of the fathers," argue Jerilyn Fisher and Ellen Silber, "only one woman allowed." At the base, such romance stories "divide girls from each other, from themselves, and from adult women." The message is clear: Girls must "relinquish ties to other women so that their energies can be harnessed in preparation for the fiercely competitive race toward men's approval.[30]

In popular movies evil women destroy and betray girls to rid themselves of female competition, to retain male desire, to be chosen by the powerful. A woman's power is derived from her cunning, deceit, and duplicity and her ability to undermine another's reality.[31] Such movies send the message that there is one *acceptable* avenue to power: be nice, stay pure, look beautiful, act white, be chosen. Come off too bold, say what you think too loudly, take up too much space, express your anger and disappointment, and you risk casting your lot with the evil ones. Above all else girls learn "the patriarchal lesson that other women are not even remotely connected to the health and happiness of growing girls"[32] and that female friendship is dangerous, suspect, or unimportant.

This message is further layered, however—as deeply racialized as it is gendered.[33] Evil women in these stories are dark and ugly, their power is derived from the mysterious and the magical and the primitive. Don't trust other women, they imply, but especially don't trust "dark" women. Such images contribute to a deep and historically based mistrust between women of color and white women.[34] On this account, *Peter Pan* is one of the worst offenders, apparent when Tinkerbell and Wendy and Tigerlilly compete for the attentions of Peter. The white boy who won't grow up is the object of desire that crosses racial lines and even human forms, causing jealousies, stereotyping, and ultimately near-deadly betrayal. Most of Disney's movies follow suit, if not representing women as evil, then representing girls as vain, chattering annoyances who look to boys and men for approval or seek to change them from beast into civilized prince.

Built into the ideal of white femininity, perfect for getting and keeping a prince, are messages about girls' place in boys' life cycle: girls are objects to own or cheerleaders to boys' adventures; they explain and protect the emotional lives of boys. On the cartoon version of *Peanuts*, for example, Linus points to the Little Red Haired Girl and exclaims, "There she is, Charlie Brown! Just take her." In stores like Penney's, AND1 basketball clothing announced: "Your game is as ugly as your girl," and "I'm gonna take two things, this game and your girl." In the ubiquitous Christmas classic *Rudolf the Red-Nosed Reindeer*, a girl reindeer is introduced to redeem Rudolf and urge him on to bravery. A story just isn't a story, even for the littlest kids, without reshaping it into what psychologist Deborah Tolman calls the "heterosexual script": the dominant story of romance that promotes boys' active desire and girls' passivity, and thus male dominance and female subordination.[35] According to Disney, for example, Minnie Mouse in the new century still doesn't make her way in the world on her own merit; she's "living la vida Mickey."

> She loves to live the Mickey life.
> She's anything but plain.
> She's got Mickey on the brain.
> Outside inside out,
> She's living la vida Mickey.
> That's what she's about,
> living la vida Mickey.

Three- and four-year-olds heard this parody of Ricky Martin's hit on the Disney channel four or five times a morning, sung against Mickey's attempts to escape Minnie's sloppy kisses, coy behavior, and shopping sprees. Girlhood, it seems, is cute, icky, and associated with chasing a boy who doesn't want you.

To be sure, this ideal of femininity has evolved in recent years. Disney's newer movies are an improvement and there are other available images and messages for girls to ponder. But even the few shows with strong girl characters feed stereotypes of girls and gender relations. Indeed, there's an emerging pattern. While the girls in these shows may be smart, adventurous, and brave, up to the challenges before them, these qualities distinguish them from excessive (annoying, petty, weak) femaleness. Their chosen qualities come at the expense of other girls, their sisters, their mothers. Boys are central and the other girls on their radar screens are, by comparison, ditsy, passive, mean, and shallow—worthy of heavy eye-rolling. There are boy geniuses but no girl geniuses. A full-page ad in the *New York Times Magazine* for the cartoon *Dexter's Laboratory* reads, "He skips grades. She just skips." "She" is "a babbling ballerina, otherwise known as older sister Dee Dee." In show after show lines drop in to remind girls of their place; an endless variation of "Yuck, that's a girl thing to say, do, wear, feel."

There are so many examples. Misty, the female Pokémon trainer who accompanies the hero Ash Ketchem and fellow traveler Brock, is clad in short shorts and crop top and worries about her "beauty sleep." She's defined in the usual female terms—"bossy" and "caring"—and pitted against her three narcissistic and scantily clad older sisters who tease her in valley girl voices. While she's accepted as one of the guys, the other girls who show up are objects of Brock's desire. And then there's Gary, a rival Pokémon trainer, who travels with his personal harem of giggly cheerleaders.

Self-possessed Helga in the cartoon *Hey Arnold!* is secretly in love with Arnold, and represents all jealous, backbiting, mean-spirited girls. Helga's mission is to take out all female rivals—usually with her fists, affectionately named "Old Betsy" and "The Five Avengers"—and decide the relational fate of the other girls in her clique. Her personal hell is home and the constant comparison to her "perfect" older sister, Olga. Similarly, part of what makes adventurous Eliza in the cartoon *The Wild Thornberrys* seem so level-headed is the contrast to her spacey, boy-crazy older sister, Debbie.

Being the kind of girl who's accepted or befriended by boys underscores a girl's power and sets her against other girls. For example, in *Kim Possible*, Kim—beautiful, thin, and sporting tight crop tops—is described as "your basic average high school girl here to save the world." She's smart enough but relies on her side-kick and best friend Ron Stoppable, a "super-brain." Her biggest threat is not evil, in fact, but the head cheerleader and if girls go to her website they're invited to choose Kim's cheerleading moves or play "shopping avenger." In *Lizzie McGuire*, the level-headed middle schooler does have a female friend,

Miranda, but the smartest person on the show is her male buddy, Gordo. Lizzie's main problem is, you guessed it, the popular head cheerleader. Reggie, the cool extreme snow/skate boarder in the series *Rocket Power* does have some girlfriends but, inexplicably, she chooses to spend nearly all her time with her younger brother and his best friends.

In the Harry Potter series, the central girl character, Hermione, is smart and brave and yet she's described as a "bossy know it all," hissing at Harry and Ron, his friend, "like an angry goose,"[36] or "cowering" in corners; words like "whimpering," "shrill," and "panicky" follow her like a house elf through the stories. She gains respect by doggedly working her way into the boys' favor; there are no other girls worth her time and energy. Indeed, Ginny, Ron's stereotypically feminine little sister, is the only other girl we know much about. When interviewed on *Dateline*, even Emma Watson, the actress who plays Hermione, couldn't distance herself fast enough from her character: "We're completely opposite," she said. "[Hermione's] bossy. She's horrible. I hate her!"[37]

So while girls are accepted, they are compromised by their barely hidden girlness or set against other girly girls. In such a climate, it becomes almost impossible to imagine a girl hero, alone or with other girlfriends, who would carry the collective imagination of all children like an Ash Ketchum or Harry Potter. In the world of media fantasy, the closest might be the *Power Puff Girls*. These cartoon mutant superheroines, Blossom, Bubbles, and Buttercup, are the result of their father's (Professor Utonium) botched attempt to create perfect little girls (he accidentally spilled some chemical X into a vat of "sugar and spice and everything nice"). To be a brave girl is to be essentially, biologically, a boy. And unlike *Pokémon* or the Harry Potter books, the Power Puff superheroines are not marketed to all kids; you'll find their pink heart-covered T-shirts and accessories only in the girls' department.

We can no longer generalize that girls learn from the media, in Katha Pollitt's words, to filter "their dreams and ambitions through boy characters while admiring the clothes of the princess." Some girls do. But others learn to filter their ambitions through boy characters and dis the clothes of the princess. It remains true that "boys, who are rarely confronted with stories in which males play only minor roles, learn a simpler lesson: girls just don't matter much."[38] Unfortunately, many girls learn that lesson too. As girls engage in boys' journeys, learn their magic, master their battles, they also learn in the process not to like girls, trust girls, respect girls, or take girls very seriously.

Girlfighting, the side effect of such disrespect and distrust, has long been depicted as funny and normal in children's movies, but it used to be pretty marginal. The only two female characters in *Muppets in Space*, for example, are self-involved diva Miss Piggy and her main competition in work, love, and beauty, actress Andie McDowell. The subplot in which Miss Piggie and McDowell fight for a news anchor job while the real action goes on, underscores to little girls just where they are located in the big picture and what they are supposed to be made of. But in this new era of girl power, girlfighting has taken center stage. Indeed most new TV shows and movies for kids have at least one tough girl character to foil the nice girls or to challenge the boys. While Jimmy Neutron Boy Genius invents things like girl-eating plants, his nemesis, Cindy Vortex, blonde, blue-eyed, and tough as nails, alternates between her crush on the cool boy and kicking alien butt. *Mike, Lu, and Og, Angela Anaconda*, and *Clifford* revolve around rivalries between tomboy girls and girly girls, nice girls and mean girls. Entire cartoon shows like *As Told By Ginger* are based on girl cliques. Fantasies of revenge, jealousies, broken promises, and secrets prevail.

And the differences between the girls matter—invariably, as we've seen, it's the girly girl who's the target. Francine, the working-class athlete in *Arthur*, for example, is often in conflict with Muffy—a rich and shallow girly girl. While the girls are friends, the young audience is made well aware that Francine, the tomboy, is the better girl—more loyal, grounded, and real. We root for Francine and we collectively dismiss Muffy as narcissistic and mean. Indeed, the nasty or annoying girl that everyone loves to hate is now endemic to kids' TV—Angelica in *Rugrats* is perhaps the poster child—but girls like her are popping up everywhere. TV shows reflect the impossible pressure on girls like Angelica to perform niceness and perfection in public and, because there is no real critique of the oppressive nature of ideal femininity or the heterosexual script, uses their justified, often covert anger against them, "proving" just how untrustworthy and deceitful girls really are.

These examples may seem trivial—but collectively they take hold. Their power is in the volume and the repetition and also in the uneven reinforcement of these messages in school and family life. In spite of all the options available to young girls today, they still meet up daily with a tired old dichotomy—femininity versus masculinity. Only now it's girls playing both roles. These simplistic constructions of gender may have little actual connection to the nuanced lives of boys and girls, but they provide an enticing fiction in which girls with feminine qualities or interests are admired by neither the boys nor the girls watching.

WHO'S THAT GIRL?

As girls move through childhood, the messages about what it means to be an acceptable girl come from everywhere, as do pressures to conform to an ideal beauty image. Consider, for example, one of the most popular book series for girls. In the 1930s when the Nancy Drew mystery novels were first published, Nancy was an intrepid, feisty detective who raced from one exciting adventure to another. In 1959 modifications to Nancy's character began and have continued over the years, so that the reader is constantly reminded of Nancy's appearance, her vulnerability, her desire for boys' attention, and her need for male help. The original version of the *Whispering Statue*, for example, describes a clever, independent escape from harm, while in the revised version Nancy is found and saved by a protector. And in the original versions of the novels Nancy was described simply as "attractive." Now we read: "The tight jeans looked great on her long slim legs and the green sweater complemented her strawberry-blond hair." Her friend Bess sighs, "You'll make the guys absolutely drool." In story after story, Nancy's bold nature is chipped away, until she resembles "a boy-crazed social butterfly,"[39] or what Jackie Vivelo describes as "a Barbie doll detective."[40] The covers of her books, rather than invoking mystery, now look like Harlequin romances or old ads for *Baywatch*.

Girls who watch prime time are "likely to see a beautiful, young, thin, white woman who is intelligent and independent but at the same time adheres to traditional gender stereotypes such as focusing on appearance and being motivated by a desire for a romantic relationship."[41] Characters in *Buffy the Vampire Slayer*, *Dark Angel*, *Alias*, and *Ally McBeal* can be strong and fearless as long as they "use their strength while wearing spaghetti-strapped tank tops and short skirts."[42] Even the women of *Friends*, one of the most popular shows for adolescent girls, periodically let us know how they re-created themselves to fit the part—Monica, once fat, is now emaciated; Rachel has had a nose job, and Phoebe has re-created herself from a tough girlfighter to a nice but ditsy girlfriend. What girls will do to fit a homogenized ideal of femininity is seemingly endless. And if changing your body doesn't work, going after other girls to elevate your chances just might. In a culture that tells girls and women that meeting a beauty ideal is all-important and they can willfully re-create their bodies, it's no surprise that they would use body gossip—judgments about failures to meet such physical ideals—as a weapon to undermine or control other girls. "Boys fight boys, fistfight," fifteen-year-old Kim explains,

> Girls will just taunt each other until they give them an eating disorder or something. . . . They're very horrible to girls. They're very good at getting inside people's heads and like playing mind games and messing them up very well. . . . Girls are very verbal and much more hurtful a lot of the time, because sometimes emotional wounds take longer to heal than physical ones. Most guys fight; that's it, it's over. But girls, once you scar them on the inside, it's not so good.

Shows like *Beverly Hill 90210*, *Melrose Place*, and *Dawson's Creek* evoke the same beauty images as part of educating girls in the heterosexual script. The world turns around what boys desire and need and good girls know what to do, where to draw the line, and how to suffer. After *90210* ended its long run, actress Jennie Garth expressed her relief about doing something different "after being the *90210* designated victim for a decade. Having been shot and raped and stalked . . . week after week . . . it was just refreshing to have some fun."

And yet, even as Britney Spears proclaims to girls, "your body is your best asset," the definition of girlhood is changing; what it means to be female is newly contested territory. Lucy Liu, one of Charlie's Angels, donned boxing gloves for the cover of *USA Weekend* as the caption proclaimed, "a new definition of American beauty." Not a new definition of the American woman, mind you, but of beauty. This is the rub. Power for the millennium girl includes the physical—she can kickbox, do martial arts, or box with the boys—but otherwise, the entrenched myths and social stereotypes about girls and women are intact. "Most of the techniques used by Charlie's Angels to attain power involve treating people like shit, being competitive, being manipulative, and being violent," notes one annoyed critic.[43] Says another: "Women are still portrayed as objects of male desire and fantasy, there are two scenes of women pitted against each other, women of color are exoticized, and big daddy Charlie still runs the show."[44] Regardless of the actual audience, we know to whom the movie is pitched when the cast is described as "easy on the eyes."[45] So girls can fight and fighting can give them a sense of power, but it does little to interrupt sexist stereotypes or the ever-increasing pressure on girls to meet others' expectations. When things go wrong for the superhero Power Puff Girls, the Townsville people chant, "Your fault! Your fault!"

The new perfection for girls is more than just being nice and kind and self-flagellating—it's nice and kind with a butt-kicking edge. *Charlie's Angels*, another reviewer comments, "is a tribute to today's woman: able, independent and cute—not so much femi-nist as femi-nice." When the Angels' scriptwriter says, "We want the Angels to be strong, but not masculine" or when a reviewer praises the TV movie *Jane Doe* because "[Teri] Hatcher's character doesn't lose her femininity and still holds her own in this action film," what they mean to say is that today's woman can be strong and independent as long as she's drop-dead beautiful, self-effacing, and nonthreatening to men. Young girls in cartoons can have that unredeeming nasty edge because they are basically nonthreatening, but adult women need to find their femi-nice side; they need to know whom to please. In her examination of the increasing prevalence of tough girls in the popular media, Sherrie Inness notes that while there is a greater variety of gender roles now open to young women, a character's "toughness is often mitigated by her femininity, which American culture commonly associates with weakness."

> Tough women can offer women new role models, but their toughness may also bind women more tightly to traditional feminine roles—especially when the tough woman is portrayed as a pretender to male power and authority, and someone who is not tough enough to escape being punished by society for her gender-bending behavior. . . . When the media *do* depict tough women, it is often to show that they are exceptions to the rule that women are not tough.[46]

The need to be, above all else, pleasing, pleasant, and subordinate to men—what Lynne Phillips calls a "pleasing women's discourse"—is readily available to girls. The magazines girls read often focus on "how to get a man," and make clear "that this should be done without seeming aggressive or 'slutty'—a pleasing woman is always discreet. . . .

Magazines communicated the pleasing women discourse rather explicitly through such tips as how to tilt one's head, smile coyly, and dangle one's foot while listening attentively to boys and laughing demurely at their jokes."[47] Reality shows like *Who Wants to Marry a Multimillionaire*, *The Bachelor*, *Meet My Folks*, *Bachelorettes in Alaska*, and *Mr. Right* all turn on these performance skills, even as the real thrill comes in those moments when the audience sees what the men don't: the competitive, slutty, aggressive women behind the scenes. I think this is why, in the final analysis, the movie *Thelma and Louise* was so controversial. It wasn't the "gratuitous violence" per se, but violence without the pleasing, redeeming romantic love of a man. Thelma and Louise chose their freedom and their loyalty to each other over their fraught relationships with the men in their lives. The further they traveled from convention, the more elusive, ethereal, clear-minded, and beautiful they became—and this was the real threat.

In this way, girls of all ages are bombarded every day with subtle and not so subtle images and messages about what it means to be a girl—a tomboy, a girly girl, a bossy girl, a girl other girls want to be with, a girl boys like, a girl who's taken seriously, a beautiful girl, an athletic girl, a smart girl, a tough girl, a fighter. This collage creates what might appear on the surface to be a rich array of choices; a new freedom for girls to be the girl they want to be. On closer scrutiny, however, the choices seem more like the refracted colors of a prism, capable of spinning a brilliant but dizzying array of options, beautiful but illusory. In the final analysis, the rich complexity of girls' experiences is narrowly labeled and voiced-over in this culture and the same old gender dichotomies hold sway: Girls will be girly girls or they will be [tom] boys; they will be good girls or sluts, nice girls or bitches. While the parameters have widened and shifted a bit, the general structure hasn't changed—both sides provide pathways to power through boys' attention and acceptance. So girls choose their weapons and face off—the girly girl, tossing her hair and staring indignantly at the tomboy; the tomboy, basketball in the crook of her arm, smirking back; each wearing a T-shirt she bought at the local department store. "Caution: Your boyfriend's at risk," says one. "In your face," says the other.

In the world of popular culture, girls are actively encouraged to choose between these and other stereotypes. Such imagery and messages contribute to a climate in which girls take on the role of policing other girls' looks and behavior, becoming absorbed with one another's failures to match up, dismissing other girls on the grounds of flimsy femininity or arrogant bitchiness, rather than questioning the dichotomies themselves and who they benefit. "Girls are, like, girls," sixteen-year-old Tamara says, explaining what it all comes down to: "It's kind of like, when a girl meets a girl for the first time, they automatically hate each other until they learn to like each other."

DIVIDE AND CONQUER

Girls begin an intense competition for a place in the social world at a surprisingly young age. Girls are quick to learn about power—who has it and how to get it—by watching, getting close to, imitating, and pleasing those upon whom it has been conferred "naturally." However, to be female in a culture so invested in boys and girls being different, while at the same time privileging qualities associated with maleness, offers a girl limited options. The fiction is repeated so frequently as to become reality: she can identify with boys—be "one of the guys"—or she can act in ways that boys find pleasing and desirable. If she's really clever, she can do both.

These options become most visible and disturbing to girls at early adolescence, when the force of the culture backs these choices and when girls' attempts to struggle and resist and live more complex lives draws public scrutiny and risks rejection from boys and girls alike. As Elizabeth Debold and her colleagues note, these are publicly sanctioned choices, the "paths of least resistance . . . well-trodden paths that women take into patriarchy. They require that a girl betray herself and her connections with women—but in different ways."[48] They are both "male definitions of the female self."[49] These choices make a girl vulnerable to invidious comparisons; each is a setup. If she tries to be one of the guys, as thirteen-year-old Jane explains, she comes off as "obnoxious and out of control," "too aggressive," "too tough," and "self-involved." If she tries too hard to be a girl guys want, she is, as thirteen-year-old Robin says, an "airhead," always "hee, hee, heeing," an "embarrassment to other girls," or she is, more simply, "a slut."[50] She is dismissed "as untrustworthy, weak, ridiculously prissy, and too nice."[51]

While she can attempt to gender pass—copying boys' behavior and endorsing boys' interests and values and judgments about girls—of course a girl can never really be a boy. Signs of her assertiveness, individuality, and competitiveness will be read differently and responded to differently—she's too bossy, rude, or mean. And by trying to be a girl boys desire, she can never really be or know herself. The competition with other girls and the potential for rejection is intense and requires a careful makeover. Both scenarios demand that she define herself in relation to an unattainable ideal and against herself and other girls. Both scenarios also set the stage for girlfighting, something all girls experience or witness in some form or another, at one developmental stage or another.

And so over time, with the help of media and sometimes family and school, and oftentimes peers, girls struggle with social stereotypes "and too often assimilate the pervasive belief that they are inferior."[52] Some take this realization out on themselves—eating disorders, self-mutilation, and depression, we know, are gendered maladies. Some take it out on other girls through fighting and ostracism; others idealize maleness and in the process disavow their entire gender, mirroring boys and men in their rejection of femininity, and by association, rejecting girls and women as weak and less important. Some bond with their close friends and reject the pressure and the ideals other girls embrace and embody. Competing with or rejecting girls becomes a way for a girl to separate, to distance herself from the inferior "others" unworthy of her friendship, adult approval, or male desire. In a culture that values masculinity and the characteristics that go with it, separating from other girls—separating from an inferior, weak femininity so incapable of attaining real power and control—is the way to gain the power of maleness for themselves.

In this way, social hierarchies and barriers to trust and loyalty among girls are formed early and nurtured over time. Since it is not "feminine" to openly want or claim power, the subterranean world of "good girls'" relationships is rife with competition that results in all kinds of painful and mean behavior experienced by girls and yet seen by no one. This is why girls are such a hard read, and why we dismiss girlfighting as irrational or mysterious. It is simply too dangerous to show your hand, to know what you know. Since "good girls" aren't supposed to say what they want, those who openly fight for power are, by definition, "bad girls" or "bitches"—girls who don't play by the "feminine" rules of relationships either because they are too much like boys or because they want boys too much.

Simply put, girls' treatment of other girls is too often a reflection of and a reaction to the way society sees and treats them. While we may not want to admit or even believe it, girls and women—by their association with conventional understandings of femininity—have less power and garner less respect in our culture. Their voices and concerns are less likely to be heard or taken seriously. Because the power they do have so often arises from qualities they either have little control over, don't earn, or openly disdain—their looks, their vulnerability, their accommodation to others' wants and needs, their feminine wiles—they too often take out their frustration and anger on each other. Girls and women derogate and judge and reject other girls and women for the same reasons they fear being derogated and judged and rejected—for not matching up to feminine ideals of beauty and behavior or for being brave enough not to care. Girls' meanness to other girls is a result of their struggle to make sense of or to reject their secondary status in the world and to find ways to have power and to experience feeling powerful.

This process of assimilation into and personal ownership of a culture that denigrates the feminine is referred to as internalized oppression—when those victimized by oppression and stereotypes assimilate the dominant views and "freely" control themselves and others like themselves. Then, as my colleague Sharon Barker says, "men don't have to put women down; they can always find another woman to do it for them." In a form of horizontal violence, girls take out their anxieties and fears about matching up to or resisting ideals of feminine beauty and behavior on each other.[53] They fight—exclude, tease, reject, and torment—other girls over things the dominant culture makes out to be very important, but in the grand scheme of things shouldn't matter that much—that is, how perfectly nice, thin, or pleasing a girl is.

In the most simplistic sense, this is the classic divide and conquer strategy—divert girls' attention from the real to the ideal; pit them against each other over trivial matters so they won't see the big picture—the institutional and cultural inequities, the societal control over women's bodies, the gendered nature of violence, abuse, and poverty. If we stay preoccupied with our own problems—and women's and teen magazines and a hugely profitable self-help book market assures us they are *our* problems—and with each other's faults, we won't notice that we are making $0.75 to the male dollar or that we carry the burden of poverty or that what matters most to human survival is secondary in a capitalist culture. If we believe we are the problem and take that out on each other we can pretty well assume nothing will change. If we don't trust each other, we won't talk. And if we don't talk, we won't put two and two together.

Such a climate of division and distrust among girls eventually undermines women's psychological strengths and their political potential. When girls internalize and unquestioningly accept the divisions we make in this culture between good girls and sluts, schoolgirls and airheads, nice girls and bitches, and when they betray other girls in order to be taken seriously or in the name of popularity, romance, and male attention, they perpetuate their own subordination, consolidate their secondary status, become complicit in their own oppression. Those girls who remain loyal and supportive of other girls resist these divisions in spite of the personal and social costs and, through their relationships and commitment to other girls, imagine other possibilities for success and collaboration.

So much of a woman's struggle to voice her thoughts and feelings, to engage in conflict and debate, to stand with other women, arises from the success or failure of her relationships with other girls in childhood—will she be punished, rejected, excluded, emotionally or physically hurt, or betrayed by other women, as she was by other girls, for speaking her thoughts and feelings, for questioning the way things "naturally" go? We need only to listen to the rhetoric of adult women's relationships and their public debates over what it means to be a good mother, a successful businesswoman, a "true" woman, or "real" feminist to understand the long-term implications of these early relationships. The pathways begun in childhood all too often consolidate and crystallize in ways that divide women and work against collective efforts toward social change.

Gender socialization as we do it in our culture prepares the ground for girlfighting. A girl of five is already well schooled in the cultural leitmotifs of girls' and women's social place in the world. By six, seven, and eight years old, she already looks to boys and men for acceptance and approval, even as she lives mostly in a social world of girls and women. By ten and eleven she may sacrifice other girls for success, popularity, and boyfriends or reject other girls as stupid and wussy. The evil thing is that too many of us are lulled into believing this must be so; convinced by sheer mind-numbing repetition of a particular social reality. We become comfortable. Change becomes threatening and difficult. We also become unimaginative and predictable and formulaic, like the many bad sitcoms we endure night after night.

That's why listening to the girls and women in this book is so important. Listening to them talk about their relationships with other girls, especially the often invisible struggle and hurt they experience, invokes the past and yet points to the possibility that history does not have to repeat itself. The fissures and fault lines girls identify can provide the information for new relational groundwork, for a different way of moving through the world, one where girls and women no longer live and enact old stories of deceit and mistrust and competition, but cross boundaries to provide one another with the psychological and social support necessary to demand they be taken seriously and treated fairly. Such a relational shift has both political and social ramifications. When we unravel the complicated nature of gender and power and desire so often at the base of girls' relational cruelty to other girls—when we alter the relational foundation this way—we prepare the ground for a generation of women comfortable with themselves, with their voices and their power, and capable of, indeed, passionate about, working together for social change.

In the next chapters I map girls' struggles to claim themselves, protect themselves, and reinvent themselves within and against the stories of femininity and womanhood they have inherited. That so much of their struggle takes the form of girls' misogynistic behavior toward other girls is both understandable and tragic. Girlfighting reveals a lot about the culture we live in and girls' desire to escape narrow and negative views of femininity. Because girlfighting is so often about keeping other girls—those who transgress or resist or defy categories—in line, it is fundamentally about maintaining the status quo. When girls go after other girls, a culture rife with sexism—and its relationship to other "isms"—and those who benefit from it are off the hook. Girls' preoccupation with the ways they and other girls look and speak and act siphons off the energy and creative power they need to form gender collectives, to reinvent current power arrangements, and ultimately to change the world in truly significant ways for all girls and women.

By unraveling the mystery of girls' and women's relational lives and revealing the corrosive impact of shallow and relentless messages about femininity, I tap the sources of girls' relational struggles with other girls. By following their voices developmentally, from childhood through adolescence, I reveal the slow evolution of a pattern of behavior that is damaging and divisive. By highlighting not only the hard parts, the misogyny and cruelty, but the places where girls resist and friendships between girls are good and healing, I seek to imagine how things might have been different for us and how we can make things different for our daughters. Only by ferreting out the cultural hand behind girls' "natural" behavior can we understand and maybe even forgive those girls who persecuted us (and ourselves for persecuting other girls), and move forward to create and support other realities for ourselves and the girls and women we love.

2

Good Girls and Real Boys

Preparing the Ground in Early Childhood

> Little girls are cute and small only to adults. To one another they are
> not cute. They are life-sized.   —Margaret Atwood, *Cat's Eye*

WHEN MY DAUGHTER MAYA was about three and a half, she announced that she wanted to be a boy. "Why?" I asked, scrambling for
trace memories of Freud's Oedipal complex. (Now how does it work for
girls?) "Because they're everywhere," she replied with the complete
and utter certainty of her age. We were looking at a *Sesame Street Parent's
Magazine*, and she began purposefully flipping through the pages,
pointing out characters and advertisements. "Boy, boy, boy," she began.
"Girl, girl, girl," I countered, although clearly she had me beat. Finally,
filled with an urgent need to prove her point, she turned to a "Got Milk"
ad—a full-page spread of a young actor in a resplendent white milk
mustache. "And him," she said. "I see him everywhere. What is he, a
country?"

The clarity of my daughter's observations caught me off guard. It
wasn't that she was so precocious—they were talking about countries
in her multiage Montessori class and what she took from that lesson
was simply that countries were really big. And it was not surprising
that, at three, she would be thinking about gender. This is the age when
kids first begin sorting through differences on all fronts, gender and
race included. What struck me most deeply was the way she had clas-
sified gender differences along power lines. She wanted to be a boy because she had noticed something special about boys—they were everywhere and they were bigger than life. In her concrete childhood terms,
she had named her social reality and also her own desire to be at the

center of a world in which boys occupy an inordinate amount of psy-chic freedom and physical space. Already, at three years old, with the help of *Sesame Street*, mind you, my daughter's attention was diverted away from herself and other girls and toward boys.

A few months later, in a brief, breathless pause from a competitive game of chase with my daughter, four-year-old Timothy, the son of one of my feminist friends, announced confidently that boys are better than girls. Anita and I stared at him in surprise; this proclamation was so completely out of character. Many, if not most, of Timothy's friends were girls and the classroom he shares with my daughter is about as good as it gets when it comes to equity issues. Anita kneeled down, held Timothy's shoulders, and looked her son in the eyes. "Do you really think you are better than Maya or Molly?" she asked him. "Well, no," he said, thoughtfully. "Do you think Mark is better than Lyn?" she asked, referring to my husband and me. "No," he said. "Do you think Daddy is better than Mommy?" she asked. "No," he said, with more certainty. "Well, then, that statement just doesn't hold true, does it?" "No, I guess not," Timothy agreed. And he was off; shrieks of laughter filled the air again. But somewhere, somehow, the seed had been planted, and the concern was written on Anita's face. "I don't know where he gets this," she lamented. "Not from me and he doesn't really watch much TV."

In spite of some truly admirable parental efforts, by ages three and four girls and boys already embody quite different social and relational histories, and the evidence suggests the chasm between them will only widen. Well before first grade, children begin to name power differ-ences between males and females in this culture, even if these differ-ences don't play out in any obvious way in their earliest friendships or their families. Girls at three and four years old already know that they need to speak to and resolve conflicts differently with boys than they do with other girls.[1] Their same expressions of strong feelings have already been labeled differently—boys are called assertive and competitive, girls bossy and confrontational. Children get the message. They pick up on the value judgments and it affects their feelings about themselves and their interactions with their friends.

My daughter and her friend Timothy both already know that "boys are better." No one had to tell them this directly. This is an assumption woven into the fabric of our culture and in their short lives they've got-ten this message in a multitude of ways. Both have been invited into a cultural story about gender that supports and gives explanatory power to this view. Young children live in the rich immediacy of the world and they are deeply affected by the messages they receive from the culture and the adults in their lives. My daughter echoes my words and ideas as well as those of her teacher, the older girl across the street, the guy at the local market. Phrases come out of her mouth that I've never heard in my life and it's not uncommon for her to say something to me with great certainty and then to ask me, in the next breath, "Mom, what does that even mean?"

Children take in not only the categories of male and female but also the feelings associated with them—the approval and support that comes when they voice or comply with good girl behavior, as well as the anxiety and fear they experience when they cross gender lines they didn't even know were there. They have to make sense out of the fact that most adults are invested in these gender categories to a greater or lesser degree and that signs of girls' self-assurance, assertiveness, and competitive nature are often labeled unfeminine and seem to bother people. Sometimes directly and sometimes subtly—by a reprimand, or a disapproving or surprised look—they are told to tone down their wild sides, to modulate their voices, to focus on "girl things" or maybe "boy things" but in a girl way. Relationally, they are told to work things out at all costs, not to be angry, not to speak bad thoughts or strong feelings. Just as five-year-olds learn not to respond to internal feelings of satiety when their parents push them to finish their plates every night at the dinner table,[2] girls learn gradually to override their strong feelings and thoughts when adults admonish them for wandering too far outside the lines of proper girl behavior.

GIRLS WILL BE GIRLS; GIRLS WILL BE BOYS

Young girls are drawn to the categories of male and female because we are a gender-saturated culture and we look at almost everything through this dichotomous boy-girl lens. *Toys R Us* has blue aisles and pink aisles. McDonald's has separate happy meal toys for boys and girls (something that frustrates my daughter no end since she always thinks the transformers, legos, and matchbox cars are a lot more fun than things like "Hello Kitty" stickers. We've taken to asking to see both toys before choosing.) TV commercials tout dolls in frilly clothes, diva dolls in sexy clothes, makeup, and jewelry sets for girls (the same old stuff now updated and labeled "girl power") and fast bicycles, power tools, and remote-controlled cars for boys (no need to call these "boy power"; that's a given). Children are learning how to name the world, and the world they are naming is drenched in stereotypes. In fact, if we want to appreciate the narrow conventions of our cultural imagination in their rawest form, we need only listen to young children categorize boy and girl "stuff." Five-, six-, and seven-year-old girls, both working and middle class, tell me in no uncertain terms that girls have long hair; that only girls can wear dresses, play with Barbies, or stuffed animals; that "girls like flowers" and "they like to stay calm sometimes," and that "girls can be pretty." Boys, on the other hand, "have to be handsome," not pretty. They have "short hair." They "like all sports" and "trucks" and are "wild" and "so rowdy." They "like fighting," "just hate makeup," and "get to wear pants all the time, unless," as seven-year-old Kaitlin says, invoking her family's heritage, "you're in Scotland with one of those skirts."

Girls explain that girls and boys are defined by their difference from each other—not only how they look, but what and where they play. For the most part, "boys play in one place and girls play in the other," explains Rachel. The worst thing she can imagine about being a boy is "playing with the girls" and the best thing she can imagine about being a girl is that you "don't play with boys." "Girls wear bows in their hair," Casey, six, explains, "and boys wear bows on their necks." Moreover, girls' sense of goodness, as distinct from boys', is characterized by their restraint in relationships and their ability to control themselves. "Girls are kind of better," seven-year-old Donna says, because they're "nicer than the boys. They're quiet. We ain't stomping around and everything like that, yelling."

Repetition ensures that these cultural categories are firm and clear. Girls are still more likely to be rewarded for not "stomping around," while our dominant cultural story of success revolves around active movement and risk taking. We've seen how the media centers boys' interests and activities. When an ad for Sunlight laundry detergent announces: "Today's lesson: girls aren't totally gross," it's clear who's speaking and what's valued. The little girl holding the frog is impressive to the boy watching because she's doing a boy thing. She's now what, only a little gross? But such denigration and marginalizing of girls doesn't happen just in the media. Because boys tend to lag behind girls in reading, educators admit that given the choice between a feminine-themed book and a masculine one, they will choose the masculine-themed book. They know girls are less discriminating of the gender of the protagonist or the themes. As one professor of education put it: "Boys read *Little Women*? I don't think so." But of course girls are encouraged to read *Harry Potter*.[3]

In this ongoing climate it's not surprising that, to six-year-old Jessica, being a boy simply means "you can do more stuff." "Once when we played with some boys and we were penguins and they were killer whales and they chased us," she says, explaining how the boys take over the playground. Elizabeth, her classmate, echoes this sentiment as she describes her desire to play baseball: "I asked [the boys] if I could play . . . and they said no, they had only boys on their team." Being a six-year-old girl, she says, means "you don't get included in most sports." Five-year-old Rachel knows how things go and uses what she knows to deal with her friends. When they are mean to her, she threatens to tell their fathers: "I tell them to be good or I'll tell your daddy," she says. "He's the boss. All the fathers are the bosses of their houses."

It's unnerving to hear such statements at this historical moment, when girls are participating in sports at unprecedented levels and when mothers are working outside the home, expecting and receiving more equity in their work and family lives. Indeed, things are not always what they appear to be. Girls make these proclamations with great certainty even as they openly contradict such sentiments in their own lives. Most have good friends, even best friends, who are boys. "I hate wearing dresses!" the girls admit. "I don't really play with Barbies much," and "I like to play basketball and sometimes baseball." In fact, many of the girls aspire to become like those they know who have the most power and the most fun. "I want to be a wrestler, like my Uncle Brian," says Jasmine. "I want to be a snowman builder," says Anika; "a basketball teacher," says Julie. While they say girls are gentle and boys are rough, these girls—so quick to repeat the stereotypes—are clearly both. In fact, so are the boys. While they describe boys as "wild" and "tough," they admit that the boys they play with sometimes like dolls and sometimes Barbie and sometimes flowers. Like a mantra, the girls chant gender rules and codes to their interviewers and in the next breath disrupt these rules with their own experiences, desires, and aspirations. In spite of the relentless public story of real boys and good girls, young girls' own lives are much more complicated and nuanced. These girls know what they want, but they also know how to voice-over their experiences to fit expectations, please adults, and perform as the right kind of girl.

Developmentally, the concrete nature of childhood thinking protects girls from being confused by such differences between the real and the ideal. Children don't have the complex thinking skills that would allow them to see or worry about the contradictions so apparent to adults. This is, in part, the explanation for young girls' healthy resistance to the narrow expectations and ideals of femininity.[4] There is a girl's experience and then there is the cultural "voice-over" of her experience, and a young girl, while she may hear what adults are saying and expecting, has no inner compulsion to integrate or resolve the contradictions between them. They simply coexist. While she may learn to lower her voice in the presence of adults, or attend to her relationships ever more closely to bask in adult adulation, or maybe just to figure out what the heck all the fuss is about, she still fights with her friends, argues about the rules, blows milk through her nose, and jumps on the couch. This is the geography of young girls' relationships: a sense of entitlement and access to the full range of feelings, both good and bad, pressure from adults and from the media to narrow those feelings to fit whatever notions of girlhood are expected, a preoccupation with what makes boys boys and girls girls, and a growing awareness of boys' power to command attention and take up space—all coexisting in a life lived intensely in the present. To adults this can seem fragmented and impossible to hold together. To a child it's life as usual. In fact, this piecing together of their experiences gives young girls' relationships a wonderfully inventive quality and a sense that all things are possible.

Indeed, girls are unapologetically drawn to the physical power boys are allowed to display. A mother laughingly tells me that her four-year-old daughter explained to her just how things would be "when I grow up to be a man." Seven-year-old Janie always takes on the boys' parts in fantasy play with her girlfriends. She'd rather play the evil male role than be a girl character. When she's asked why, Janie is baffled by the question. "Boys get to do all the exciting things, like race car driving," she says with certainty. Her girlfriends try to talk her out of her choices. "Girls can be anything too," they say, repeating what their parents tell them. Janie's parents tell her this too, but she's not convinced. She's an astute observer of the world around her. The token girl or woman she sees doing what are more typically exciting male activities does not fool her. She wants to be at the heart of things. Using the phrase to her full advantage, Janie decides that if a girl can be anything, then she'll just be a boy.

It's understandable that girls would be drawn to experiences that offer them power. Power is exhilarating and liberating. It can come from being a responsive and compassionate person or it can come from intellectually or physically pushing the limits or both. The problem is that we place these human qualities in opposition, culturally sanction one or the other by assigning it a gender and color-coding it, and then, often in the guise of cuteness or humor, denigrate or trivialize one gender and praise and reward the other. It only makes sense that girls would pick up on this difference and that it would affect their feelings about themselves and about other girls. While some girls wholly embrace the cultural story of femininity, others actively work to reject it and the girls who embrace it. "We don't like to play with Sunny," Emily says. "She's too girly."

So here it begins. Our cultural obsession with gender differences and with "opposite sides" combined with the centering or valuing of experiences associated with maleness begins to affect what and who girls really value and want to please, and this sets the stage for girl-fighting.[5] The larger point here is that girls' friendships (and boys', for that matter) too often rest on and derive meaning from gender roles and stereotypes that are anemic, out of relationship to the complexity of their lives, and that work against their best interests. Girls are not just "being girls" when they exclude other girls because they're not nice or too bossy; they are responding in the best way they can to voices in their social environment—voices of teachers and parents and the media that override or pull them away from this complexity and give their social reality an order of a particular kind. While adults often disagree with each other and even with the media, the repetition of one public version of femininity has a considerable effect on how girls size up other girls and how they treat them.

On the one hand, we can celebrate the fact that girls can be "girls" *and* girls can be "boys." In fact, many parents of sons wish for such freedom for their boys. But the girls themselves point out the problem. Girls who want to be boys—or want to have the power and freedom boys have—pick up more than skills. Because the boy role is defined by and gains power through its opposition to and denigration and rejection of the girl role ("girls are gross"), girls pick up value judgments about other girls that are deeply divisive.

PRINCE CHARMING

At the heart of such divisiveness is the romance story. One way we ensure that boy and girl roles remain distinct and that male behavior remains central is by promoting traditional assumptions and views about romance. Whether girls and boys are friends, whether boys tease girls or girls chase boys, adults cannot seem to hold back their compulsion to overlay future romance on these relationships. When my daughter was just born, a friend, whose son was but six months old, giggled with delight that "maybe someday they will get married." This jives with the equally compulsive pairing of girls and boys in cartoons, movies, and stories aimed at the youngest children. Whether it's Sally and Linus, Mickey and Minnie, Dennis and Margaret, whoever and Prince Charming, girls and boys are romantically paired early and relentlessly. Not surprisingly, then, many of the seven- and eight-year-olds I listened to already had boyfriends and ideas about love and romance that mirrored this wider culture.

For these young girls romance is strictly heterosexual: Seven-year-old Kaitlin, who has a boyfriend, is already absolutely certain that "You can have a boyfriend, you can't have a girlfriend. You can have a friend that's a girl, but you can't have a girlfriend, but you can have a boyfriend though. . . . You can't be in love with a girl. . . . You can love her, but—you can care about her, but you can't *love*, love her." This compulsive attention to heterosexuality starts to constrain and channel girls' feelings toward other girls long before romance or sexuality have any real significance. Real love, *love* love, is reserved for boys only. The overall message girls receive is that boys are central; the love or attention of other girls is, by comparison, secondary.

Romance is not only about boys, it's about certain kinds of boys— "real boys," boys who are on the opposite end of the gender spectrum from girls. Kaitlin tells me that she is not interested in "one of those calmed-down boys . . . who likes to play with Barbie." Her boyfriend, by contrast, is "funny" and "wild." Part of his boyness seems to be that he gets in "bad moods" and he's "grumpy." To Kaitlin he is unreadable and inaccessible a lot of the time. "I'll say, 'Why are you in a bad mood?' and . . . he had no reason to be in a bad mood. He was just in a bad mood." In the face of his silence and disinterest, like Belle in Disney's *Beauty and the Beast*, Kaitlin seeks him out and pushes him to open up and say what's wrong. The reason for Kaitlin to have a boyfriend, it seems, as distinct from friends who are boys, is to practice her role in the romance story: pulling out the emotion in a distant, unreadable, and moody boy.

For Kaitlin and other girls her age, there is a connection between their romantic interest in boys and boys' emotional and physical elusiveness. In fact, the girls enjoy the game. "We always call Jimmy a bad boy," Jessica giggles, describing the pleasure she takes in chasing Jimmy and trying to kiss him. "We just like to make fun." Romance is connected to pursuing and being pursued and these girls like to do both. The problem is that the chasing game often depends on tacit knowledge of girls' inferiority. It is one of those rituals that sociologist Barrie Thorne observes designate girls as pollutants. Boys run from girls because girls are icky, they have "cooties," they threaten to give you "girl stain." While the girls feel quite powerful in their ability to make the boys run away, the result can be painful and confusing, precisely because the boys are playing a different game, with different rules. Romance is the last thing on their minds.

Seven-year-old Jessica, her long bangs filtering my view of her dark flashing eyes, describes a typical "romantic" scene of girl chasing boy: "And like yesterday, I was chasing Tyler and he, um, caught me by the stomach and lifted me up and squeezed my stomach so hard and it hurted yesterday and now it hurts now." For too many of these young girls, "romantic" pursuit of boys is connected to being physically hurt. Indeed, without the adult or cultural overlay of romance, these games might simply be about strength, courage, and competition among children, male or female—that is, who can run the fastest, get to the top of the hill first, and stay there. But with the frustratingly familiar adage, "If a boy chases, teases, or hits you, it's because he likes you," adults offer an explanation for violence that's tied to relationships with boys, even if a boy never sees it this way.

Seven-year-old Melissa knows this adage by heart. As she struggled during our conversation to understand the fact that her "boyfriend," Donald, someone "who be's, um, nice to me," would also call her names and even hit her, she suddenly remembered, with delight, her grandfather's assurance that "if boys chase you then that means that they love you." In truth, Donald and Melissa have a complicated relationship. At her school I saw them everywhere together—in line for lunch, on the playground; Donald, in jeans and a T-shirt, poking and kicking out at invisible foes; Melissa following him in her smudged homemade Laura Ashley–style dress, baggy white tights, and scuffed shoes. In his interview, even when asked directly about girls he knew, Donald did not mention Melissa by name. Melissa, on the other hand, talked about Donald all the time:

> In school do you ever just get mad about things?
> Every day.
> Every day? About what?
> Some part of every day, 'cause of Donald. That one!
> What makes you mad about Donald?
> He says swear words, and sometimes he punches me and he
>   pushes me and all them other mean things.
> Mmm. Why does he do that?
> I don't know. He's just a mean person.
> And what do you do? What do you say to him?
> "Stop it, I don't like it. . . . Please leave me alone."

After a time, Donald resurfaces in Melissa's interview, but now as the boy who "loves" her. And again later, when asked to tell about one of her friends, Melissa chooses Donald:

> Donald? Tell me about Donald.
> He says swear words; he be's mean, but he only does it to show
>   people up.
> And why do you think he wants to show people up?
> I don't know.
> What is it that you like about Donald?
> He be's, um, nice to me.
> He's nice to you?
> A little.
> A little? Sounds like sometimes he isn't and sometimes he is?

Melissa is annoyed by my last question. She knows this about Donald, but can't explain his behavior. "I can't read his mind!" she exclaims to me. But she knows he loves her. Indeed, she is certain that if someone treated her badly, Donald could be called upon to protect her, to "pay them back." "Guess what Poppa says?" she asks me. "If the boys chase you then that means that they love you." "Hm," I respond. "What do you think about that?" "Weird," Melissa admits.

It's disturbing to hear the degree to which connections between romance and violence are already entwined in young children's friendships. And I found myself taken with Melissa's complicated response to Donald. To Melissa, Donald is boyfriend, protector, and harasser; she expresses her anger at his meanness even as she professes her love and dependence on him. While at seven, Melissa names her different feelings and responses to Donald; while she tells him directly to "stop it, I don't like it," and even calls her grandfather's advice "weird," such views of romance, so well supported by the media and the adults in kids' lives, threaten to voice-over this complexity and call the whole contradictory thing "love."

Girls learn from the media and sometimes from adults that they should be preoccupied with what boys think of them (even though in real life boys this age aren't thinking about them all that much, which of course reflects the power imbalance.) This means figuring out the mystery of boys' feelings and behaviors and giving boys' desires and their elusiveness particular significance. If being with boys means either being like a boy—giving up less important "girl" things in order to play what the boys want to play—or hanging with girls, but being the kind of girl a boy might someday choose as a romantic partner, then girls' desires and experiences are secondary.

At the most basic level, boys and girls absorb the message that they can't be just friends—we've told them so often and in so many ways that they are too different. If girls play with their friends who are boys, they almost always agree to play sports or other physical activities with them. It's just much riskier for boys to play dolls or dress-up than for the girls to play basketball or space aliens. Within the category "girl" there is room for the tomboy—the sports-minded, competitive girl, and so it is easier for the girls to move into boy territory, to give up what they might want in order to relieve boys of the relentless pressure they feel to live by the boy code.[6] But boys pull away from girls for their own reasons—too much is at stake, especially for the boy who feels pressure to be a "real" boy uncontaminated by girls and girl stuff. In the traditional romance story overlaid on girl-boy relationships, such male reluctance can be explained and overcome if only a girl will try harder and give up more.

Deeply held views about gender and romantic intentions overlaid by the media and adults thus turn girl-boy friendships into something they are not, so that genuine friendship in which one can express feelings and engage in a range of activities becomes girl-only territory. The irony, then, is that this apparent all-girl territory so many psychologists tout as "the wonder of girls"[7] is defined from the very beginning by its difference from boy territory, from the power boys have in the physical world and by its relationship to the larger cultural story of romance and desire for boys' attention. This means that girls' friendships with other girls, as wonderful as they can be and as important as they are, will be measured time and again against two prevailing ideals—being like boys or being liked by boys; being girls who do what boys do or being girls boys want. As these two culturally sanctioned choices become more defined and encouraged, betrayal and competition, rejection and exclusion will be focused on those girls who challenge these pathways or threaten a girl's status and power by being a better, more successful traveler on one road or the other.

VOICE TRAINING FOR FRIENDSHIP

If a cultural story about boys' power and girls' subordination is at the heart of girlfighting, as I think it is, we should begin to hear the rumblings of trouble in the youngest girls' stories of friendship. Because girls exude a bold, assertive, and entitled sense of themselves, a finely tuned sense of justice, and a tendency to "speak their minds with all their hearts,"[8] they receive a lot of instruction or voice training from significant adults in their lives, as well as from the culture in the form of the media, about the ways good girls or nice girls *should* speak and should sound.[9]

Girls as young as three and four years old develop ingenious ways to respond to such instruction. For example, sociolinguist Amy Sheldon finds that girls develop a "double voiced discourse" to resolve their arguments and conflicts. This allows them to balance their own needs with cultural voice-overs that tell them good girls should be caring and put others first. Sheldon illustrates the creative tendencies common among young girls when she records a conflict over a plastic toy pickle between two four-year-olds. It's worth noting that this short exchange is excerpted from pages and pages of conflict—the girls spend a lot of time working this one out. They do not give up easily.

SUE: Lisa wants it! (the pickle)
MARY: I cut it in half, one for Lisa, one for me, one for me.
SUE: But Lisa wants the WHOLE pickle!
MARY: Well, it's a whole HALF pickle.
SUE: No it isn't.
MARY: Yes it is, a whole HALF pickle
SUE: I'LL give her a whole half. I'LL give her a WHOLE
   WHOLE! I gave her a WHOLE one.[10]

Both Mary and Sue insist on their own positions, illustrating that sense of unapologetic entitlement of young girls. Each is also responsive to the other in ways that open the door to new possibilities—if one could just change perspective, a half pickle could be a whole and everyone could get what she wanted. Mary and Sue stay with the battle, each asserting her wants for so long that we almost forget that the point of the conflict is to appease another girl, Lisa. While they are both strong-willed and forceful persuaders, the girls' solution is relational and inventive because they have already gotten the message that, as Sheldon notes, "conflict must be resolved, but a girl cannot assert social power or superiority as an individual to resolve it."[11] The girls already know that they can't just assume a dominant position, grab the pickle, and give it to Lisa. That would be mean.

   This is a lesson girls learn early and learn well. Four- and five-year-olds matter-of-factly name the reality of their friendships in ways that are shockingly frank and direct, at least from an adult perspective. When her friends don't give her anything to play with, five-year-old Rachel says nonchalantly, "I just say to them that they are not being a friend to me." When Jessie threatens to go home because her friends are not including her, one friend says, "just go home." Explaining why she and her friend are fighting, Jasmine says, "I said she was a bad person. . . . She got really mad." "We get mad. I get mad," Donna says, thinking about a time she fought with her friend. "She said, I hate you, that one time." Describing her problems with her best friend, Tremaine says, "She's mean to me. I do mean stuff to her too. Like we push each other and stuff . . . 'cause we get angry, we get so mad."

   But even as they fight openly with their friends, admit their anger, own up to their pushing and shoving, girls are tuning in to the reactions of adults to their conflicts, to their open confessions of meanness, to their feelings of anger and sadness. Friends shouldn't fight, eight-year-old Elizabeth explains, not because fighting is wrong or someone could get hurt, but "because the teacher might hear them and then she might get mad at them." Adults are watching. Girls thus learn to balance their needs and desires with expectations that they should be nice and good and cooperative. This capacity is a strength of young girls' relationships—most of us would agree that creating a "whole half pickle" is better than just grabbing it. The problem is when they are so encouraged to get along and give up their own needs that they feel they must maneuver below adults' radar to get them met.

This disapproval of disagreement and squelching of conflict by adults is important because it begins to set the tone for girlfighting. Feeling anger and the desire to aggress, as the psychologist Sharon Lamb says, are part of being human.[12] Girls fight, they disagree with each other, they compete. But if they get the message that such human emotions and reactions are wrong or forbidden, they simply do them in private—they move their strong feelings underground or their behavior out of adults' sight. Listening to groups of three- and four-year-old girls arguing, for example, Sheldon notes that as conflict escalates, the girls' voices get softer, not louder. Sheldon reports on two four-year-olds, Arlene and Elaine, pretending they are nurses caring for their sick children and fighting over who gets to give the shots to the children and where:

> Arlene persists; she intensely, directly, and threateningly orders Elaine to stop: *Now don't you dare!* Arlene doesn't shout but instead mutes her voice by lowering it. As the confrontation reaches its peak of insistence, the girls' voices get lower and lower with anger, not louder and louder. . . . Elaine directly orders Arlene in an even lower voice:
> ELAINE: (voice lowered more that Arlene's but equally intense) Stop saying that! (pause) Well, then you can't come to my birthday party!
> ARLENE: (voice still lowered) I don't want to come to your birthday party.[13]

Other researchers in psychology find that girls this age are more likely to "relationally victimize" their peers than are boys.[14] This means that girls learn early to use covert tactics like threatening to damage or control a girl's relationships with others or to ignore or exclude someone they are angry with. While we associate gossip with older girls, preschoolers already use gossip to build a sense of solidarity with their girlfriends and to set up "we against others" scenarios. "Go! We want her to go away!" one girl says to another. "We don't want Alison here to bother us again," her friend agrees. "We're very mad at her," says one. "We are very mad," agrees the other.[15] The ultimate threat when a young girl feels the wrath of another girl is not being yelled at or hit, but excluded: "You can't come to my birthday party."

In this way, adults' expectations that girls be nice and cooperative and avoid loud conflicts becomes a kind of voice training for friendship and sets the stage for a more opaque, but no less aggressive, form of girlfighting. Girls become more attentive to behaviors that involve the manipulation of relationships.[16] Exclusion becomes a huge issue for the youngest girls. It is the preferred strategy for expressing anger with other girls because it is an acceptably quiet, appropriately feminine way to resolve conflict, to assert your feelings and keep other girls in line. That is, it doesn't attract the attention, and therefore, the judgment and ire of adults that open arguing and fighting do. And the irony of course is that for those socialized to care about relationships, exclusion is the cruelest punishment. Even preschool girls know the dangers of social ostracism and they engage in protracted power struggles over inclusion. In connection with their pretend play, some preschool girls are already skillful in verbally engineering the ostracism of other girls and some have learned to resist being ostracized or left out by making themselves socially desirable—that is, by being especially good at appearing nice.[17]

This is the early form of what psychologists call "relational aggression," a kind of aggression more typical of and more stressful to girls than to boys. Relational aggression is often indirect and thus difficult to prove. Because open conflict and competition are taboo for "nice girls," girls simply find creative ways to disguise their disagreements and conflicts. Even girls as young as three and four learn that their best recourse when they are frustrated or angry or when they feel competitive or jealous is to rely on subtle, relational forms of controlling others—at least when adults are around.

What we might think of as fickleness in girls' friendships is often, in fact, a sign of the double-voice discourse Sheldon talks about—the effort by girls to get what they need and also to respond to another's needs. And, like snowflakes, no two relationships are alike. Indeed, the cultural and relational contexts of girls' relationships can have a profound effect on the ways girls negotiate and balance their friendships. Much of the work on relational aggression and conflict negotiation has been done on white and middle-class girls. We have every reason to suspect that working-class girls and girls of color get different feedback about conflict and the acceptability of their direct expressions of anger in their homes. Growing up working class, direct expressions of anger were pretty much normal in my house. I felt the pressure to tone down my voice and to take my strong feelings underground only when I began attending school.

So even while girls talk openly about being hurt, feeling sad and angry, they know they are less likely to attract attention or cause trouble if they exclude others rather than express their anger more directly and openly. In the midst of such covert threats of exclusion, rejection, or withdrawal, girls learn to read the social world of their friendships and peer relationships like naturalists.[18] If you can't decide whether a girl is nice or not, seven-year-old Cloe suggests that you "watch how she acts to other people." Girls pick up nuance and learn how to read the subtly encoded messages contained in their friends' sharp looks and turned bodies, their raised eyebrows and supportive glances. Young girls are building a repertoire of relational experiences and hoarding a wealth of information about how to get their point across to each other without attracting the negative attention of adults or incurring the wrath—the rejection and teasing—of other girls.

This practice accounts for the off-again, on-again quality of girls' relationships, the ebb and flow as girls fight and make up on a daily basis. "Who's your best friend?" I ask Madison. "Sometimes it's Tara, sometimes it's Nicole, and then it's Chelsea," she responds. "Sometimes I get in a fight with, like, one of them, so those two are my best friends. And then I get in a fight with two of them, so that person's my best friend. Sometimes I get in a fight with all of them, so I need to choose new ones right now. . . . I suppose I could go make up with one of 'em so I'd have at least one." It's pretty typical to hear a five-year-old yell to her friend at the top of her lungs, "You aren't my friend anymore. I hate you!" in one instant, and to hear peals of hysterical laughter the next.

In spite of their apparent off-again, on-again quality, young girls' relationships have staying power. Girls can fight and make up, fight and make up because they know their friends will be there the next day. They are practicing, discovering their persuasive power, exploring the range of acceptable emotions and the possibilities in their friendships as well as finding ways to be "good girls" who can also express "bad" feelings and desires. But if the adults in a girl's life and, through the media, the weight of the culture, define good girlness as a certain way of talking and being and looking, she is going to learn what not to say and hide the parts of herself and her relationships that don't match up. This struggle to match up is likely to be played out with her girlfriends, not only because they are going through the same thing, but because she will be caught in the throes of comparison with them.

Differences and disagreements are part and parcel of everyday life for six- and seven-year-old girls. Friends fight, they say, "'cause they see things different," because "they think different," because "we're not all the same. Every person is not the same." Fighting between friends happens but such fighting doesn't negate love, anger doesn't override joy. But it's important to appreciate the impact of messages repeated to girls over and over again about what it means to be a good girl—nice, kind, sweet, attentive to others, calm, and cooperative. Because conflict *is* a problem for most adults, girls hear the party line over and over: "communicating is better than fighting," "be nice," "don't make anyone mad," "don't make a ruckus or a mess of things." We begin to hear the results of this repetition when girls translate differences and nuanced feelings into gendered notions of "nice" and "mean," "good" and "bad," and when the voice-overs or cultural stories about nice girls start to mute girls' realities. Talking about her best friend, six-year-old Barbara sighs as she explains how Rachel's "a friend to everybody." "That's pretty nice," her interviewer comments, "to have people that are friends to everybody." "Yeah," Barbara responds wistfully. "But Rachel never sits beside me. . . . She don't like to." This difference between the ideal Rachel who's a friend to everybody and the real Rachel who isn't a friend to Barbara may coexist now, but when the nice or ideal girl story gains enough weight and power, Barbara may start to lose track of her reality or blame herself for being less than ideal.

This is the voice training for girls' friendship, the voice over their voice.[19] The irony is obvious. First we tell girls to attend to relationships, and then we expect them to take their own strong feelings out of relationships to protect the feelings of others or to maintain a cover story of girls as nice and "friends to everybody."[20] We ask them, in this sense, to work at relationships that do not feel authentic or real to them. Relationships, friendships, they learn, are not simply what people experience together, alive and inventive as they feel, but something else—

something that conforms to adult expectations, something that reflects the dominant cultural view of what a good girl should be.

When adults voice-over girls' voices with platitudes and stereo- types, things can get strangely discordant. Girls begin not to trust their strong feelings or to feel ashamed for having them. For example, while it's true that "it's good to say you're sorry," or to "always share," when such advice is given without appreciation for the specific context or re- lational scene it can also be dangerous and disingenuous. Is it good to say you're sorry when you have been treated badly or unfairly? Is it good to share when you had something first and someone else de- mands it? Is there never a time to question or disrupt the ways things go? The danger of such gendered platitudes as be nice and kind, sweet and apologetic, is that they so often challenge a girl's reality and she be- comes confused about what she really feels and what a real relationship is. In this light, the word friendship is too often applied to something that doesn't feel like real friendship, precisely because the thing called friendship is contingent on not fighting and not being mad and not making too much noise. That is, you can't be in a truly genuine rela- tionship when you are not allowed to have or express common human feelings. Instead, girls are so often taught that friendship is a relation- ship where everyone is always responsive and everybody is always happy and everybody signs their letters with love or dots their I's with hearts—even when they don't feel like it.

POLICING RELATIONSHIPS

The areas where young girls feel the greatest pressure to act in certain ways in order to be liked and included and desired become the very areas in which they begin to police and fight with other girls. That is, girls become relational traffic cops, maintaining order, ensuring that so- cial rules and regulations are obeyed, and preventing other girls from transgressing the good girl code they are led to believe is so important to maintain. With the growing pressure to be a good girl, a model girl, however that is defined in their families and communities, comes the anxiety of failure, of not matching up.

Five-year-old Harriet, watching a video of her swimming class, comments not on the skills she had just displayed, but on her stocky friend: "Deidre looks fat." When a friend, Jane, asked Anneliese in

private whether she thought another classmate, Carrie, was fat, An-
naliese was bewildered. When she didn't immediately respond, Jane
encouraged her: "It's okay, Carrie says she's fat all the time. Tell me
what you think—pinky swear, I won't tell Carrie." When Anneliese said
then, yes, she thought Carrie was fat, Jane immediately ran over to Carrie to tell her what Anneliese thought of her.

These comments and interactions are about much more than
weight, but given the emphasis we place on girls' bodies and the importance of being thin, it's not surprising that this would be the way
girls express their insecurities, desire for attention and approval, and
their anger. Girls carry these anxieties and feelings into their relationships, in part because it's easier to see and name the failure in someone
else than in oneself and because it is profitable to do so—it elevates
one's own status. This is what girls are after when they report other girls
to their parents or teachers: "Mia just told me I couldn't play with her";
"Lori is being mean to ReAnn"; "Tiana won't share her toys with me."
Girls tell on other girls not only to receive fairness, but to receive adult
approval and love for being a different kind of girl—the kind of girl
who is inclusive, nice, neat, who shares; the kind of girl who matches
up to the adult's ideal. Reporting other girls' bad behavior provides a
sense of personal power that comes from being the right kind of girl, the
socially desirable girl.

Listening to girls talk about who they are and are not friends with
and which girls are bad or mean, conjures up an image that's awfully
familiar: an image of white middle-class femininity. Indeed, this is a
process of enculturation. It is thus easy to imagine the girls who do not
match up—working-class girls and girls of color who may have different definitions of what it means to be a good girl or to be feminine, or
white middle-class girls who have been encouraged to resist such a limited view of "good girl" behavior or appearance—who "brag" or talk
too much about what they are good at, who are fat, who are "bossy,"
tough, or too assertive in their relationships.

Renee, who is African American, remembers how hard it was for
her biracial daughter, Domonique, to be in a mostly white public school.
When she was seven Domonique would come home crying, because
the other girls "would ostracize her, they wouldn't play with her. She
would come home just getting in my arms crying every day. She had di-
arrhea; she was really upset." While Renee would say to Domonique,

"You've got to stand up for yourself," she knew in her heart that it was more complicated.

> She's a little girl. And she wants friends and she wants to be happy, you know. To have people be so mean and turn their backs on you, it's just not okay. It was mostly white kids, and I found it was the little white girls that I just wanted to strangle because they'd be like, "Well, I'll be your friend from 10 to 2." I'm like, excuse me? From 10 A.M. to 2 they'd be your friend and then afterwards they wouldn't? I'm like, I don't think so, that's not what a true friend is. Or they'd come to Domonique's house and [say], "I'll stay your friend if you give me this or give me that." And I'm like, uh, uh. I prayed my daughter knew not to be so shallow. Over the years she hasn't let herself down.

The ways girls deal with conflict and difference are rooted in gendered and racialized patterns taught by and modeled on their parents.[21] Domonique's "friends" were negotiating their power in the ways white middle-class girls are taught; they subtly and indirectly set the terms for social ostracism. They were asserting their power by carefully negotiating the terms of access and inclusion. To Domonique, caught in a mostly white school context, it's a cruel and chilling experience. She is reminded through exclusion and offers of friendship carefully meted out in timed chunks, of the power and status of the other girls.

Renee thinks that Domonique was punished by the white girls and also by her white teachers because she wasn't "a cookie cutter student and I'm not a cookie cutter parent." Renee was direct in ways that made the white women teachers and administrators in the school anxious: "If I think you're wrong I'm going to tell you. And get used to it." As a result, "they all just kept saying that Domonique thought she was special and this, that, and the other." In other words, neither Renee nor Domonique fit the white version of nice and good. Both were too full of themselves, too confident, too direct and bold. They needed to be shown their place, taken down a notch, but in a "nice" way.

"Cookie cutter" is Renee's code for white and middle class. White and middle-class femininity is defined by conflict-avoidance, by "niceness"—although as we can clearly see, white girls can be as mean and nasty as anyone, maybe more so because of the pressure to appear so nice on the surface. Girlfriends are chosen because they are "nice," by which girls mean "they help me," "they play with me," they "say 'I like you.'" On the other hand, girls who are not nice "tattle-tale on people," "push and shove," they brag, or they are "real mean," or they boss other girls around. This makes perfect sense at first glance—of course girls prefer a friend who says "I like you" to someone who "pushes and shoves" or is "real mean." But the problem comes when such girls label any outspokenness as "mean" or signs of self-confidence as "bossy" or when they buy into a definition of relationship that has more to do with ideals or expectations than genuine human connection.

Because so much value is placed on being nice by the adults who educate girls, this word becomes, for white girls in particular, a power word, a code word for those who most closely approximate a cultural ideal, and thus niceness becomes a means to judge all girls against a rather narrow standard. In this way being nice picks up and contains all that is associated with being an acceptable or good girl in the dominant culture. As a result, it is a prime motivator for relational aggression. In our interviews with seven- and eight-year-olds, Carol Gilligan and I found that girls used "niceness" to judge the overall quality or goodness of other girls. It becomes a reason for liking or not liking, inclusion or exclusion, and thus threats of not being nice become a form of social control.[22] And while white middle-class girls are more likely to internalize this term and judge themselves against it, girls of color and working-class girls who are raised or schooled in predominantly white contexts learn its power, learn to perform niceness for the right people or pay the price.[23]

But as we have seen, while girls may perform or tout the absolute value of niceness, they do not always feel nice or act nice in their relationships. What's striking in listening to seven- and eight-year-olds talk about disagreements between friends is that they seesaw between the ideal of niceness—that voice over their voice that says, in Faye's words, "everybody should like everybody else"—and the real activity of their relationships—the fact that, in life people have "different opinions," that fights break out because "sometimes people don't like your opinions" and "try to have their own way." After all, says Claire, explaining why two friends might have different feelings about another girl, "different people like different things than other people do. Like you can't just say, you probably like her, too, just because I like her." Jane agrees, "You can't like everyone. Some people like some people, and some people don't like some people, and . . . I don't know anything else."

While the girls seem pretty comfortable with both truths and, as Gillian adds, people can disagree "because it's a free world!" it becomes harder and harder for girls to admit the not so nice parts of themselves or to stay with themselves if they have less than always nice and kind feelings. If a girl was mean, Andrea admits, she "probably wouldn't admit that she was mean." While the girls often tell it like it is—say what they like and don't like in their relationships—it becomes tougher to own and stay with that knowledge. While Dana admits, "I like friendship a lot, but, well, there are some people I don't like," she risks being called mean if she says so to the wrong person.

Repeatedly, the white girls I've listened to say that admitting they dislike a person is the same as calling that person mean, and to call a person mean is itself a sign of meanness. Being mean is about being too self-centered or "selfish." And since "it's better to be nice than not nice" because "you get more friends and relationships," the choice is clear. But just as the "Just say no!" drug campaign is grossly simplistic and effaces the different pressures and realities of kids' lives, the mantra "just be nice" serves to override the complexity of girls' thoughts and feelings, the reality of difference, and the hard work of relationships.

When she was three my daughter would say, "Let's play. You be bossy and I'll be sassy." At five she told me she was worried about bossing or bragging too much because other girls wouldn't like her, they would think she was not nice. Here again is a most common usage of the word nice: to control other girls. A girl who knows and talks about what she is good at is at odds with what a nice girl ought to be—self-effacing and concerned for others—and so other girls are made anxious and attempt to pull her back to the fold. There is already, as we can hear, an emerging language and cover story that says if you want to be an acceptable girl, well liked and included, then you don't pull yourself out of relationships by drawing attention to yourself. Girls read such renegade or rogue behavior as mean and hurtful and threatening because the one who brags has blown her cover and she risks betraying all the other girls who need and want that cover to ensure acceptability and love. The bragger must be taught a lesson; for her own good she must know this will jeopardize her position in the group of good girls. "I really don't like Tina at all," Jenna complains. "Because she brags and stuff, and gets real mean." Jenna goes on to describe how she responds to Tina's bragging by using her own powerful place in the friendship to control Tina:

Like if I don't give her something, then she says, "Please, I won't be your friend." And then I finally give up and I just say, "Tina, just leave me alone, alright?" And then she still doesn't and I feel really mad at her. She likes me the bestest and she doesn't want to leave me alone. And guess what? Sometimes she always tries to be the teacher; she tells us what to do and stuff. I feel really sad, and mad at her too. I choose to just walk away from her. But she still follows me. And I feel really mad at her and I say, "Tina stop! I do not like you following me!" But she still doesn't listen. She says, "I don't want to listen to kids." That's what she says. And I don't want to listen to her either. And she's always wrong and she's just mean that way. . . . At least I can read better than her, too. Her mother's really mean too, because Tara did *not* step on her sandwich and that's what she even told two teachers. And *her* mom got mad at Tara's mom. 'Cause Tina always tells lies. If she does that when she grows up, she'll hardly have any friends but Rachel, 'cause Rachel's her only friend. She just says that she has lots of friends but I know she doesn't 'cause I only see her playing with Rachel.

Tina's bragging and bossy behavior leads Jenna to catalog a number of other relational violations and personal failures—bossing people around, meanness, lying, not listening, having few friends and a mean mother, and even poor reading skills. Tina, who is white and working class, is literally and figuratively just too much; she is excessive, doesn't know the good girl code of ethics. She is "not nice," meaning she's out of bounds. Tina unknowingly challenges the good girl cover story and threatens the safety at the heart of it and so she makes Jenna and the other girls very anxious. Jenna attempts to teach Tina by showing her the consequences—by walking away, getting mad, not listening to her, and even putting her in her place by doing a little competitive bragging herself.

Disconnecting from or excluding girls like Tina, who are acting in threatening ways, has a powerful effect. We know this because young girls are so open about their feelings when they are left out or left behind. As Karen says, when people leave her out, "I tell them no because they really hurt my feelings and they might do it again." When she's asked about a time when she wasn't listened to, Abbie doesn't hesitate to tell her story. "Sometimes my friends do that," she says, "like when I say, 'Chelsea, I want to talk to you,' she goes on talking with Nicole, 'cause that's who she likes best. She hardly likes me. And Meg likes Nicole better than me. . . . It makes me feel sad. I wish they would like me the same as their other friends." Abbie doesn't say anything to her friends, however. "I just go off playing with other friends," she explains. But still she wishes she could say something, something like "I want you to listen to me, please. And I don't think they would listen to me though."

Abbie knows that speaking up can put her in further jeopardy. Emmie struggles too when she hears that her friend, who promised to invite her to a sleepover, decided against it. "It makes you mad," Emmie says, "because it's not really fair." She chooses not to speak up for fear that "they, they don't ever invite you." The threat of exclusion is powerful and girls often give in to their fears of being all alone and without friends. "We can't agree on something so we get in a fight," Mary explains. "That almost always happens when Tara comes over. She's kind a like, 'if you don't like this, I'm not gonna be your friend anymore.' . . . so I do it . . . because she's one of my best friends." "I have to follow Frannie's rules [at recess]," seven-year-old Rosalind explains in a plaintive voice. "If I don't I won't have anyone to play with and I'll be all alone."

Young girls are taking in and reflecting our dominant cultural views of femininity. Inserting themselves and ensuring they get what they need, they make full use of the avenue to power made available to them: their relationships. They police and protect and ensure the continuation of this culture by excluding and rejecting and ostracizing "other" girls who don't match up. Girls whose families and cultures do not share these values and ideals come face-to-face with their normalizing power when they attend school, that official gatekeeper of the status quo. Here girls are too often educated in a femininity stripped of color and texture, a kind of one-size-fits-all notion of girlhood.

Of course, different girls react differently to such gatekeeping. But the very idea that there is such a definition of the good or nice girl eats at genuine relationships. Girls find themselves fighting for adult approval and competing for attention with other girls around a very narrow set of characteristics. Already girls know that to aggress, express anger, or compete publicly would ensure exclusion and disapproval. So their remaining option if they want attention is to tell on the bad girls who do these things, to put other girls down, to comment on their shortcomings, to reel them in with threats of meanness and exclusion if they threaten to take too much time or attention. If they do this well, if they cover their real intentions, then in the eyes of adults they look like the good girls. It is a thin line to walk and a balancing act few can sustain for very long.

A CASE IN POINT

To fully appreciate the intricacies of girls' friendships, one has to immerse oneself for a time in their rich complexity, to see the relational world as girls see it. The struggle to be loved, to be heard, accepted, and included is such a complicated drama, lived in a particular time and place, filled with the praise and admonishments of adults and the deep feelings of the girls themselves.

Nancy, Meghan, Jill, and Susan are white second graders in a small rural working-class Maine town. Their public school classroom is pretty typical, except for one thing—there are nineteen boys and just the four of them. These four girls find themselves closely bound together in this context, which perhaps infuses the hurt feelings, fighting, jealousies, and also the support and protection they reveal with more significance.

On the surface, the girls are great friends. Yet their respective answers to a seemingly simple question, "Who is your best friend?" is the first sign that things are not entirely fine between them. Meghan, tall and energetic, her long black hair pulled back with a ring of sparkly butterfly clips, answers without pause, "My best friend is Jill. She's nice. She's always caring about me." And Jill, her clear blue eyes sparkling, enthusiastically returns the favor when she's asked the same question. "Meghan!" she replies. "She plays with me a lot. . . . She's really nice to me. And she's kind and she doesn't treat me like I'm stupid." Susan answers the question with enthusiasm as well, but her response foreshadows trouble. Like Meghan she also chooses Jill. Swinging her legs in unison she describes her best friend as someone who "loves cats and . . . came over to my house once and we played with my kitten." Nancy, her brown hair pulled high into pigtails, wisely doesn't commit: "Well, I have three best friends," she explains. "One's name is Meghan, and Jill and Susan. And they're nice to me and we have a lot of fun together at recess and I invite them over and they invite me over."

The girls talk easily and frequently about the joys of their four-way friendship—the time they stole M&Ms off Susan's birthday cake, the tricks they've played on their brothers and sisters, the pets they love, the fun games of chase and freeze tag, and the secrets they share. Each girl acknowledges the weird off-kilter gender dynamics in their class and how it makes them feel. "Sometimes I wish there were four boys and the rest were girls . . . because there are like two million thirty-five boys and four girls!" Jill exclaims dramatically. Well aware that they are outnumbered, they tell stories of supporting and protecting one another. "We always get chased by David," Susan explains. "One time we were doing this thing, we were sending a letter and I wrote one to Meghan and David. Meghan was sitting right next to David and he kissed her and she told Mrs. Swan and everybody started laughing at her . . . and she ran out in the hall and she was okay out there because Jill went right out there and talked to her."

Unlike other girls their age who have boyfriends and talk about romance and marriage, these four girls seem overwhelmed by the sheer number of boys in their class and take no pleasure in such fantasies. The boys, Jill explains, are no fun to play with at all because they are "nasty and mean. . . . They play street fighters." "They have very mean days," she adds. "They push and shove a tiny bit more than the girls do. . . . We get hit and pushed around a lot . . . by boys."

Boys, in this case, provide opportunities for the girls to bond, to be brave and protective. Sometimes the girls hit back and sometimes they chase the boys off. But surprisingly, these shows of aggression do little to interrupt messages they've received about gender. In spite of their open criticism of the boys' behavior and their active resistance to being pushed around, the girls describe being a girl in rather stereotypical ways—girls are "nice," they say, and they "don't fight." Moreover, they pass value judgments on other girls for being too "girly." "Girls are really delicate," Nancy states unequivocally. In fact, the worst part of being a girl, she explains, is that "you get, you get real delicate when people hit you, you like fall on the ground and stuff, and you don't like that. And start screaming when people are chasing you, like boys. I hate that." Instead Nancy admires her older sister who, she says, is into "boys' stuff" like soccer and karate.

By their own description, these girls fall between the cracks of the usual definitions of girlhood. They are neither wimpy nor delicate and are certainly not always nice, and fighting verbally and sometimes physically is a daily occurrence. Given the choice, they distance themselves from the victim position—the girly girl who screams or falls when people chase her—in favor of "boys' stuff." Of the two stereo-types—girly girl and tomboy—this at least provides them some self-re-spect. And it locates them somewhere closer to their daily reality be-cause, quite simply, the girls do fight and fighting is a sign that some-thing is real and at stake in the friendship. "That's what friends do," Meghan explains, sighing when her interviewer doesn't seem to un-derstand. "They fight. Like if you weren't someone's friend, then you probably wouldn't fight with them unless they were really mean to you. Friends are supposed to, they fight, you know, because that's, when you fight with your, with your, like when you fight with somebody who's truly your friend." This explains, she says, why she fights with Jill so much and not very much with Susan.

The problem is that fighting is also dangerous. Nancy, in fact, wor-ries about all the fighting because it can go too far. "If we didn't like each other then we wouldn't be real friends, and if we kept on fighting every day . . . we wouldn't be real friends." It's the making up that pre-occupies Nancy and she makes it her responsibility "to try to cheer a person who is mad" or make the "person that hurts somebody's feel-ings . . . say they're sorry to the person." The ebb and flow of strong feel-ings is important to Susan as well, although she has the perspective of a seasoned veteran: "Sometimes we can get mad at each other, but we come back to friends the next day, because we forget about it. . . . We argue but then we get back to being friends again. . . . Sometimes it takes a while to get back together when you have an argument," she explains. "Me and Meghan have been friends since kindergarten, and we keep on fighting, and we come back to friends again the same day."

While it seems that fighting comes with the territory of their close friendships, bad feelings do linger and these seven- and eight-year-olds are already well rehearsed in masking their strong feelings. There is more at stake, perhaps, with so few girlfriends to rely on; the risks of being left out or left behind are much greater. When asked if she'd ever pretended to like someone when she really didn't like them, Nancy re-sponds immediately:

> Well, yes, because they were being nice to me and . . . it was Meghan
> that happened. Because she got all mad at us, because she got out on a
> . . . on a game and then she says, "thanks a lot you guys, you got me
> out." . . . So she starts pushing us and stuff, and then the next day she

says hi to us, and gives us all kinds of hugs and then she comes back to being our friend again. And, and then, and then I try to make her think that I'm still her friend, but I'm really not.

At the time of the interview, weeks later, Meghan had still not said "her apology." "I'm still mad at her," Nancy fumes.

The fighting among the girls takes certain forms across their friendships and reveals different motives and anxieties. The relational struggles, it turns out, are primarily between Meghan and Susan, both of whom named Jill as their best friend. Meghan is forceful and direct and Susan sees her as mean sometimes because "she treats us like she is our boss and stuff like that and so, that's why we're half her friend." Yet even bossy Meghan sometimes hides her frustration and masks her feelings. "Like I'm hugging Jill and stuff," Meghan admits, "but I don't like her that much." Susan is in the wings and Meghan can't afford a fallout with Jill.

Nancy, who sees Susan as "one of my best friends," also has trouble with Meghan. Asked if she ever wanted to help somebody but didn't, Nancy replies, "Yes, Meghan. Because she deserved it. . . . She was being a jerk and she told me to help her. And I said no, because I told you . . . I asked you to please help me, and you go, 'No.' So . . ." It turns out that, in fact, Meghan and Jill collude sometimes to exclude Nancy, who then turns to Susan for support. Again, because there are just the four of them, this exclusion is particularly frightening: "I get so mad because those are my only three friends," Nancy admits. "So I couldn't play with anybody . . . so I sat down and I was thinking of them . . . and then they come up to me . . . and they were being really mean to me and I didn't want to get up." Nancy talks about how all this feels to her. It's "like somebody really like hurt you and hurt your feelings real bad and you don't like it, you were really, really angry . . . and you would go, 'Come on, play with me please. I have no other friends, you girls are the only ones here that are my friends.' That's what it feels like."

These four girls need each other. Their friendships provide them protection from a seawall of boys. But even this cannot prevent the pairing up, the hurt and exclusion, and it may even exacerbate the fighting. They take the intensity of their feelings out on each other, even as they mask these strong feelings to preserve their relational safety net. Can they really afford to be honest with one another in this context? While the girls angrily resist the boys' chasing, pushing, and kissing, they already measure each other by the female standards of niceness and the male standards of strength and possibility. To be girlish is to be delicate and wimpy; strength is a boyish show of physical prowess and athleticism. But to be too assertive, to be a bossy girl like Meghan, is to be outside the realm of good girl behavior and is cause for concern. Already they know the power of niceness to mask or cover over the strength of their feelings and the complexity of their relationships.

Girls this age see and name the difference between what they feel and think and want and what others say girls ought to be like. In a social world in which they are expected to narrow the range of their feelings and modulate their voices, young girls are amazingly creative in finding ways to get their point across. Sometimes they break out altogether in an attempt to disrupt old categories, as when seven-year-old Mary imagines the gender-bending "zuts" from outer space—"maybe they'll be people with long hair down to here that are boys and play with Barbies," she says. More often girls move back and forth between gendered stereotypes and their own realities. At seven and eight, being a girl is about being "pretty" and having long hair, but it's also about fighting with your friends and refusing to play with people who treat you badly. And for Julie it's simply about the freedom "to play by myself and stuff." "It's good to be free," she says.

But girls also know there is power available to those who buy into cultural ideals and notions of good girlness and they see that masking what they want and what they know to be true can buy them attention from adults and also friendships with other girls who desire that same feeling of power. While approximating a feminine ideal promises adoration and love, approximating a masculine ideal can buy respect and distance from weak or "wussy" girlness. These are the culturally sanctioned choices and, unlike boys, both are available to girls. But a culture that consistently refracts individual differences through narrow gender stereotypes makes it harder and harder for girls to stay with the reality of their everyday experiences and to stay connected with each other in a way that's fluid, open, and responsive. It's very hard to hold onto the other parts of yourself when at seven years old you're labeled a "delicate" girly girl for liking dresses or for being "calm," or when you're considered a tomboy if you're bold and don't mind getting your pants dirty.

What accompanies girl things and boy things, as we've seen, are a whole set of opposing behaviors and expectations. References to heterosexual romance and prince charming are ubiquitous and connect femininity to passivity or construct girls as potential victims of active male desire or aggression; dominant views of femininity require girls to shut down their anger and to be pleasing and caring toward others. Dominant views of masculinity require them to separate from anything feminine and to criticize things girlish. These voice-overs threaten to contain girls (and boys) and they quite understandably get anxious and suspicious. How will they reconcile such stereotypes with their reality without giving up things that are fundamental and important—the power and certainty that comes with knowing what you want, the capacity to say what you like and don't like, at times forcefully and with self-righteous anger?

Built into these gender stereotypes is a whole host of dos and don'ts and the resulting frustration and anger girls feel gets taken out on other girls, either the girls they compete with or the girls they'll have nothing to do with. It's no surprise that girls fight over who's nice and who isn't, who's loud and who's calm, who's too pleasing and who's too much, who's thin and who's fat. They are practicing, trying out idealized femininity and proving to those around them who are invested in this "Reality" that they can match up and are worthy of praise and love. Similarly, when girls like Nancy distance or decontaminate themselves from "the worst part of being a girl," they are operating out of the same system—just from a different standpoint. Our narrow views of gender limit girls' imaginations and the possibilities open to them, so that the complex and interesting relational weave of their daily lives becomes channeled into tired, predictable patterns.

Girls who resist or don't match up run the risk of being cut off from other girls—labeled bad, bossy, or mean. The alternative is to embrace the ideals, at least publicly, and to protect yourself by being the arbiter of good and bad. The best defense is a good offense and girls who know and embrace what it means to be a good girl in school and other public places have the moral high ground. Moreover, they have the power through adult approval to persuade others to this position or to punish those who don't make the grade. Those with less power or less interest in this performance learn the hard way. Controlled by threats of exclusion or rejection, they learn to read the relational world like naturalists, self-protectively masking their feelings at appropriate moments and calling the whole nasty unreal thing friendship. Or they learn not to like or respect their gender and see the great benefits of acting tough or picking fights with the "delicate" girly girls.

It doesn't have to be so. The very fact that young girls can be so direct and open about their thoughts and feelings ensures that there is a lot of public debate about just who does and doesn't match up and who does and doesn't care. Girls take themselves very seriously and are quick to point out unfairness to other girls and to adults. This capacity for conflict is something adults should support and encourage. Notions of good and bad, nice and mean are on the table and the debate is on. All the elements for a healthy resistance to the narrow ideals of femininity and to sexism, racism, homophobia, are present and available and ready to be nurtured in girls: self-respect, openness, determination, clarity, honesty, and capacity for anger and critique.

Needless to say, the voice-overs we're more likely to offer girls do not provide a good foundation for female friendships. If girls can't stay with themselves and the reality of their experiences, they can't stay with other girls. If being a girl means effacing their anger or performing niceness or acting tough to be taken seriously, girls can't trust other girls to be really present in their relationships—to see what's going on and to be fair or responsive. When is a girl real and when is she fake? Things are already getting dicey by second grade as girls move back and forth from the real to the ideal. "Mindy has the number one slot," seven-year-old Gail says about her best friend's relationship to her, "and KayAnn and May are fighting it out for number two." If a girl knows that choosing the voice-over of feminine niceness and compliance buys her the number one slot, she also knows that other girls know this. There is, then, a seed of uncertainty, and possibly mistrust, germinating at the heart of girls' friendships. As we see in the next chapter, this uncertainty can grow and divide girls in more consistent and obvious ways.

3

Playing It Like a Girl

Later Childhood and Preadolescence

I'm standing outside the closed door of Cordelia's room. . . . They're having a meeting. The meeting is about me. I am just not measuring up, although they are giving me every chance. I have to do better, but better at what? . . . From behind the closed door comes the indistinct murmur of voices, of laughter, exclusive and luxurious. . . . "You can come in now," says the voice of Cordelia from inside the room.

—Margaret Atwood, *Cat's Eye*

BY ALL VISIBLE ACCOUNTS, I lived in a great neighborhood—there were tons of kids my age. We had the freedom to run and explore that so many small-town kids had before fears of kidnappers and child molesters took root in our collective imagination. Neighborhood games of freeze tag or red-rover or hide and seek went on well after dark until, in some loosely predictable fashion, our parents called us in for baths and bed.

But the layer beneath the visible was more complicated. There were Lisa and her cousin Charlotte and then there was me, a late-arriving and unrelated interloper. There were also Jackie and Cindy and Tracy, but somehow they were not on my radar screen in quite the same way. It was Lisa and Charlotte I coveted. And so, for reasons that were never quite clear to me, I clung with all my might to the tenuous threads of a triangle that shifted allegiances daily. I knew only that I was tertiary, except of course when Charlotte and Lisa fought with each other—then I was sought after with a vengeance. But I knew deep down that much as I wanted and needed them, I would never reach the secure status of best friend. I was nine-year-old Elaine behind the door in Atwood's novel

Cat's Eye, listening, waiting to be invited in, not sure what I had done this time to deserve such treatment.

Then I met Connie DiCenzo. We were both invited to Lisa's ninth birthday party, a slumber party that brought together girls from the public school, like me, and Lisa's friends from parochial school. Connie was Catholic, which was the only conceivable reason why, in this small Maine town, we had never met. I was captivated by her. She was everything I admired—tuned-in, wonderfully smart and creative, a budding artist who saw things in the world I'd missed and named things I'd felt. As we all trudged down the hill through the January snow to the bowling alley that afternoon, Connie and I dropped back to marvel at each other. That night when a big fight broke out over the Barbie dolls, we sat it out, still enthralled. It was love at first sight.

Over the next months and years our friendship deepened. We soon discovered we had the same volatile families, the same astrology sign, the same likes in clothes, in books, in attitude. Talking and walking became our chosen activity. We would set a departure time from our houses and meet half-way at Ruth Clark's store where we'd buy cokes, barbecued potato chips, and peanut butter cups and walk randomly around town, lost in conversation. In the summer, when Connie moved a half hour away to her camp on Pleasant Lake, we wrote long rambling letters to one another, hand delivered by my older sister and her older brother who, miraculously, were dating. Covered with hearts and signed with Xs and Os, these letters were lifelines out of the treachery I suffered in my neighborhood. Somehow it just didn't matter so much anymore. Without my intense need for their love, Charlotte and Lisa lost their hold on me.

Something quite miraculous happens between girls at around nine and ten years old. The world of friendship deepens and ripens in ways that are truly expansive. Harry Stack Sullivan, a psychiatrist who wrote decades ago about the importance of relationships in children's lives, suggests that a close intimate relationship with a same-sex friend at this age is akin to the first experience of genuine love.[1] Indeed, those writing more recently about girls agree that "the intensity of friendship is equal to that of any romance."[2] It's the first time a child fully sees herself through another's eyes, the first time she truly experiences mutual validation. The pleasure and joy are palpable. As ten-year-old Valerie says of her friends, "When they're around me they just act so bright. I mean, I guess like, they have a light bulb inside them, something inside them that lights them right up."

Friendship is so important because this is the time in a child's life when feelings of loneliness emerge. The delight in difference we heard in the younger girls' voices begins to give way to concerns about what is "normal" or "regular" and fears of being an outsider. Sullivan suggests that anxieties about being left out and alone are so powerful that children will put themselves in uncomfortable or painful situations to avoid them; rather than have no one, they will seek out friendships with people who do not love or validate them in kind. The feelings of "wholeness, homecoming, and delight"[3] I experienced when I met Connie were ballast against morbid feelings of being different and fears of being all alone.

Such fears cannot be overstated. Everywhere in their interviews nine- and ten-year-old girls talk about the experience of being left out and alone and they allude to the ways they adjust their behavior to avoid this most horrible of outcomes. "With friends," nine-year-old Tina says, "you can't have a battle or anything." The reasons are clear. "If you have friends," Dana says, "you're never alone. You always can feel that you always had, like there's something you can depend on." "When a friend makes me feel bad," Rita says, "is when she goes away and starts playing another game, and like makes me feel so like alone, like nobody likes me and stuff." "And sometimes," Jane explains, "you like get in trouble for just doing something [to get on your friends' nerves] and it makes you feel really uncomfortable because then you feel like you're all alone." Unlike the outspoken younger girls, threats of getting in trouble or being excluded for openly "battling" or annoying people make "it kind of difficult" or make "it hard to tell" friends what they really feel and think. Suddenly, not only what you say but how you say it matters because what you have to lose is so fundamental and important.

Because of these anxieties and the need for acceptance and inclusion, this time in girls' lives—nine and ten—deepens the social fissure between private and public, between what you feel and what you say out loud. Out of this split emerges a dark underside to girls' relationships. Accompanying this new preoccupation with being seen as a "normal" girl others can love and want around is the anxiety of difference and the risk of punishment for being transgressive or unfit for friendship. Girls who don't fit the accepted norms seek out others for affirmation and love. In an essay on friendship, ten-year-old Victoria writes:

> Some girls that were unpopular like me made a club. Ever since then I know that when I'm sad or depressed I can count on those three girls. Before that I didn't know what was going to happen. Like my puppy just got ran over. I called Danni and she really comforted me. The next day two other girls called me. The callers were from the other members of the Leftovers. I liked the way it felt to feel wanted. Though we are leftovers in the school cafeteria, I know I'm liked. That feels *great*. Sincerely, A Leftover.

Of course, what it means to be "normal" varies across social contexts and depends on such things as race and class. But as we've seen, there are feminine ideals promoted by our culture through the media and encouraged by adults in girls' lives. Girls who are different or not "normal" because they call feminine ideals into question by being too full of themselves or because they look different or dress "weird," produce anxiety because they remind other girls of their own potential failure to match up. Such girls must be improved. They are tested and teased as a way to reassert or reaffirm the "normal" and to make the social world understandable, predictable, and safe. The irony, of course, is that reasserting the normal or the ideal makes so many girls feel unsafe, sad, and defensive. "They are teasing me again because I am still the shortest," Nina protests, "but I am still normal."

Normal can now mean fitting a predefined standard of what a girl should be, whereas for the younger girls it simply meant the typical or usual goings on. So while fighting between girls still happens all the time—as Piper says, "all friends have to fight, cause it wouldn't be natural if people didn't fight"—it is no longer considered "normal" from a public point of view and adults remind them daily that "good girls" shouldn't fight with their friends. And so when Rita and her friends fight, as they so often do, they also feel compelled to fix themselves, to "figure out that we can still be friends and that we shouldn't fight. . . . We just talk and then we get back to playing, like normal, like we were before." Arguing, fighting, or disagreeing are all still part and parcel of friendship, but the lines are drawn—fighting should not be seen or heard. Younger girls knew this at some level, but girls this age begin to embrace it. It is a dangerous abnormality; something that gets you in trouble because it interrupts the desired harmony and threatens good girlness or targets you as "one of those kind of girls." Indeed, nine-year-old Shelley knows that from the point of view of "normal . . . the best thing that can happen is we could like, we never got in a fight." In reality, she says, "that never happens with us girls."

Normal refers to how a girl looks as well as how she acts. In predominantly white contexts, a girl of color can be made to feel the pain of being an outsider. After hanging in for a time at a mostly white school in which her biracial daughter, Domonique, was treated badly by both the white girls in her class and by the white teachers, Renee, whom we met in the last chapter, transferred her daughter to a more diverse, but still primarily white, school—the only option in her city. Things are better but not perfect for Domonique, now nine years old. "Domonique wants friends so badly," her mother explains, "that she's willing to do whatever [the white girls] want . . . because she just wants to be accepted and part of the group, you know what I mean?"

Ironically, however, it wasn't harassment from her white classmates that surfaced after the school transfer. Renee explains:

> In Domonique's class, she was having a problem with this girl. Now I didn't even know who she was, but when I talked to the principal, I said, "She's a dark-skinned girl, isn't she?" They go, yes she is. It hadn't occurred to them that I could be knowledgeable of the problem between two girls of color. But you know, I've seen this before, this infighting in our own race. She hates Domonique. You know, Domonique has what they call the "good hair,"—of course I hate that term, that means you're implying that the rest have bad hair—but she's got long straight hair that comes down past her shoulder blades. She's very, very fair.

Renee was sure skin color and hair texture were at the heart of the matter.

> [This girl] came to the school and she was new. She was new, everybody made over her. Well, then Domonique came to school and everybody made over Domonique. . . . [This girl] got jealous and then everything just kind of spiraled out from there. . . . She'd kick [Domonique], she'd hit her, she'd tell her she wanted her to go back to her old school

and she wishes she never came here. You know, just mean things. She told her she hated her hair; she told her she hated her skin, all the things that you know just aren't true.

The white teachers first thought it would be best to sit the girls together at lunch, to encourage a friendship, but Renee felt otherwise.

I'm like, no, you don't understand. It's deeper than that. I had to educate them a little more about this. I had to make them understand that it's not just two girls not getting along; it's more of the deep-rooted problem we've had within our race. Dark-skinned versus light-skinned girls and once we started looking at it that way, things started moving a lot faster. They're in the same class now; they don't like each other, they don't talk to each other but I'm okay with that. And Domonique seems to be okay with that too.

Domonique is lucky to have a mother who understands the significance of history and the impact of our culture's homogenizing image of beauty on her child's daily interactions. Renee is aware that there are narrow beauty ideals in American culture, "generally based on a particular combination of hair texture and color, skin color, facial features, and body size and body shape."[4] Black girls who internalize negative feelings about their looks can judge themselves and others against these standards and contribute to a climate of division and distrust.

Renee also sees the limitations of superficial signs of nice girl behavior and the pretense of friendship. In contexts in which girls this age are made to feel that they *have* to get along, *have* to be friends, *have* to be nice, they begin to push their strong feelings, like anger, out of sight. The underside of pink and sweet and innocent and perfect *must* be the whispering, the derisive laughter, the judgment and exclusion and rage. Such basic human feelings as anger and frustration and displeasure must go somewhere.

When there is pressure not to show anger or dislike, girls—particularly white middle-class girls—begin to fuse their anger with more acceptable feminine emotions, such as sadness. In the younger girls these emotions are very distinct. For seven-year-old Nancy, for example, "mad is the opposite of sad. . . . I'm mad first and then I turned more sad . . . because I had, I didn't, I wasn't playing with anybody." Now, just a year or two later these feelings are almost indistinguishable. Since

girls' outrage is so often a response to separation and relational viola-
tion and since direct anger is not permitted, sadness emerges to soften
the edges of their rage. There is no word in the English language that accurately reflects the complexity of this mad-sad feeling. Girls and
women report that they often cry when they are angry and that this response is seen as manipulative and weak. In reality it's an adaptive response that holds the complexity of girls' strong feelings within the constraints of their public expression.

Let's stop and think about what's going on here. As "normal" gets
defined and asserted in ever more narrow forms, girls begin to compete
and fight over who best fits the norm. They do so because fitting the feminine norm is highly rewarded with attention, love, friendship, even
good grades. A homogenizing image of beauty is reflected on TV, in
magazines, and among advertisers, all of which insure an association
between images and products and "fantasies of becoming what the
white culture most prizes and rewards."[5] The anxiety, stress, and distress that accompany this competition for the ideal get played out between girls and begin to occupy a lot of their time and energy. Girls begin
to find fault, to fight with, criticize, and invalidate one another. Such behavior leads to increasing mistrust and separation from other girls.

When "normal" for girls is defined as not fighting or "causing a
ruckus," but being "nice" and "making everything better and stuff,"
signs of meanness or anger or strong feelings get girls in trouble with
authorities. Girls either become troublemakers or take their anger else-
where. Often it takes root in the underground, either in secret conversations or transgressive behavior with people they trust or in diaries
and journals, only to surface in well-disguised forms. Girls mask their
strong feelings, hone their creative tendencies to express what they
want indirectly, and communicate their desires and anger in more subtle relational ways. The stakes are high. With awful feelings of separation and loneliness in question, all bets are off. All's fair in love and war,
and this is a war for love. Secrets begin to be whispered, notes passed,
cliques formed.

DIVIDING THE CANTALOUPE

Descriptions of girlfighting by nine- and ten-year-old girls inevitably
lead to comparisons with boys. "Boys don't talk when they get in a

fight," Rita observes. "If they get in a fight . . . then like the minute after they get in a fight they'll like go back together and start playing again." Girls, on the other hand, talk and talk and talk. "Girls can communicate with one another and they can understand each other," Jane explains. "Right," agrees Tina, "and they can really understand them and feel how they're feeling and it's like when you're a girl you can tell another girl something more than you can tell a boy. Even if they were like your best friend, you would want to tell a girl because they can understand you and know how you felt because they're a girl too."

Girls fight more than boys, nine-year-old Lisa says, because "when you know more, you fight more." Knowing more—and I think she means knowing more about what's going on with other girls emotionally and relationally—gives you power. It means knowing things others might not want you to know and thus knowing how to hurt others. "Because you know about it and you don't think that's true, or possible, or something," Lisa explains. "So you might get a little excited with it, because let's say I didn't want Karen to say something and she did. I wouldn't feel good."

Perhaps not surprisingly, given increased pressure not to say what they really feel and think lest they be targeted as not nice and are excluded, all this talking girls describe doesn't necessarily lead to support or coalition building, but often signals emerging divisiveness. "Sometimes a lot of girls will gang up on, like, say there's ten girls and three of them believe in something and the other people believe in something else," ten-year-old Hattie explains. "So the group with more people will gang up on this group. And then there's a fight." "I used to say girls always had more friends than boys," nine-year-old Erin admits, "but I don't think so now." "Mostly girls have groups," Dana explains, "and boys have this, yeah, all the boys are one big thing or it's kind of like a whole cantaloupe. It's one whole cantaloupe, and that's the boys, and then there's the split cantaloupe in like quarters, and that's the girls."

What's interesting is that to the untrained eye, the girls' cantaloupe can *appear* quite whole, mature, and appetizing. Indeed, some psychologists look to girls' ability and willingness to mask or hide their strong feelings as a sign of their emotional and psychological maturity relative to boys. But behind what Dana Jack calls the "pastel, pink feminine mask" of nice and kind are anger and anxiety that grow out of proportion because they are kept under wraps.[6] So while girls successfully mask their strong feelings, winning adult approval for their nice, good, "mature" behavior, they begin to pay a heavy price, both psychologically and socially.

BEHIND THE MASK[7]

Listening to when and why girls this age mask their strong feelings tells us a lot about what is going on in their relationships and about their growing awareness of what it is okay for girls to say and do to each other. In some cases, hiding their feelings protects girls from the embarrassment of difference and protects their self-esteem and dignity when they've been left out or taunted. Ten-year-old Naomi, clear-eyed and intense, hides her hurt feelings "when somebody won't let me do something . . . they won't let me play with them and stuff," by "just standing there watching them, pretending I wasn't sad." Instead of saying anything, she says, "I just go find somebody else to play with . . . or I just walk around doing nothing." It's just too risky to call "friends" on their mistreatment. "Friendships can get so mixed up, I sometimes get lost and pulled under," Lee explains. When you don't know for sure what has happened and why, your best bet is to "ignore it," do nothing, "just get over it," pretend you didn't notice. Explaining her response to a picture she sees of two girls talking while a third girl watches from the sidelines, nine-year-old Tobie touches on the fears that keep some girls from voicing their feelings and thoughts: "She invites some friends over," Tobie explains, pointing to a girl in the picture:

> The friend who invited her over and the other friend started playing games, jumping rope games for only two people, leaving her out. So she said an excuse like, "I'd better go take care of my brother," or "I have to go set the table for my mom," like that. And then instead of doing that, she'd walk way out in the big field in back of her house and think. I guess she'd feel uncomfortable telling them the truth 'cause she isn't brave enough to tell them. Maybe her friends would make fun of her and they'd tell everybody at school and at school they'd exaggerate it. They'd think she was a crybaby or a big sissy.

When girls *are* brave enough, they may find they don't have the support of other girls. When Brittany, a popular girl at their school, criticizes and orders other girls around, Nikki, ten, decides to speak up. But first she seeks out her two friends for support and a little coalition building. "They promised to be good friends with me. . . . They said they would stand up for that too. It was against this other girl and I was standing up for something and they said they would too 'cause we had like, gone over to each other's houses and discussed this." But when Nikki takes Brittany on, when she diplomatically says to her, "You've become a really good friend, but it seems like, I think that you've been ruling over us and stuff, and I just, I don't really like that. And I think that some other girls have been feeling that way too," her friends abandon her. She's gone too far, risked too much. At recess, in fact, one of these "friends" aligns with the popular girl against Nikki, telling her "all this stuff about me." "Brittany was popular, so Sasha was happy to give information," Nikki explains. "I was like, how could you do that?" The cantaloupe is divided; mistrust and betrayal between girls emerge because the benefits of selling out other girls outweigh the costs.

Girls can hide their real feelings or feign feelings they don't have to ensure they get what they need from others. Piper says her friend "can get on my nerves" because "she jokes too much. It's like, 'Piper you're so ugly. I hate you so much' and then she goes, 'I'm kidding, I was only joking.'" Teasing, joking, or even acting nice when they feel angry protects girls from the risks of damaging relationships and thus being all alone. Anna, ten, explains that when a friend wouldn't play with her, she "pretended not to be angry and that sometimes changes [my friend's] mind, 'cause she tried to get me angry—but I really was deep inside." Judith, nine, tells about how when her friend, Laura, "got mad at me. . . . I pretended I wasn't her friend." This enraged Laura further— "She got wicked mad!"—which gave Judith the upper hand in the friendship. Tea, also nine, explains why she hides her feelings with a group of friends: "If one of their friends got really hurt or something and I didn't like that friend, then I would be happy but I didn't want them to know it because then they would probably dump me because I didn't like their friends or something like that." Anna, too, "sometimes" fakes her feelings for the sake of inclusion and to cover her jealousy when another girl "hangs around with my best friend." She found that pretending she was sad when she was happy worked with this girl, because "when I was happy she just, she'd like take away my friends so I'd be mad. . . . She'd just go away and take it somehow." When her friends "try to keep their friends away," when "they're like, you know, you're not my friend or anything," Anna feigns a response to retaliate.

"I pretend I'm not their friend to get back at them. . . . Sometimes it's the best thing."

What these nine- and ten-year-old girls are telling us is that when direct expression of strong feelings and desires place them at risk for being labeled bad or mean or give others reason to reject, betray, or hurt them, they have to find other ways to say what they feel and get what they want from each other. As a result, things are often not what they appear to be; the relational world of friends and peers becomes treacherous. Creating or maintaining a sense of uncertainty or ambiguity is, in this case, protective and necessary for social survival. Here, in the relentless pressure to be a "normal" girl who looks beautiful and acts pleasing are the roots of long-standing notions of girls and women as deceitful, manipulative, and untrustworthy. Piper explains what happened when some friends "got really mad at me and like they wouldn't speak to me and I'm like, 'What happened?' And Georgia goes, 'You know,' and I'm like, 'Not exactly.'" Nothing is clear or predictable and one can't be sure if people are "really real." Girls are telling us that deep social significance and meaning are attached to actions adults barely notice, like "ignoring" others, "doing nothing," and "hiding feelings." They are telling us that what they are encouraged to call love and friendship is contingent on the disappearance of core parts of themselves; that acceptance and inclusion by others is connected to self-effacement and fraudulence.

SEEING THROUGH A DARK GLASS DIMLY

The nature of girls' friendships and peer relations is now undergoing a sea change—what was once fairly transparent, even in its contradictions, is now more likely to be opaque and unreadable. The relational world has become what psychologists Terri Apter and Ruthellen Josselson call "the social cauldron of girls' friendships" where girls must develop "a rich sensitivity to the meanings of even minor infractions."[8] It is difficult to know what is really going on and so girls who want to be loved, accepted, and to fit in must now put an inordinate amount of their energy into reading the social world of girlfriends and learning how to negotiate this world in subtle and indirect ways. This is, in part, what girls are doing when they spend so much time figuring out who is friends with whom. Listen to Piper describe the group of girls she hangs out with. The conversation started when she described a fight with Meg. Not that simple:

> Kit's best friends with Gloria. Well, not best friends. She's best friends with Shannon, Gloria, and me. Me and Gloria are best friends. And Kit and Shannon. Shannon doesn't think Kit's her best friend, but Kit thinks Shannon's her best friend. See, Shannon isn't like totally best friends with Kit, but Kit's totally best friends with Shannon, or one of her best friends.

"Who's Shannon's best friend?" her interviewer interrupts. "I think either Joyce, or Lynn, or Vicky, or someone." "And what about Meg?" the now puzzled interviewer asks. "Oh, Meg's is Lynn. And Summer's is Lynn. And Lynn is Meg's and Kayla's best friend. Or it seems like it. And Vicky." The proverbial cast of thousands. This is more than just fun, however, and more than a reflection of the intimacy of girls' groups. Embedded is a message about which girl can be trusted to be a real friend and whose reality dominates the social scene. The fight with Meg indirectly involves Piper's social standing with the entire group of girls. Humorous to us, perhaps, but to Piper this is an anxious negotiation.

Because we have conditioned girls from day one to attend to relationships and to others' feelings, spoken and unspoken threats of being talked about, ignored, excluded, or left all alone have a powerful impact on girls' voices and behavior. Caroline, now fourteen, remembers the power other girls had in third grade to control and manipulate. "We had a club," she remembers. "And we had this one girl who—she was the leader—and if you didn't do what she said, you know, you were out of the club. And so everyday people would be out of the club. You followed the leader. You had to do whatever she said or you'd be worried about being her friend at all." One day this girl decided the club should go into the music room, which was forbidden. Caroline refused and paid a high price. "I didn't go in; they told me I wasn't in the club anymore and then the teacher heard about this, and he told the girls that we couldn't have the club anymore and everything just went wrong and everybody hated me because I was the one who didn't go. It was bad. I felt really bad because everyone blamed me."

Often the threats are less clear or straightforward. Jill, for example, feels an unnamed pressure not to sit with her "really good friend" who is a boy, because she knows through some kind of osmosis that if she does this "my friends won't really want me around." Ten-year-old Nikki, who is typically outspoken, isn't sure what she would do if she saw one of her friends being hurt because she knows without anyone really telling her that she could be targeted next. "I'd feel really bad for that person," she explains. "And sometimes I am, like I do stand up. But other times I'm kind of scared to, or I don't really want to, like lose my reputation or something. Maybe he or she would start spreading rumors about me or like getting people that he or she knows and like hate me too. So that might intimidate me."

Girls begin to watch ever more closely to discern intention and meaning because expectations can be subtly encoded. Ten-year-old Caitlin talks about how a girl who is angry with her "accidentally tripped over my foot." Mia, also ten, talks about accidentally saying things she doesn't mean because owning her anger is so dangerous: "Sometimes I give her a hard time and I try not to, but it just walks out of my mouth sometimes and I just try to stop myself and I just keep doing it." Girls develop indirect forms of relating their disapproval to one another. When Valerie's friend, Rita, gets "really bossy," for instance, Valerie lets her know how she feels indirectly but clearly: "I just, if we're by a chair I'll just, like this, and sit down." "With your arms crossed?" her interviewer observes. "Yes, kinda ignore her and she'll try to make up with me again. It usually works." Gloria explains how this indirectness works to warn other girls not to start conflicts or be too disagreeable: "Like if you do something to this girl in my class, if you disagreed with her, then she'd ignore you for the rest of the week. She'd give you dirty looks and if you looked at her, then she would immediately grab the person next to her and whisper in her ear loudly."

Girls have been well prepared for these relational "skills," as we have seen. "The silent treatment," so common a strategy for white middle-class women, is honed through years of practice. Here in the third and fourth grades, in the context of increasingly careful scrutiny and threats of judgment and exclusion, silence becomes drenched in meaning. And that ubiquitous power word "nice" now comes with all kinds of encoded rules and parameters—one doesn't want to be too nice or not nice enough. Like the old picture on the Cream of Wheat box, where a model holds the cereal box of a model holding a cereal box of a model holding a cereal box, ad infinitum, there's a world within a world within a world, but in this case each is progressively more complicated and subtle. The art of passing as a good girl or a girl who is liked and included is contingent on not looking like you're pretending or faking your feelings when you are; not showing that you want something too much when you do. As Tea says about her socially marginal friend, Anna: "She's nice except she's kind of, sometimes she's a little too nice." Or as Andrea says of some girls who are not liked, "Sometimes they just push it too hard and they just follow you around and try to do everything with you."

Not surprisingly in this uncertain landscape, the issue of loyalty now emerges big time—who can be trusted to hold and keep secret those thoughts and feelings now unacceptable for public consumption? Knowing is important. But it's hard to know. With pressure to mask strong feelings and keep secrets—the logical, adaptive response to increased scrutiny and social control—comes the need to know who your friend really is and who will sell you out. Anna likes her close-knit group of friends because "they'll keep your friendship. They won't let you down and if you don't want to go outside and they do they won't say you're not my friend anymore. . . . They won't be mean and all that to me." Tea says that she and her friend Nora spend a lot of time "kind of telling each other secrets that, like, we don't want to tell other people." Victoria talks about her best friend with total devotion: "We do everything together. We hardly get in fights and if we do, we get in fights for a little while and then finally, we just sort of, we forgive."

Girls this age who are more outspoken and willing to risk conflict look to their friends to protect them when they are treated unfairly in public, an experience that is all too familiar. Falsely accused of a misdeed by her teacher, eleven-year-old Megan is angry with her friend for not setting the record straight. While Megan chooses not to say anything at the moment because "everybody in the class would be on her side and everybody would be against me," speaking to her friend about her disloyalty is important: "I would feel proud of myself, that I spoke up for myself. . . . I would feel good that I stood up for my rights. . . . If I didn't," she muses, "then I would be getting pushed around all my life." What defines a good friend, says Caitlin, also eleven, is that "you really stick together and you tell the truth to each other and be faithful to each other."

But maintaining loyalties is risky in a world where alliances shift and it's difficult to really know what is happening between people. Telling secrets, ten-year-old Mia says, is "kind of like blackmailing . . .

without the money part." Instead of money, inclusion, acceptance, and protection are on the table. Such emotional blackmail is one way girls this age control other girls who are getting out of line because they cause trouble, call attention to themselves, or don't behave appropriately.

While the younger girls were certain about what it means to be a "proper" girl or boy, despite their own frequently "improper" behavior, by the time they are ten girls talk about shifting realities and the consequences of crossing lines that no one has clearly or publicly defined. Amelia, for example, struggles to make sense of the distinction between her own observations on the playground and what her "friends" tell her. "We were playing out in the playground . . . and I asked like everyone that was a good friend to me if I could play with them and then they were like, 'No! Because we're playing something with somebody else and we already have enough people.'" Amelia sees that this is not the case, but their excuse is said nicely enough and sounds reasonable. What are her friends really saying to her? Has she misunderstood? Are they mad at her? Are they seeing something she is not?

For Amelia and others, the line seems to shift without warning and at the whim of those with social power. In response, some girls struggle to improve, to adapt, to become shape-shifters, relational chameleons, female impersonators—pretending to be the kind of girls others seem to want. "If I knew why a person didn't like me, I would change it," Gabriella says flatly. But other girls meet the pull of expectations armed with questions and critique. If the strength of the younger girls was their outspokenness and sense of entitlement, the strength of girls this age is their capacity to know what feels good and real to them and to wonder, talk about, struggle with those experiences or messages that seem unfair, false, or out of relationship. "A lot of my friends aren't friends at all," ten-year-old Helena admits. "They try to act cool and they swear and do bad things on the bus just to get attention. . . . There's one girl in my class that doesn't have many friends because she acts like a cool hot shot. Now she's taken up giving things to people just to be friends. . . . That's the worst kind of friendship." Friends "should like you just the way you are," Cara says. Friends aren't people "who want to be with another [popular] person so they dump the one they really care about" or someone who "pretends to be like" girls they admire. While these things happen a lot, girls this age see and name the compromises such betrayals demand.

Things often shake down differently for girls who stand in a different relationship to cultural ideals of feminine behavior. Nikki, who is African American, is likely to speak her mind at the risk of sounding "rude."

> Like if they've always been holding a grudge against one person because one day they acted like teacher's pet or something, then they should just say, "Well, I feel like sometimes you're acting like the teacher's pet and it really gets on my nerves." Or if you're stealing all my friends, if that was a problem, then like someone said, "You're stealing my friends, like all my good friends are becoming your good friends." Then maybe they should talk it over and the other person hopefully would listen and maybe . . . become better friends and they'd all be one big crowd.

Piper, too, is clear about her thoughts and feelings. "As you know," she says, "we get mad with Amina sometimes. We don't yell out at her all the time. Just once in a while, 'cause you have to let her know you're mad at her, without hurting her feelings." Ten-year-old Jana, who describes herself as "smart, light-skinned, a little short," has an urgent sense of justice. When a friend mistakes her laughter at another girl as laughter at her, Jana tries to explain. Her friend won't listen, and while the other girls who "all laughed too" are quick to apologize, Jana refuses. She knows the relational risks, but won't sell herself out:

> She made up with them before she made up with me . . . because they all said sorry and at first I didn't think that I had to say sorry, because I wasn't laughing at her, I was laughing at the other girl. But then I told her, she finally listened to me, after like three days, and I told her that I didn't have anything to be sorry for, because you misunderstood me, and so we made up and started talking.

Girls who receive guidance and information in their families and communities about how to survive a sexist, classist, and racist world are more likely to question the way things go, seem less afraid to speak their thoughts and feelings publicly, and are generally less terrorized by rifts in relationships.[9] Jana's philosophy that "everybody gets an equal part of something . . . everybody should be equal," is a philosophy that includes herself. Clearly messages she has received about fairness and taking herself seriously have shaped this view and it filters through to her friendships. Indeed, her resolution of the problem with her friend—though it took longer and required a lot of attention—made for a more genuine connection.

GAMING—IT'S NOT THE GAME, BUT HOW YOU PLAY

The ways girls negotiate and resolve conflicts in their games tell us a lot about their social lives and about cultural and racial differences in girls' fighting and conflict negotiation. "Conflict is as inherent in the games of girls as it is in their everyday dealings with one another," says anthropologist Marjorie Harness Goodwin.[10] Games also tell us a lot about patterns and concerns that cross what we usually think of as cultural divides.

The first thing we need to appreciate about traditional girls' games like jump rope, hopscotch, and four square is that the way they're played and the intentions of the players are as important as the rules. Like many things related to girls, what you think you see may have little to do with what is actually going on. The seemingly simple rules of such games leave a lot of room for complicated negotiations and interpretations; they provide the loose scaffolding for subtle communication among friends, for power plays, and for deeply meaningful conversational strategies. Through games, girls in third, fourth, and fifth grades learn and teach one another about power, relationships, and the social order. And games provide girls with acceptable opportunities to aggressively police that social order.

Not surprisingly, white girls describe their conflicts and competition in pretty specific terms—it's mostly about being nice and mean. Each move is coded, layered with meaning. How does a particular move advance or derail friendships? What feelings or loyalties underlie decisions to resolve a dispute one way or the other? Linda Hughes, in her study of Foursquare, found that white girls coined the phrase "nice-mean" to describe how being nice to their friends translates into being mean to others:

> The problem for players was that it was not possible to be "really nice" and still "play the game" of Foursquare. In practice, almost anything players could do to "be nice" to one person was by definition "mean"

to somebody else. If they were "really nice" and didn't get anybody "out" this was not only boring, but also "mean" to players who were left standing around waiting to get into the game. If, on the other hand, they tried to "be nice" to players in line by helping them get into the game, they had to "be mean" to somebody else by getting them out. . . . If "being nice" in the game could also be "mean," then perhaps that meanness was not "really mean," but something else entirely—in their own words, "nice-mean."[11]

This is a perfect example of how a children's game is influenced by cultural expectations and messages. In this case, through their talk, arguments, and disputes over the rules, these girls practiced and played out what it means to compete as a nice middle-class white girl. But it says something more—about how the performance is often different from the reality. The girls in Hughes's study used a stereotypically feminine rhetoric of "being nice" and "being friends" and not "being mean" to support aggressive competition between players and "to overlay a complex team-like structure on a game that called for individual competition." Being "nice-mean" provided the framework for aggressive competition in their game, as it pretty much does for white girls' competitive relationships in general.[12]

On the other hand, in her conversational analysis of a group of black working-class girls—"the girls of Maple Street"—playing jump rope, Marjorie Goodwin finds quite different gaming strategies and ways of dealing with conflict. "The structure of black girls' games, as in their dramatic play," she contends, "tends to promote the feeling of solidarity rather than competition" through the attention to turn-taking and basic rhythms and singing or chanting in unison.[13] Like the white girls, these girls created and re-created their social order from moment to moment, but they focused more on who has the power to interpret the rules or make changes and not so much on the relational intentions of the players.

Goodwin underscores cultural differences again in her study of a group of Spanish- and English-speaking second-generation Central American girls in Los Angeles. Unlike the white middle-class girls in Hughes's study, these girls openly competed for first place in a round of hopscotch and they openly bragged about their successes. They enjoyed the position of judging others' actions and playfully teased or lightly pushed or in other ways tried to unnerve other players when they were preparing to jump. "Although the game is played with the intent to win, it is richly overlaid with multiple types of framings and textured nuances, including laughter and joking. Having the last laugh, by outwitting those in the audience judging one's performance, results in considerable enjoyment for players, and seems as important as winning."[14]

These cultural differences are important to note and consider in any conversation about girls' conflict negotiation and forms of girl-fighting. But equally important are some telling similarities. In all cases, the looseness of the game rules encourage both interpretation and judgment and a focus on the subtle cues that come from bodily movements and facial expressions. In other words, the game itself doesn't detail where a girl is positioned within the hierarchy or group, as is often the case in "boys'" games. Girls make such distinctions based on additional criteria—their relationships, a girl's appearance or demeanor, her behavior at the moment. In spite of the appearance of simplicity, girls often elaborate a complicated structure of informal dos and don'ts. For girls, "gaming" is more important than the rules themselves.

Such games give us a window into differences and similarities in language as well. Whereas white girls are more likely to use hesitant speech or to modify their thoughts and feelings than are girls of color, girls in all the above studies used less direct speech like "let's" and "we gotta" and made more attempts to soften the force of their speech than did boys. And across the board, girls were more exclusive in their relationships, tending to play in smaller groups (although there are exceptions to this as well) and establishing relative positions within these small groups by barring certain girls from play or creating coalitions of two or three against one.

The point, of course, is that there is no typical girl and no one way girls fight or resolve conflicts—at this age or at any age, in their games or in real life. And yet, that certain patterns hold sway across these groups is important, because the ways girls are similar tell us something about the force of gender socialization and its complicated intersection with race, ethnicity, and class. Exclusion and judgment, attention to body, ritual movements, and group choreography, a focus on the group over individual competition together with the interpretive detail brought to individual moves and intentions within their games, shed light on the ways girls fight and compete with each other for real.

LIVING THE PERFORMANCE

As girls move toward early adolescence, they get harder on themselves and harder on each other. The reasons why are complicated and social scientists studying girls' development note this time and put forth all kinds of theories: it's the result of hormonal changes, gender roles become intensified at this time, the dominant culture and its expectations of girls and women become more explicit and desired. My own view is rather eclectic. As girls become visibly like women—as their bodies begin to change, as their faces mature, and as boys begin to enter the picture to confirm their emerging sexuality—they confront a fresh wave of pressure to be "good" and desirable women in the conventional sense. Adults invested in girls' conformity or concerned with their safety wish to control them, other girls compete with them, boys desire them, and media messages, refracting and commodifying dominant views of beauty, are aimed at them.

Girls this age are moving into a culture that takes women less seriously and values them most for their physical beauty and their compliance. At the same time girls hear that "they can be anything." This is a precarious time precisely because there are so many contradictory messages. Girls have an intense desire to be recognized, to be heard, to fit in, and yet they know what happens when they speak their minds, take up too much space, break away from what others expect of girls and women. Cliques and clubs are enforced with a new intensity as girls try to deal with what has become a treacherous relational scene—girls policing other girls in an attempt to secure their own social power and to protect themselves from those with the power to reject and exclude them.

As girls move into the culture, as people react to their changing bodies and as they confront new expectations and demands and messages about what it means to be "normal," accepted, loved, and listened to, reality begins to shift. Girls begin to name the differences between the reality of their experiences, their thoughts and feelings, and Reality with a capital "R"—the ways girls should look, act, think, and feel if they want to be the right kind of girl. This is a different sort of naming than it was for the younger girls who held both realities and lived with the contradictions. And while girls are distinguishing real from ideal, genuine from false, there is increasing pressure to choose—and the choices, girls are well aware, have serious ramifications.

For white middle-class girls this is an especially confusing time, since their families, school, and the media often collude in a construction of white femininity that is very different from the way girls have experienced and known the relational world of childhood. They are expected to modulate their voices and narrow their possibilities in order to fit in or not make waves. White middle-class girls this age talk about themselves, their thoughts and feelings, as "endangered" or "jeopardized," describe their voices as "muffled," and suggest in various ways that it is disruptive to know what they know, and dangerous to speak their knowledge publicly. They talk about knowing when they are being themselves and when they are pretending, performing, or impersonating the right kind of girl in order to keep their relationships with boys or satisfy others' views of appropriate behavior.[15] Girls of color are more likely to have families and communities that nurture their critique of white femininity and support them when they publicly claim their realities. Their struggle is not necessarily with the seamless collusion of their families, communities, and the wider culture (although this can happen too), but how to move through disparate worlds with a sense of integrity and hope.

The pressure to meet cultural ideals of femininity comes at a time when girls are beginning to think in more complex ways. They now see and name the gap between the ideal and their more complicated realities, even as they realize there's so much support for the ideal that the real becomes, for too many, associated with personal failure. For those who are already well practiced at hiding the "bad" parts of themselves and faking their emotions to get what they need, it becomes ever more difficult to hold onto the real. And anyway, if one looks just at the extrinsic rewards, who would want to?

The divisions between girls now take on the gendered language of the culture. Girls associate themselves more openly and consistently with masculine or feminine traits, girls who hang with boys or value male qualities or "girly girls." And for those who take on feminine notions of girlness, there is a ready-made and convincing language of judgment and criticism. Tobie adopts it when she complains that

> all of the girls in my class are sissies. They're totally sissies. Well, see, they can't run. They don't like to play sports. They sit out and give the gym teacher a hard time and they think they're smart. And they cheat on spelling tests and other tests. One of them is a crybaby. So Mel and

I, a lot of the time we play tag. We play with the boys and they don't. We're nicer to a girl in my class that they bullied.

Calling other girls "sissies," "crybabies," or "wusses," refracts girls' anger or disappointment through a culture that denigrates the feminine—we all know such names refer to nonboy or "girly girl" traits. To draw on this language elevates Tobie to the status of boy, gives her a kind of power and moral authority; she stands above the complaining, whining, crybaby girls.

Cliques and clubs, secrets and whispering and note passing, and, in some cases open fighting, intensify at this time. Perfection means the best, the most beautiful, smartest, purest, finest, and there is little room at the top. Girls know this because they see it everywhere in the most obvious places—if not on TV and in movies or in books and magazines, then in the social hierarchies at their own schools. The girl at the top—adored by teachers, loved by peers—must have everything in just the right amounts and must please the right people.

So girls are learning, through pressure to meet such ideals, to see themselves as others want them to be, rather than to experience and feel and think as they are. To be objectified as a girl is not a new thing for them, but to own it—to actually experience oneself as an object—is new. And part of experiencing it, owning it, is generalizing it to other girls— that is, learning to police others, to judge others on the same terms. Thus, girls at the inside edge of early adolescence develop skills the adult women in their lives have perfected, such as what psychologist Dana Jack calls the "Medusa's stare," a form of relational aggression that asserts control over others.[16] Just as they are objectified by the culture, girls are developing the skill of putting other girls in their place through staring, looking, judging.

The Medusa's stare is unmistakable to the person receiving it—it moves her from the subject of her own story to the object of another girl's hostility or judgment. The observed, in her surprise, might say, "What? What did I do?" The answer invariably will be, "Don't look at me, I didn't *say* anything." The intent of the girl who stares is not clear or aboveboard and so the look can either be mistaken or, if intentional, denied. It is a powerful tool, easily misinterpreted by the uninitiated with dire consequences. Nikki uses "dirty looks" to warn another girl that she is "playing teacher's pet" a little too well. One girl writes:

"There is a girl who rides my bus, and she hates me. I mean, she absolutely despises me. She threatens me and says she hates me right to my face. She hates me because on the very first day I rode the bus I looked at her. Sometimes I get so scared that I don't even want to go to school. I'm scared that she will beat me up, or worse."[17]

Increasingly, staring, whispering, back-stabbing, and exclusion point to the anxiety and pressure girls experience and the degree to which they feel both threatened and constrained by other girls. Gloria describes how girls in her fifth grade tortured a new girl in their class.

> Well, when she came no one really liked her, and they do that at all schools when you go to a new school, and you don't really fit in 'til a couple of weeks afterwards, but she never fit in and it just kept going on and on. And all these clubs were formed against her and they would put a red cross on their hands and they have to show the person they are part of the club and they can come to their house and something like that, and you could come in. And Saturday they would have these meetings and everything. This is what I have been told. They would say mean things about her and they would draw pictures of her and have her do weird things, like standing on her head and her brains falling out and things like that, and then sometimes they would give the pictures to her, and sometimes you would find them on the floor and she would see them like that. So it was really bad.

When the teachers found out what was happening, they called a meeting. "Everyone had to say I'm sorry and hug and everything," Gloria said, "and then we had to promise to be friends again." On the surface it seemed to work—"she walks down the hall with us . . . and she feels comfortable about calling people about assignments and things like that"—but, really, who knows? Like the teachers at Domonique's school, these teachers underestimate girls' capacity to perform niceness when they're being watched.

Riva, now in eleventh grade, remembers back to fifth grade when "there were three girls that really hated me, and there was a leader of those girls that was just evil, and I came to school one day and it was the book sale time of year and they were putting Mr. Peter's books in the book sale boxes." Riva watched in amazement because "usually I was the leader of these types of things."

Later that day, everybody was taken out of math class to talk with my teacher and the principal in the hallway, and I was the only one not taken out. . . . [It was] one of the most excruciating, nerve-wrenching times of my life, because . . . there'd been a lot of talking all day that actually had made me very nervous, and I remember during lunch a lot of people were looking at me, especially the girls that didn't like me. And I was in this math class . . . and about ten minutes went by, and then I was called out in the hall, and the principal said, "Excuse me, I have to go to a meeting" and she was angry at me, and my teacher took me by the arm, and took me into a hall closet downstairs, that was like a bookstore room, and he shut the door, and he moved me so that the back of my head hit the back of the book things, and he said, "What did you do?" and he twisted my arm, and he gritted his teeth, and he said, "What did you do this morning?" and I said, "Nothing, I came to school," and he said, "I don't want any lying from you. I want you to admit what you did," and I said, "I didn't do anything, you know, I didn't do anything wrong today."

Riva discovered later that the three girls who hated her—"preppies" with good-girl reputations—had placed the blame on her and then persuaded other girls to agree with them. She was suspended for five days, labeled "a liar," and grounded "for a long time."

Girls this age become active participants in what Paulo Freire calls "horizontal violence," a primary characteristic of what's been called internalized oppression or what Mark Tappan terms "appropriated oppression."[18] They internalize or appropriate cultural messages about what it means to be a "good" girl—messages that have great power and thus invite constant comparison and competition—and take out their own failure to meet these ideals on other girls because they don't have the power to take them out on others. No one wins, because jealousy directed toward those close to perfection is as divisive and damaging as the rejection of those who don't have a chance.

Not surprisingly, then, as girls move toward early adolescence, the repertoire of relational forms of aggression increases, as does the terror of not knowing how to read the relational cues. Anika, ten, describes this "weird feeling" of not knowing when she's done something wrong. "I've had it before," she begins, "but I don't know how to explain it. Like it's almost terrified, but you are not all 'whoops,' you know, it is like answering a question you know very well, wrong, or something you had worked on for a long time, and you get it wrong. You feel that weird sort of feeling, like why did I do that, confused sort of." As a result, Anika finds she cannot speak her anger or express her feelings directly.

> When you are really mad at somebody and you want to say something really bad, but you can't, you just can't. It's like it comes out of your mouth and you forget what you are going to say or I don't say something because somebody says a real good idea and everybody agrees and mine is like the exact opposite and you don't want everybody to leave you out and say, "Oh, that's horrible, why we don't want to do that." Or they won't want me in the club since I don't have good ideas and you sort of get afraid to say it. And sometimes you get afraid to say things like I hate you . . . when you're mad at somebody. Because a lot of times they get really mad and it really terrifies you because you feel like they are going to tell somebody and they are going to get almost the whole class on her side and it would be one against, I don't know, ten.

In these cases Anika says, "I don't feel very good. I feel like I'm making this whole fight, that is really turning out to be a mess." In the face of such confusion and fear, girls band together, both to protect themselves and to gain social power. The depth of their need and desire for such protection and power often goes unseen because so much has gone underground—so much is whispered, passed from girl to girl like an invisible electrical current. "When me and my friends have a fight," Anika says later, "it is usually pretty private. A lot of people can tell you are ignoring each other, but it's usually pretty private when you fight." The private nature of fighting means friends can leave you all alone and, in Carrie's words, "talking into space."

Secrecy protects girls from being targeted by other girls, but also from the unwelcome interference of their mothers or teachers who are quick to put an end to their conflicts. When Brianna fought with her best friend, whose mom is good friends with her mom, she didn't let on.

> When I got home my mom asked how it was and I said it was great, and I didn't want to say anything because I didn't want to have her go into like "we should go over there and talk to her," and everything. I just wanted to leave it alone, so I didn't tell her . . . yeah, and have my

mom say, well, get into this long talk about why didn't you do this and were you mean to her and was she mean to you and everything and so I didn't get into all that . . . . because I knew we would be back together and we would be friends again soon.

THE "PERFECT" POLICE

As girls come to know and name the signs of female perfection—popularity and beauty, as well as academic or athletic excellence—fighting and competition are intensified. "Our class is like, sometimes people get mad at people that are too popular and stuff, and then we like get in fights and stuff," eleven-year-old Rebecca explains. "Just people were popular, and some people didn't like it, so everybody got in a fight, and I don't know, they were acting snobbish and stuff . . . whispering together and stuff like that." Melanie agrees: "See if some people are really smart, or they're really good athletes and stuff people will, sometimes they don't like them as much. . . . I hate it when this girl does this, because she always has this grin, or she thinks like, well I'm the best writer or something and she might always get As or something like that."

Signs of perfection raise anxieties. A girl who flaunts her excellence is universally condemned—she is gossiped about, rejected, or teased. "One girl . . . she thinks she's so cool, she knows everything," Cameron says. "And she really doesn't because well, I'm not going to say what kind of grades she got, but, um, she didn't do that well, and so she likes to brag a lot and we don't." Cameron separates herself and her friends from such a girl, confident that the woman listening to this story is on her side. A girl who brags is a threat to other girls in part because she breaks the unstated rules of femininity by either ignoring the prohibition against standing alone, outside of relationship, or by aggressively taking what ought only to be graciously and self-deprecatingly received. Bragging rejects the tacit rules of relationship and the "egalitarian ethos" to which so many researchers of girls' friendships refer,[19] an ethos that affirms (and sometimes declares) we are in this together and that we share knowledge and agree on how to negotiate the world.

Bragging is also a threat because it's a blatant, unapologetic attempt to be noticed, to want and to have power. It heightens the vulnerability girls are beginning to feel as they move into a culture that treats females as secondary, as subordinate. Bragging indicates that there's a girl out there no one can control or police—she has the potential to disturb the way things go and to join and identify with those who have power. She needs to be brought into line. The braggart is thus condemned, rejected, or shamed for her blatant desire for attention and disregard of others' feelings, as well as for her betrayal of other girls.

Popular girls are often the target for others' gossip because they are, by their very nature, as one girl says, "too big for their britches." Even if they are nice, even if they work to convince others that they are non-threatening, they stand apart because they are desired by boys, coveted by girls, and liked by adults. As in our cultural stories and fairy tales, they are the chosen ones: the one the glass slipper fits, the one fit for a prince. This means, by comparison, that other girls are rejected for not matching up, they hold the status of ugly stepsisters. When girls target popular girls or when popular girls exclude and reject other girls, they are appropriating, enacting, and reproducing these stories of good and bad girls. The story works by covering over more complex realities and putting a pretty face on narrow and destructive cultural stories of femininity.

Nikki, an ever-astute observer of other girls' behavior, gives us a sense of how such horizontal violence—girls against girls—works:

> One girl is popular and so everyone is like, "Oh, can I sit next to you, oh can I sit next to you?" And once someone got in a big fight and I could tell that some of them thought that the other person was right, but they just followed along with her. I guess they were afraid of that popular person in their class, because if they don't then they'll have the popular girl against them, plus the rest of the crowd, even if the rest of the crowd doesn't feel that way. She just has the power to . . . maybe it's some insecurity in her, the popular girl, like, if she loses her friends, like who will she have? And so she acts big and stuff, to make people scared of her.

Nikki can't imagine that the popular girl would actually covet her place in the hierarchy or that she may feel great about herself and confident in her relationships. She must really be insecure or afraid or full of false bravado. In this way Nikki feels justified keeping her distance. Dismissing this popular girl, talking about her, deeming her unworthy of the power she wields, is Nikki's way of feeling good, saving her own sense of pride. The problem is that this is a fairly short-sighted coping strategy, an attempt to gain some personal power by doing just what the fairy tale dictates.

Fifth grade is a hotbed of such social alliances and rejections. As I listen to girls talk about their social lives, I hear story after story of the role clubs, cliques, and groups, both popular and unpopular, play in policing other girls' behavior. There are simply "too many cliques," Lilly complains. Cliques provide protection, elevate one's status, and teach outsiders a lesson: "Last year," eleven-year-old Julia says, "people didn't like me very much, and they would make clubs against me, they would say, let's make this club against her because we don't like her or something." What Julia learned was that she needed to improve herself because the people in the clubs "thought I was a different person, but I'm really not." Kate describes the teaching and policing that goes on in many cliques:

> Okay, there is a girl here. . . . She has this group that she thinks is pretty and nice and very smart, and she takes them into her group and teaches them not to like certain people and then she uses other people to get information out of some people, but then, that's what some people think, that is what we think she does, that is what some people think that don't like her, and so she's just mean, she thinks, "I'm so pretty and she's ugly, why should I like her?"

There is a clear jockeying for social position and power in these girls' groups. The gaming that goes on in play becomes all too real as girls paint a vivid picture of the ways gossip and exclusivity undermine any sense of solidarity. Diane talks about how her class "took to two groups . . . some people went with their friends on one side and the other groups went with their friends on the other side . . . and another girl . . . she kind of went from group to group, and she would go to one group and listen and then go to the other group and tell." Anika talks about how the cliques change her class from a "tangled up" and "together" group of girls "into a long string of fights." The script is all too familiar—the stories and media images of girlfighting have filtered their way into girls' social lives. Exclusion, gossip, and acts of betrayal become painful power plays and as girls become more and more myopic, the larger cultural framework that supports girlfighting fades from view.

The line between good girls and bad, nice and mean, popular and unpopular is not a line girls created, but one they've absorbed from the wider culture in which they live and one they're expected to maintain and anticipate wherever they go. Moving to a new school is scary for Miranda because she wonders "is everyone going to hate me because I'm so ugly and they won't like me very much." Such anticipation means girls are on the alert for missteps, always hypervigilant. This is why deciding whose invitation to accept or whose house to play at, on the surface so minor, becomes something just short of apocalyptic—it can make or break your social standing or your reputation; your decision can be read as intentionally mean or a sign that you are too full of yourself.

Girls this age are responding to something quite real—those who strike out on their own, who make their own decisions apart from other girls, who refuse to participate in teasing or taunting other girls, or who commit the terrible sin of daring to relish their own achievements pay a heavy price. It's unfair, Jamie says, that when she refused to admit that a girl she liked was mean, "they started making fun of me . . . for saying that she was nice." When Andrea refuses to participate in a conversation in which her friends might say things like, "Well, somebody's so dumb, and she just doesn't know anything and she never studies for her tests and she walks weird and she's ugly and stuff like that," she knows she's in for trouble.

> Sometimes I feel that my friends won't like me or something, so I sort
> of go along with them, but sometimes I say "I don't know," just to
> cover it up, 'cause I don't know what to say, but I usually think, "Well,
> it's not their fault if they can do things good and stuff." . . . And some-
> times . . . I would say, "Well that's not always true," but I wouldn't dis-
> agree with them totally.

Andrea's fear is that "sometimes the friends that were talking about people—sometimes they might just go on talking, and then later they'd talk about me . . . and spread it around and then no one would like me." Knowing from experience "what it feels like to be the person that everyone doesn't like," Andrea feels a lot of anxiety in these situations. Brie, too, fears that her friends will "leave me out when they are doing something" or "might all of a sudden whisper about me or something." Indeed, the potential for treachery is everywhere, built into the cultural messages girls have received and now play out with each other.

As girls move into adolescence, they begin to fight—physically and verbally—over boys. Donna describes her response when she introduced her friend to a boy, only to have her friend reject her: "I introduced them and then she started acting wicked mean to me and I told her I didn't like the way she was acting, so she pulled my hair and then I pushed her down to the ground and we just started fighting." Indeed, as we will see in the next chapter, boys add a new dimension to girlfighting. While girls in later childhood have been absorbed with each other for the most part, boys and their desires of course have always been present. The romance-saturated media is never far away and neither are parental hopes or cultural messages about how to look and act and be to please boys. Negotiating relationships—especially friendships—with boys proves to be complicated, as girls struggle to find something authentic between the anxieties of their girlfriends, the pressures boys feel to act macho in their presence, and the messages of compulsory heterosexuality all around them. As ten-year-old Anna says, "There is a girl in my class who is not being treated very nicely by any of the other girls in my grade. I finally found out why the girls hate her: she hangs out with boys at recess."[20] And as Donna complains. "Well, I mean, like in our class like if I sit by a boy or if we talk or we hang out or we're good friends or something, like everybody's like, 'oohh, you're going out.' And I mean that's a pile of shit. God you can't sit by someone!"

It isn't surprising, or it shouldn't be, that as girls become more fascinated with and more convinced by the "normal," (and thus more freaked out by the abnormal) girlfighting reaches a new intensity and takes on additional significance. Over and over again these girls express their desire for "everybody to be nice to each other and get along well," for people not to be mad at them or disappointed in them or blame things on them or hurt other people's feelings. They don't want to be left out, to be all alone, to be treated badly; they want to be in the club in the worst way. All this is evidence that girls are learning to take on what "normal" girls need and desire and they are made anxious by any transgression of what "normal" girls do and say.

But normal is a contested term. That is, whose version of normal has the persuasive power in any particular context or culture? Much of the girlfighting at this age is about invoking and protecting and perpetuating whichever version of normal is most convincing to girls. The media has much to say about this. Just as girls resolve conflicts in their games, they use culturally relevant forms of control to bring other girls in line. Threats of rejection, teasing, joking, and criticism are designed to bring other girls in line, to improve them, or to underscore just how bad they really are at being "normal" girls. Cultural differences notwithstanding, girls have been given space in and control over the relational world and they take their job very seriously.

It's not a stretch to connect what girls are doing to wider power relations, and to a prevailing misogyny in U.S. culture. Girls this age are beginning to accept and reject, reward and punish, like and dislike other girls because of their association with or failure to meet or rejection of certain cultural definitions of girlness or femininity. So the hatred of other girls because they are girls—too girlish, or not feminine enough—emerges now in the form of group structures like clubs and cliques and exclusive games. There are now systems of support or rejection in place; there is justification beyond the whim of any one girl. When girls reject or hurt other girls for bragging or being too much of an individual or feeling too good about themselves or not playing by good-girl rules, they are unwittingly mirroring and supporting a status quo that has long controlled and trivialized girlness and femininity. The club or clique can, with much cultural justification, bury an individual girl's strengths or trivialize her femininity, associating her either with pathology or with weakness and contempt, just as the culture has traditionally done. These are well-worn pathways to feelings of superiority and power for girls and women, placing them in good stead with those invested in maintaining the status quo.

Girls' misogyny is not just a white girls' problem, as we will see, but white girls are especially seduced by the status quo because it affords them special protection and security. That is, good white girls who play their cards right are promised good white boys, the eventual power brokers. White women and girls have much to gain by taking in and taking on the special role of educating others like them to be good. Those white girls and girls of color who are different, who refuse or resist, threaten to reveal the awful compromises perfect girls and good women have made. They threaten to reveal the fraudulence, the failure, the psychological and relational damage. Such "different" girls must be brought down, separated out, silenced, or made to fall in line through threats of exclusion or loneliness.

But at what cost? As girls begin to take their anger and frustration out on each other, there is less and less space and opportunity to consider what's happening. Some girls, however, do see and name the price of this divisiveness. "If we could put all our talents together," eleven-year-old Lilly begins, hope flickering and then faltering, "we can't, but if we could, we'd like, you know, it'd just be no holding us back." Beyond the hurt feelings, the suffering, the pain of not matching up or fitting in, there is the possibility of real social change. But, as we shall see in the next chapter, the advances of early adolescence and the culture of middle school make this possibility difficult for most girls to realize.

4

Dancing through the Minefield

The Middle School Years

> The Elephant then said, "Daughter of the dragon, I too am under a
> spell. I know how it may be broken—but I choose to live as a
> changeling." . . . "When the times are a crucible, when the air is full of
> crisis," she said, "those who are the most themselves are the victims."
> —Gregory Maguire, *Wicked: The Life and Times of
> the Wicked Witch of the West*

I WAS LYING in my parents' hammock reading, when my thirteen-year-old niece ran up and threw an open copy of *Seventeen Magazine* in my lap. "Look!" she said, disgust in her voice. The word "slut" jumped off the page in large, hot pink letters. The picture of a girl confronted me, her head tilted to one side as she gazed directly, pensively, into the camera. Her long blonde hair brushed her shoulders, her white T-shirt branded her "X-girl." Beside her, two girls of color, dressed in dark retro clothes and black sneakers, stood together, furtively checking her out. The article's title continued: "What's with that word? What does it really mean? And why are so many girls using it against one another?"

The article was by Peggy Orenstein, author of *Schoolgirls,* a wonderful ethnography of early adolescence. "Wow, Jen," I said. "I bet this is good." "No," she said, "*This!*" She flipped the page and I felt her distress. The camera had panned out, clicked again; I saw the scene from another angle; a boy was standing behind X-girl, leering at her; the other girls were now staring openly, their arms crossed. "Explain yourself," they seemed to say.

I scanned the open magazine page and it hit me. In fact, it wasn't the article that had Jen upset, but a Converse ad on the opposite page.

I'm not sure, in hindsight, if she actually caught the full connection between article and ad. In the ad two girls, one black, one white, were huddled together at a small table, laughing, conspiring; another girl in the background, somewhat out of focus, walked toward them; she had big hair, her low-cut, tight, gold dress covered a feminine hour-glass shape, she was wearing spiked heels. The two girls at the table, leaning over coffee cups, were in casual "cool" clothes, a short skirt, a crop top, shiny purple pants, they were prepubescent thin, their long legs were lit to accentuate the black Converse sneakers they were sporting. The caption read: "Carla and Rachel considered themselves open-minded, non-judgmental people. Although they did agree Brenda was a tramp."

Beyond the calculated choice of juxtaposing Orenstein's article and the Converse ad (after all, the cool girls photographed for the "slut" article were wearing sneakers of the same color and style as the cool girls in the Converse ad), one cannot miss the obvious lesson here. Certainly my thirteen-year-old niece, the age of the typical *Seventeen* reader, didn't miss it: "Watch your back: girls are brutally tough on other girls."

Why does Converse know this ad will sell their sneakers to adolescent girls? Unlike the photo accompanying the slut article, there were no boys present in the ad. But boys do not have to be present to exercise power; the photograph invoked the male gaze. Brenda, the "tramp," was dressed seductively and her open mouth, pushed-up breasts, and spiked heels suggested her audience and her availability. But she was also gesturing with attitude, elbow bent, index finger pointed straight up, and walking toward the two cool girls, so that her open mouth also suggested that she was addressing them. Brenda was defiant. She was a threat. She knew what she was doing and what was going on at the girls' table, and she didn't care.

If you could see the picture, you would see how subtle all this was. Brenda's dress reflected the red and gold mural on the wall behind her. Dark and shadowy, the mural appeared to depict both the sensuality and angst of entwined human bodies. The position of Brenda's arm and hand drew attention to an extended hand in the mural, so that together they framed the ad; they were of a piece, the background to the two girls' friendship. Against this dangerous, sexualized other, these two girls stood out, bright and clear and safe; they transcended Brenda's full-bodied sluttiness. But since their friendship was founded on the rejection of Brenda and girls like her, it was a tenuous bond.

What was not so immediately apparent were the social class and racial overtones. Girls of color were complicit in the exclusion in both the ad and article photographs—an interesting reversal of reality. Brenda, like X-girl, was white, but more obviously "cheap," outside the lines of social acceptability, in excess. She either did not care or she did not know how to walk the fine line between being appealingly popular and slutty. And because she was unapologetic, she deserved to be talked about, laughed at, rejected. She was asking for it. Of the two girls huddled together, the white girl was most expressive, the instigator; the black girl, while in it, was a harder read—her expression was ambiguous. But clearly they had a secret and the very possibility of their cross-racial friendship depended on the rejection of Brenda. In their collusion they adopted a superficial multiculturalism that reconfigured the battle lines: gender and proper sexuality, not race, were of primary concern.

The message we're supposed to get from this ad goes something like this: Converse shoes are your ticket to popularity; if you wear them you will be cool enough to cross racial lines, you will have a modern multicultural boyish-athletic-asexual or safely sexual identity, protected from fear and ostracism. These shoes are your ticket to the big secret; buy them and avoid becoming objectified and used by boys, glared at and rejected by girls; you will be safe from Brenda's sluttiness, her ignorance, her excess. Buy them and you will be Carla and Rachel, desired, invited in.

Because the ad would have the girls who read *Seventeen* join in the rejection of Brenda, to see this rejection as basis for friendship, it co-opts them in this version of girlfighting. It is, in fact, Carla and Rachel who create the *real* anxiety here. Carla and Rachel, cool, in control, popular, mean, justified, as feared as they are longed for. The fact of the matter is that in this ad, no girl is admirable and nothing is stable or secure. Know this. Watch your back.

Converse, of course, isn't alone in its astute awareness of what adolescent girls most fear and want. A few years earlier, Candies shoes conveyed the same message. Under a picture of two girls laughing together at a slumber party, their caption let us in on the secret: "She was the only girl in high school that didn't own Candies. . . . Maybe that's why she never had a date." And Sun-In, perhaps the most recent product to exploit adolescent girls' fears in this way, shows a full-page spread of a conventionally gorgeous, thin, blonde, blue-eyed girl staring provoca-tively at the camera. "Four out of 5 girls you hate ask for it by name," reads the copy. "Stop hating them. Start being them."

"Advertising has always sold anxiety and it certainly sells anxiety to the young," reports Frontline in its exposé *Merchants of Cool*. These ads bring the old "don't hate me because I'm beautiful" message to early adolescents, where the struggle to fit in and feel normal is at its peak and played out between girls, sometimes in the cruelest ways. "In middle school everything's about friends; it's all about friends," Hailey asserts, as she argues that teachers should give up trying to teach and just help kids get along. Anxiety runs high. In all these ads, girls are whispering, conspiring, excluding, and rejecting other girls. The subtle power plays, the third- and fourth-grade clubs and cliques, take on a whole new intensity in early adolescence.

Girls who write to *New Moon Magazine's* on-line voice box know this happens and how it feels, because they have experienced it:

MOLLY, 13: I was friends with some "popular" girls. Then, in sixth grade when we entered middle school, everything changed. All of them, even a couple of girls whom I had been friends with since first grade, began to ignore me. I was very hurt.

ANDREA, 14: Being popular is a big thing, even in small schools. You know who's in the "in" crowd and who isn't, and girls especially make other girls who aren't in their group feel horrible and low about themselves.

MEGAN, 13: I think girls are mean to other girls because they're insecure. They build up their self-esteem by hurting other girls.

EARLY ADOLESCENCE: A GIRL'S EYE VIEW

The middle school years are hard on all kids. Early adolescents are mov-ing into a truly complicated culture rife with mixed messages and con-tradictory expectations. "We're growing up," twelve-year-old Aviva says, "and everything is new." It's a time when gender-related expecta-tions are intensified—boys are pressed to be traditionally masculine, girls to be conventionally feminine[1]—and studies show that the boys and girls themselves approve of and actively construct such gender distinctions and expectations.[2] In their search for signs that they are normal, that they are the "right" kind of boy or girl, adolescents this age look around and grab the "best," least ambiguous examples—if not from their families and schools, then from MTV, magazines, music lyrics, or movies.

Labeling people, putting ideas and other kids into neat categories, gives the illusion of control and order in the midst of chaos. There are jocks, nerds, preps, posers, gang-bangers, wannabes, wiggers, princesses, stoners, brainiacs—a distinctive list for nearly every school. At one point Lydia, a white lower-middle-class girl from central Maine, describes the groups in her school as popular, regular, and the cast-outs or spit-upons; at another point she refers to them as the royals, the knights, and the peasants. In Aviva's Quaker school in Brooklyn, New York, there are the "popular, the semipopular, and the unpopular" people, while in Karin's private school in the Midwest there are the "popular people and the smart people." As a form of protection against the hated "preppies," Iris and her friends in New York City label themselves the "Evil Threevil." In Power Puff Girls fashion, they take on individual identities: "I was like Funky Evil, Roxie was Psycho Evil, and Nora was Smarty Evil."

Girls seem both open to and vulnerable to such labeling, perhaps because in our culture girls tend to be branded in either-or terms: good or bad, madonnas or whores, nice girls or bitches. To girls, whose bodies are changing earlier than boys, who face pressures to be good women, who become objects of others' desire before they have half a chance of being subjects of their own experience, such labels come fast and furious. Middle school-age girls thus spend a lot of time and emotional energy dancing through the minefields of prohibited behaviors. They cannot be too smart, too fat, too thin, too sexualized or sexually experienced, too angry, too full of themselves, too much their own person. In such a potentially dangerous context, where one slip can spell disaster, simply being one's complicated self is risky.

Finding or creating an "other" girl to gossip about, reject, or tease becomes a way for girls to measure their own worth in comparison to others, to assuage their fears and anxieties about not matching up or fitting in somewhere. It is also a way for girls to keep their reputations pure by hanging the "bad bits of femininity" on other girls.[3] By defining themselves against other "bad" girls, a girl's claim *not* to be what she fears most—rude, full of herself, a slut, a bitch, a dyke—appears more convincing, both to herself and to others.[4]

Gossip, teasing, or correcting other girls' behavior is also, quite simply, a way to establish consensus and hold friendships together. It is perhaps not surprising that the time girls spend talking with friends nearly triples between fifth and ninth grade,[5] or that this increase coincides with an increase in teasing and relational cruelty.[6] Girls' relationships are more intimate than boys'; they are also more painful and difficult. Finding a peer group and fitting in is perhaps the most important achievement of early adolescence.[7] Having a safe place or home in a social scene saturated with possibilities, anxieties, and daily flux offers girls a sense of security and power.

The development of a self-observing ego, one of the hallmarks of early adolescence, is another enormous achievement. It widens a girl's perspective, allows her to be more deeply compassionate and self-aware, provides the capacity to be a critical consumer—it also allows her to develop a highly attuned sense of how she appears to others, to see herself as boys and other girls see her. This age marks a genuine crisis as psychologist Erik Erikson defined it: a moment of both opportunity and danger.[8] For girls the opportunity is marked by a wonderful openness to different perspectives, and from this openness comes a deeper compassion and desire for intimacy. The danger arises when girls are pressed to give up their own voices in the service of others or to align with a dominant culture that effaces or renders marginal their cultural values and experiences. Maritza, a Latina sixth grader who wants to be a writer because "it's like you can be a time traveler," reveals this newfound awareness in a story she's written of a girl whose father is going off to war. The father "was trying to comfort [his daughter] when he told her about his own fears of going," she explains, "but really she was just mainly surprised and she hadn't realized that he could feel like this too. That other people could feel like this." And yet the daughter's sudden awareness of her father's feelings seems to override her own fear and sense of loss. Knowing "how scared he was," and that "he needed to do it fast," Maritza explains, "she didn't get so upset, or she didn't show it."

This is the legacy of a lifetime of socialization to attend to relationships or to match up to others' ideals. The capacity to appreciate different viewpoints becomes not a moment when the world of possibilities reveals itself and a girl is encouraged to listen to her own voice as distinct from those around her, but a time when she is pressed to be ever more deeply attuned to the thoughts and feelings of others. Liza, white and middle class, describes this newfound ability to read the social world as "kind of like being bilingual, being able to speak all different languages in that you can communicate with other people by seeing both sides of the story." But the point of this language acquisition is not so much to ensure that her own voice is translated properly; rather, it's to prevent conflict and make sure that she doesn't "hurt" others. Liza's cognitive abilities are spent learning to speak and interpret social languages so that she can be more "discreet," and thus avoid or manage the imminent struggles that threaten her connections with others. "You have to keep your eyes open at all times," she says, "you can't just ignore something. . . . You have to be omniscient. You have to be able to see everything, not just the physical appearance, or how well they can do something—you have to be able to see inside them in a way" if you don't want to "disturb" your friends.

As we have seen, since childhood many girls, especially middle-class girls, have been pressed to care about relationships and to avoid conflict. The pressure intensifies to become what Carol Gilligan refers to as a "crisis of connection" for many, as others' expectations and judgments make it difficult to hold onto what they feel and think and want.[9] "No one wants to hurt anyone or make a fool of themselves," Lara, who is white and middle class, explains. The answer, it seems, is to take it slow, to be wary, to "try little experiments" before committing to anything or anyone. Fools rush in. "Take things gradually and, you know, you can see how they act," twelve-year-old Neeti, South Asian and upper-middle class, advises. Morgan, also middle class, concurs: "If I had done something, been myself, and they didn't like it, that would have ruined everything." This means that girls turn their attention outward; to see themselves as others see them. Surviving early adolescence for these girls often means "keeping your eyes open and being friends with everyone."

Such an approach not only makes for an exhausting social life, but also fuels gossip and forms of relational aggression. It does so because for girls to be less than ideal, to be hurtful or unresponsive to others is a source of public shame. Shame, argues psychiatrist James Gilligan, "is the primary or ultimate cause of all violence. . . . The purpose of violence is to diminish the intensity of shame and replace it as far as possible with its opposite, pride."[10] Gilligan is writing about male physical violence, but I think shame motivates girls' relational violence as well. When conflicts or disagreements arise, how better to avoid them than to pick on someone else altogether; how better to shore up one's self-pride and reestablish shaky group solidarity than through the emotionally violent targeting of an outsider. Moreover, if fitting in is all-important, then having an exclusive group is a sign of power. Through gossip, teasing, and other forms of rejection, girls establish the rules and boundaries of such groups while they remind each other indirectly, but forcefully, of the shameful consequences of noncompliance.

Reports of exclusivity, meanness, and cruelty crop up everywhere, it seems, as girls and often their mothers struggle to make sense of the power plays between girls and the relational scar tissue they leave behind.

One mother writes about her daughter's exile and their "season in hell":

> This time last year, my happy, friendly seventh-grade daughter was voted off the island. The stars aligned, the dice rolled, the ballots were cast and she was "it." She went from being a member of the "in crowd" to becoming its designated exile. She was talked about, hated, despised, not invited, ridiculed, but mostly, most cruelly, ignored. . . . Even the fringe girls, those not quite in the clique, started avoiding my daughter. Under strict orders from the reigning queens to not speak to, look at or, God help you, sit near the victim, they complied until finally, the cheese stood alone.[11]

But some girls offer a more realistic version of themselves and are less preoccupied by societal ideals of femininity, which protects them from such shunning rituals of white middle-class girls. Sharon Lamb heard African American girls express a less idealized view of their thoughts and feelings than white girls when they were asked about their aggressive behavior. Whereas the white girls could or would not admit to bad feelings and spoke about their aggression as if it came out of nowhere, African American girls spoke in more balanced, realistic, and open ways about their aggressive feelings and actions.[12] I heard this balance also in interviews with both girls of color and white working-class girls. Twelve-year-old Tatiana, African American, describes herself both as "sometimes a bully" and "a caring person sometimes." Linda, also twelve and African American, describes a friend as "somebody who knows what's wrong and what's right and they know when to do right and when it's necessary to do wrong." At the risk of being seen as immature by other students and disruptive by teachers, a group of white working-class, middle school girls in Maine openly claimed their voices and versions of femininity in school. They were kind and they were tough. Being their loud complicated selves could get them in trouble, but it was better than being victims or invisible.[13]

GIRL POWER

So what are girls doing and how did it get so bad? How did the subtle power plays, the third- and fourth-grade clubs and cliques, become full-blown emotionally violent "girlie bullying," as "exiled's" mother calls it? What are the girls in the magazine ads and in real life whispering about and why? When Valerie Hey studied the notes adolescent girls furtively pass in school, she found that over 90 percent of what girls wrote concerned their relationships with each other; only a few concerned boys or boyfriends.[14] While Hey, like the girls in her study, took the notes and note passing seriously, she found that the girls' teachers didn't. Girls had succeeded in taking the most important, most forbidden parts of their relationships underground and enacting their anger and forms of social control beneath adults' radar, like stealth bombers. Having their notes regarded as silly or "little bits of garbage"[15] ensured privacy and full control over their relationships. They were free to say and do what they would, and thus notes "winged their way uninterrupted back and forth across the public space of the classroom."[16]

Girls are whispering, passing notes, spreading rumors, and gossiping about "who we like and who we don't really like," because these are proven, subterranean methods of communication, and because in their secrecy and invisibility is the power to contain and control other girls. "You never know what they are saying," twelve-year-old Melanie says of girls in her urban white working-class neighborhood, "and if they are talking about you, they never tell you. I tell them it isn't fair and they don't care." The intensity and vehemence with which girls gossip is connected to their own shame of not matching up to the ideal of what it means to be a girl. Shame moves them to choose undetectable ways to police others, to keep them in check, to improve them, or threaten them to stay within normal good-girl range, or to justify their rejection by underscoring their difference or "otherness." At the same time as girls are doing these things, many are functioning above ground as nice, polite, lovely girls—after all, they know from years of experience that this impersonation of a nice, perfect girl is what adults are interested in and what they will reward.

Years of experience, television viewing, and observations of adult women have prepared girls for these strategies and have taught them to enact on each other what they have endured on a daily basis. Girls' acts of hidden, horizontal violence are motivated by feeling the weight of expectations, the shame of not matching up, and the inability to openly protest or resist without being labeled a troublemaker or disruptive or bad. It's just easier and safer and more profitable to take it out on another girl, to pick on someone your own status or lower.

In spite of the increased prevalence of physical fighting in the media and in their lives girls' power is still for the most part located in the private, the personal. Girls rely on their power to affect or *move* others much more than their power *over* others—of which they have relatively little. These "powerful poisons of intimacy," as Hey calls them, hurt most because they come, often unpredictably, from those you would expect to be your allies.[17] Girls' power plays function so effectively because of their uniquely invisible and intimate nature.[18]

SHE WHO WOULD BE QUEEN

Girls' peer relationships at early adolescence are framed not in established hierarchies of power and privilege, but in cycles of popularity and isolation that shift and change in sometimes unpredictable ways.[19] While popularity may be thought of in vertical terms by girls and boys alike, for girls it is experienced more as the center of a web of relationships; the closer you are to the center, the safer and the more powerful you become. One wants to be inside, included, chosen, in on the secrets. Like the threads of a web, or the sticky insides of a honeycomb, intricate connections secure those at the center. But I imagine the dynamics to be more like the infrared radar beams that protect precious jewels in a museum. Alliances and loyalties overlap in invisible and unpredictable ways and a girl has to carefully pick her way through relationships so that she doesn't trip over something or someone and end up in the relational equivalent of Siberia.

This unpredictability keeps girls on their toes, especially if they are working their way to the center. Reality can shift without warning. "You thought you were real good friends," twelve-year-old Eva explains, "and they come over and say mean things to you . . . you're stupid or something and you don't even know why, and you didn't do anything and they are just mad at you because their friends are mad at you." Performing a certain kind of compliant femininity or masking bad feelings are often conscious self-protective strategies white middle-class girls employ. "I do all the things they like," Olivia says, "so they will like me more." "If you're not like nice," Danielle admits, "they'll get mad and we'll have a fight and so you're kind of always pressured to be nice because if you're not nice then you won't have any friends." A desire to be popular leads girls to "pretend to like someone more than you do," or to find themselves "constantly smiling and laughing and talking about things that you don't know anything about." When she's around a popular girl who "considers everyone who isn't in her crowd to be weirdos," Neeti says, she feels "sort of weird, so I try to act like I'm better, and then when I'm with normal people I'm back to my regular self." Neeti says, "I stutter because I'm nervous and I can't look directly at her." Twelve-year-old Brie, playing it safe, says: "I just smile all the time."

At Alice's private girls' school, niceness is a litmus test. "If you're popular," she says, "it just means that you're nice." To become accepted, however, new girls endure a form of relational hazing particular to elite girls: How nice can you be in the face of bad treatment? How much can you take before you get angry and blow your cover? "The kids would test," Mollie explains, "they would see how far they could go. So if the class did stuff to them and they did it back then the class wouldn't like them." If being "super nice" is critical to becoming popular, then hiding anger is very important. When her friend says, "Adele's mad at me," Adele backs way off. "I go 'No, I'm not!' And inside I'm like, 'Yes I am. I hate you. I hate you!'"

But popular girls are not always nice—quite the contrary. Popularity often means feigning niceness, a cover for intense feelings of competition and jealousy. Moreover, niceness might get you to the center, but meanness keeps you there. Power corrupts. Jenna, white and middle class, explains:

> If you start being popular and you start out being nice, you can totally warp and like turn into some mean person, ya know, like—and that's

the one reason that you get really popular. Like if you be mean to others and tease them, and then the other—people who are teased start being scared of you and they're scared to talk back, but meanwhile the people, the other popular kids, they're like, "Oh, that's so cool." You tease this poor kid and you're popular and that's so awesome.

Meanness is especially effective as a group threat. Kendra doesn't want anyone to be mad at her, not because she's afraid of disagreement with any one girl, but "because they are all going to be mean." Don Merten, exploring "the meaning of meanness" among a clique of popular seventh-grade girls dubbed "the dirty dozen" by their teachers, found that, in fact, the girls used meanness to protect themselves from the relentless pressures they felt to be "super nice."[20] They had cleverly discovered that being mean allowed them to hold onto their popularity and desirability without the risks of being called stuck-up or toppled from their position by the envy of other girls. Because competition and conflict were unacceptable for girls in their school, open meanness to other girls broke the straightjacket of the nice-girl code and became an ingenious way to hold onto their power. No one dared to mess with them.

For some girls, though, being calculating and mean is the pathway to popularity. "You can use other people to get popularity," Lila explains. Some girls "try to get all the dirt on someone and then tell it to everyone," says Anne. "I heard other people saying that you had to be nice to be popular but that's not always true," Jill argues. "You can be really mean and tease the people who are nice and aren't popular and you can be even more popular." In a context in which most girls play it safe and try to be "nice" because they want to be liked, girls like fourteen-year-old Anita, white and working class, hold court. "I act tough. I say to some people, if they bother me I threaten them. . . . I found that it works if you threaten them and then they are afraid of you, and then they do what you want them to do, or they just leave you alone."

Once popular, girls maintain their place at the center by flaunting their status openly and also carefully patrolling their borders. "It's the way she acts," complains fourteen-year-old Zoe, white and working class. "Everything that happens, her little fan club, which is everybody, always has to agree with her. It's just like, 'I don't like you, so stay away from me.'" Kristin and her group of white middle-class friends found this same attitude in their school. "Deidre was walking down the hall with a bunch of friends, with Cassie, and I dropped like a book or something . . . and Deidre picked it up for me, and I was like 'thanks,' and Cassie goes: 'don't talk to her.'" "It's like prejudice," Lydia adds. "I mean," Kirstin admits, "some people I'm like afraid of. There's this girl, she's like a real bully, and she always asks me for the answers . . . and I don't want to give her them . . . but I always move my hand for her . . . she has a lot of power. Like she's really popular, and she—" "Well, she can get to the popular people," Lydia interrupts.

In Ruby's urban public school, the popular girls

> always pick on everybody else, so they know they are the tops. . . . They're popular, touchy feely . . . always playing, hitting, playing with the other person's hair, hugging, and stuff like that. . . . Everyone in the eighth grade knows them, they play around. It's like the two girls and then all the boys are all over them, be always touching. . . . They play too much and then they go around smelling each other's hair and . . . they think they're better than everybody else.

One can almost feel the sexual energy and see the overt displays of intimacy and exclusivity. As sociologist Barrie Thorne notes, "the lives of the popular often become public domain."[21]

This means that the most popular girls become the target of vast amounts of gossip and condescension. Much as Lydia and Kristin and their "regular" group of girlfriends talk about and hate the popular girls, their envy is palpable. "She's like the popularest girl in the school," Kirstin says sarcastically, making a face. "She's so nice and sweet and athletic and pretty and smart." Since in their school smart girls and popular girls circulate in different groups, the popular girls are reduced by Kristin and her friends to the lowest common denominator—the "hee, hee, heeing girls," "mindless airheads," concerned only with their looks and boys, an "embarrassment to other girls." Kristin and her friends could not stop talking about them and could not stop desiring to be them.

QUEEN OF THE HILL

In some cases girls literally fight their way to the center or, in the case of physical fighting, to the top of the hill. While most girls think that "girls talk and boys have another way of expressing" themselves, girls fight too and, according to reports and the girls themselves, more often than they used to. As Erica, who's white and middle class, says, "I think there's a lot of physical fighting in girls, because like now I guess people don't really talk it over . . . like if you're mad and there are people around you or there's no one around you to like talk or anything, then you can lose it and start fighting."

Girls are sometimes called "brutal," "mean," and "tough" and they get "carried away" and "lose it" at times. In fact, according to Brandy, white and working class, "girls can fight just as bad as boys, but they fight better, because they don't get the little wussy punches, you know, they really punch, girls do, they have the power." From Brandy's perspective, "boys are soft-hearted. . . . Women in general are tougher. . . . I've noticed changes in a couple of my friends. They got more tough and are sticking up for themselves, not taking any guff from anybody."

Girls talk about resorting to violence and threats of violence to seek revenge, to protect themselves and others, and also to keep peace. Fourteen-year-old Becka, white and working class, justifies fighting because "they'd gang up on us and try to kick Shannon, like throw her against the wall and everything; they totally hated her for no reason at all." "I act tough," Anita says. "I threaten them, but I never carry my threats out because I can't stand to see people hurt." When she sees two kids arguing and insulting each other on the bus, Anita says, "'I say if you don't shut up now I'm going to come up to you and beat you up. You will not believe how much you are going to hurt.' I never really do anything more than that. . . . I haven't hit anyone in my life. I go after them and they run away. I can't stand hitting or hurting people."

There is, it seems, a certain resonance to physical girlfights, or at least to the ones girls are willing to describe. Along with their justification for picking a fight or defending themselves, girls often convey their regret for causing another girl pain or hurt. "I was screaming," Norine says, "and then realized I felt really bad and kept apologizing because I hit her really hard." Tatiana's description of herself "as a bully" but also "a caring person" allows her to fight and threaten when she needs to, but to hold a certain line. It's rare that a girl talks about fighting without expressing a mix of emotions, some sadness or shame or reluctance along with the rage and righteousness.[22] Ruby, African American and working class, talks about fighting this way:

There was this girl named Marti. . . . it was me and my cousin and another friend of mine . . . and we were like [downtown] and so the girls was like, she was working, she's underage and we went and told on her. So we came back and my cousin is the type of girl that likes to fight, so she was over there telling her, "Yah, your mother works the street," and arguing with her to get her mad. So then my cousin was like, "I can't fight her because then I will go back to [the youth center]." So she said, "Why don't you fight her?" And I wasn't in the mood for fighting, so now she said something to aggravate me, so we sort of argued and then my cousin pushed her. . . . She fell down and she jumped up and hit me. I didn't do nothing to her. . . . And I gave her my shot. . . . I didn't really want to fight her, but I gave her my shot and I guess you could say that I was sort of pushed into it. . . . She was too scared of my cousin so her reaction was to get to me. . . . We could have avoided that and I sort of liked this girl. I don't really know her. . . . I think we didn't have to fight just to prove we were bad or anything.

Ruby wasn't looking for a fight. She says she had to fight "because it's like, if you walk away you're chicken," and because she "sort of protected" her cousin. This was also about self-respect—about not letting an insult go unanswered. "Because who is going to sit there as you talk about their mother and be calm? Nobody is going to." All these reasons, and yet Ruby gives us more than anger; she tells us that the girl she fought was "scared" and sort of likable. Ruby describes herself as part of the "quiet group" in her school and thinks people should "respect each other more," and "not put people down and take them for what they are."

The one arena I find where girls are unlikely to express regret is fighting over boys, and fighting over "guys" is a pretty common experience. As Simone, white and working class, says nonchalantly, "We used to fight a lot over guys. A guy would come up to me and she'd like him and we'd get mad at each other, or the other way around." Donna, thirteen and from rural Maine, describes her response when she introduced her friend to a boy, only to have her friend reject her: "I introduced them and then she started acting wicked mean to me and I told her I didn't like the way she was acting, so she pulled my hair and then I pushed her down to the ground and we just started fighting."

In most cases, physical fighting or acting tough and invulnerable is not a means to popularity for girls, at least within the school system. In school, popularity is the result of not only peer acceptance and admiration, but also adult approval and school-sanctioned status. Fighting can, in fact, ensure a girl's outsider status and girls sometimes fight as a way to separate themselves from white feminine ideals and behaviors they see as "wussy" or weak. Indeed, when girls talk about fighting they often invoke comparisons to boys and male power. Working-class girls, like Angela, "try not to show" hurt feelings because "I feel like a wimp when I do." The association between femininity and wimpiness and masculinity and toughness is important. Girls talk as though fighting like a boy is the ultimate expression of freedom, the rejection of all constraint and fear. This is arguably more about the girls' own fantasies and desires than about boys' realities, but it is a belief that sparks girlfighting. In any case, when girls imagine themselves being boys they say things like, "I would have told them to bring it on," or "If I was a boy I could beat on somebody, maybe another big boy, I'd kick the crap out of him 'cause all the guys think they're tough. I'd go cause trouble."

It's important, however, not to assume that teasing about sexual and romantic behavior or the ritual teasing more prominent in working-class white and black girls' peer groups is always about power struggles or signs of competition for status or precursors to physical girlfighting. While such teasing may look and sound harsh, it can be playful—a way to socialize others into the group, a way to practice self-defense strategies, a way for girls to protect themselves against male ridicule, even a way to dissolve competition over boys.

Girls attribute what they see as an increase in "fist fighting," as opposed to "talk fighting" (or what one middle-class white girl refers to as "pleasant fights") to the media. "We kind of get that from magazines and TV, like pushing each other," explains Edie, who's white and middle class, "but it's a lot more than it used to be." Indeed, a glance at TV shows like *Buffy the Vampire Slayer, Dark Angel, Alias, Birds of Prey*, or movies like *Charlie's Angels; Crouching Tiger, Hidden Dragon;* or *Tomb Raider* would support her argument. Beauty can also be the beast. Femininity in the new millennium is contested territory.

But it's also old territory. Whether we're talking about mudwrestling or soap opera hair pulling or Jerry Springer–like name-calling, girlfighting as voyeuristic and erotic is not lost on the girls either. It's certainly not lost on Julia, white and middle class: "Guys like to stand around and watch girls when they physically fight and make a catfight or whatever and they think something will happen between them. But like if there's no one to stop them, then it becomes more; people do that more often and then they get hurt and then it keeps happening."

Regardless of whether a girl detests it or desires it or both, being at the center or at the top looks safe and secure and powerful from the outside. But popularity among the popular girls is often treacherous and unstable, in part because it relies so much on fraudulent and competitive relationships and in part because it is motivated by fear—fear of being left out, of making mistakes, of not matching up, of being invisible, pushed down, or pushed out to the margins. Being popular looks great from the outside, but it isn't always liberating for girls; it can be tightly constraining and even threatening. Because of intense competition to get in and stay in, girls in such groups can be especially mean to one another. And the one at the top is most vulnerable, the clear target for any girl inside or outside the group. "Everyone feels, I mean competes, to be the best, like coolest," says Mia. Ironically, being the most popular can cost a girl her individuality, loyalty, genuine connections with others, and security. The price middle school girls pay for their inclusion and social power is constant scrutiny and group conformity—they are "in" if they play the game and follow the rules just right.

GIRL-SLURS: SLUT-BASHING, FAT TALK, AND THE BITCH

Whether you are in the popular group or on the outside looking in, on top or scrambling to be there, the incentive to create an "other" girl is enormous; it is the way a girl either maintains her popularity or justifies her insider status, the way she can claim to be good, normal, attractive, tough, cool. As nineteen-year-old Sarah explains, thinking back on her experience at early adolescence, it's also motivated by fear:

> In early adolescence, the fear of rejection is intense; it is as if everyone, even those who are popular, are being held over a pit of lions just waiting to be dropped; waiting for the moment when they will be the victim. I was terrified of the lion's pit of ridicule and was constantly scratching and clawing to keep myself above it, even if that meant tossing in others to save myself.

While most of their time and intimate conversations are with girl-friends and girls write "long conspiratory notes," Maritza says, an effective way to gossip involves slam books—notebooks in which girls record their frank and often cruel opinions of other girls. Maritza explains:

> Well, you write the names of all these people first, and then sometimes you'll say prettiest, ugliest, smartest, most likely to succeed, uh, stupidest—whatever—in the back. And then you pass it around and people will go through it and write what you think of everyone.

These days notes and slam books have given way to e-mail exchanges and instant messaging, all the more attractive because they cannot be easily traced if discovered. Exiled's mother found out about the "smear campaign" directed at her daughter when she discovered a batch of e-mails her daughter had saved on the family computer. "The electronic missives went beyond mean to breathtakingly evil and they were attached to extensive buddy lists."

This written record of girls' flaws and faults creates a kind of low-level surveillance that produces a lot of anxiety. How does one know whom to trust? Like informants to the KGB, the watchers and judgers hope for protection and safety, but of course their activities perpetuate the status quo and their subordinate place in it. That is, they are judging other girls against dominant cultural ideals of femininity: on how well they contain their sexuality and negotiate heterosexual romance, conform to white middle-class ideals of beauty, and collude in passive, nondisruptive, "nice girlness."

Slut-Bashing

In her provocative book *Slut!* Leora Tanenbaum reports the enormous power girls have to change the course of another girl's life with one simple accusation. Being labeled a slut by other girls or by boys doesn't necessarily have anything to do with sex or sexual behavior, but is a way for girls to seek revenge or to control another girl who is too different or too popular or threatening in some way. It is, as Tanenbaum says, "an all-purpose insult for any female outsider,"[23] a stand-in for something else altogether: "how well she fits into the American ideal of femininity."[24]

When Tannenbaum interviewed women who had been accused of being sluts in adolescence, she heard an unfortunate refrain: how cruel girls could be. "Nearly every 'slut' told me that girls had either engineered the ostracism themselves or were more hurtful than boys."[25] The personal pain comes from the experience of betrayal—that other girls would attack one this way—and that friends would recoil or back away for fear of being the next target.

Slut-bashing reaches epic proportions in middle school because girls' bodies are developing in a culture that is simultaneously sexually obsessed and sexually repressed. Girls' bodies are looked at, objectified, and desired by boys and men at the same time that they invite judgment, anxiety, fear, and attempts at protection and control by girls and women. The cruel ostracism girls can direct at those who develop early physically arises out of anxiety and their own fear of being different, of not fitting in, of being targeted for reasons beyond their control. When girls' bodies become public property—something people comment on, play with, look at; when, as twelve-year-old Robin, white and middle class, says, "you walk down the hall and all of a sudden part of your anatomy is in somebody else's hand"—it becomes terribly difficult to maintain personal integrity and control.

Girls know they are one mistake away from being labeled a slut themselves and they know a culturally sanctioned double standard increases the risk. "If a guy did something," Tessa from rural Maine argues, "he's considered a stud; if a girl did something, she's considered really bad." "If a girl sleeps around," Adrianna, her friend, agrees, "she could be a slut. If a guy did that his friends would say, 'cool.' The girls don't do stuff because society holds them differently." Girls are, indeed, "held" differently—their sexuality is contained more and their desire is nearly unspeakable.[26]

In a culture in which a girl who has sex is a slut and a boy who has sex is a stud or player, reputation is everything. And in a culture in which even "best friends decide that you aren't cool anymore and they don't want to be friends anymore," it's hard to count on anyone to stick up for you or "have your back," as girls say, if you cross the imaginary line into sluttiness. It makes perfect sense that girls, in such unpredictable circumstances and under the threat of harsh judgment and rejection, would defend themselves and secure their own good-girl status by casting aspersions on other girls.

Tanenbaum comments on the "subtleties of emotional cruelty" girls display.[27] A girl's power over other girls comes from the way she conveys that she can make their private knowledge public property. In other words, a girl can use the social damnation of girls' bodies and the cultural double standard around sexuality for her own purposes. Such a threat is enough to make most other girls fall in line. Those who don't are in for it.

A girl has to be very careful not to upset the delicate balance she forges between being cool, being liked or desired, and being a slut. A big part of maintaining the balance is not to upset anyone—girls or boys—lest she endure the worst kind of revenge. Twelve-year-old Sandy, white and working class, knows this well as she tries to decide how not to offend a boy she doesn't want to date:

> Well, you see I was afraid that if he got mad at me, he might find someone else to like and tell them something about me that was not true . . . and I didn't want, you know, the girl that he likes whispering to someone else, "blah, blah, blah," something bad, not very nice, not true. They could whisper something to one of their girlfriends and I don't want any rumors going around that I am something that I'm not. . . . I figured if I could just pretend to be what he thought I was [his girlfriend], then I would sort of ease out and just become his friend and let him meet someone else new. . . . Well, it's hard because you are between a rock and a hard place. You know, it's like if you turn this way, if you are trying to go to sleep and there is only a hard rock for you to sleep on and then over there you say, maybe this is better but that's just a whole bunch of little bitty rocks and it is very uncomfortable, so either way it would be bad. But this way, I think I did something because at least I am not lying on a hard floor and I am not lying on hard pebbles either. I am sort of in between. . . . I just felt normal.

What's "normal" for Sandy and other girls her age is negotiating the "in between," finding that place of least discomfort, fitting in, feeling safe. This in between state gets harder and harder to orchestrate because signs of purity are both not cool and necessary. Dressing in spaghetti–strap tops, low rider jeans, and miniskirts has to be balanced by carefully downplaying sexualized behavior. Until recently, Britney Spears herself—all bad girl tough and sexual; good girl sweet and smiley—insisted weekly that she was still a virgin. The costs of implying otherwise are obvious (Britney has paid the price in record sales) and a girl spends a lot of time attending to people and relationships simply as a means of social survival. But her responsiveness to others is often wasted time and energy since what it buys her is, at best, uncertain and tenuous. There is no guarantee that she or her reputation won't be attacked anyway.

"The capacity of girls to reposition other girls within the regime of the male gaze is a *general* capacity of girls' friendships," Valerie Hey argues.[28] Repositioning other girls from subject to object, from girl to sexualized body, serves to chasten a girl, allowing her to claim her purity and goodness. It also places her in the driver's seat; she has the power—backed by the weight of the culture—to simplify, objectify, and dehumanize other girls. For girls at early adolescence, this means looking at other girls and judging them through male eyes.

In so doing, however, girls forswear their connections to other girls and deny the oppressive experiences and the social contexts that contribute to their own "catty" behavior. Talking about guys at a party, for example, a group of white working-class girls are quick to put down another girl who was, as Stacey says, "playing hard to get. The bitch." When the boys begin to bet on whether this girl "would do it" with the boy she was with, some of the girls try to join in:

> STACEY: Yeah, he said . . . "Come on, I've got five bucks riding on this!"
>
> SUSAN: No!
>
> STACEY: No, he said that to her. 'Cause him and Charles had a bet.
>
> RACHEL: Yeah, they did. And I did too, but I didn't have enough money, so they wouldn't let me bet.
>
> STACEY: Yeah, me neither. I only had eleven cents.
>
> DIANE: Well, who was betting who?
>
> STACEY: Charles and Jon. Charles won.
>
> RACHEL: He's so nice. He's really cool.

In this instance the girls fully accept the boys' reading of the reluctant girl's refusal to have sex at the party—she is "a tease" and "a bitch"—and identify with the boys' behavior by trying to join in on the joke. Reading the boys' refusal to let them join as an issue of money rather than power, they ignore the boys' attempts to exclude them. Instead they further separate themselves from the other girl and align themselves with these "cool" boys who were "sitting there swearing in the car," bragging about who "could kick the piss out of who."

What this move to reject other girls' experiences for boys' construction of reality yields, of course, is not real power. All the posturing and imitating in the world doesn't give a girl the cultural currency of a boy or ensure that she won't be the next bitch or slut; it just gives her the status of a male "mini-me." In the meantime, she's cut herself off from herself and other girls—the real source of her power. There is, of course, the power to be chosen by boys as girlfriends and the competition on this turf is intense. But this, too, is an illusion, albeit a highly desired one held in place through the rejection of all those other girls who have failed to make the grade and get the guy.

Fat Talk

Fat talk is the term Mimi Nichter and her colleagues use to describe the "I'm so fat" discourse among girls and how it facilitates their social relations.[29] Girls' awareness of others' bodies starts early. When we were watching a video of her swimming class, my daughter, then five, commented not on the skills she had just displayed, but on her stocky friend: "Deidre looks fat." Her deadpan delivery surprised me more than her comment. My explanation that we all have different bodies and isn't that cool, was lost on her because her comment was not evaluative really; it was an observation of a difference that hadn't yet, but soon would, make a huge difference in her and her friend's life.

The evidence is astonishing. By age six children show a strong preference for thin figures and ascribe positive attributes to them; by ten and eleven, children rank drawings of obese children the lowest of all those they are asked to evaluate, including children with severe disabilities.[30] As many as 80 percent of girls at early adolescence are dieting at any given time,[31] and while 78 percent of teenagers overall are dissatisfied with their weight,[32] they are more likely to feel dissatisfied at puberty, when they experience a natural "fat spurt."[33] For white girls in particular, failing to meet the dream of becoming Barbie or Britney is devastating[34] and can lead girls to be deeply competitive and jealous of one another. Beautiful girls invite envy and jealousy; "I hate her," girls say, "I want to hurt her," "I could just kill her."[35]

Girls have a "unique capacity to 'get beneath each others' skin by establishing powerful judgments upon the surfaces of each others' bodies," Nichter comments. Anger at another girl's actions or ill-treatment quickly translates into physical critique: "She's ugly," "She's fat," "Did you see her thighs?"[36] For girls of color, more accepting of a range of body types, such judgments tend to focus more on skin color and hair.[37] "Who does she think she is?" a group of black and Latina girls ask about a Haitian girl who has bleached her short black hair. "Blonde ambition," they chortle. "Usually if [girls] are mean and they don't like somebody and there's one person who everybody gangs up on," thirteen-year-old Cheryl explains, "then they'll probably say things about her like, 'Oh my God, did you see what she's wearing? Oh, oh, oh, did you see her butt? Oh, I know! Doesn't she look ugly? Ohhh! Look at her hair!'" Like slut-bashing, such body gossip serves the purpose of creating solidarity among girls. But solidarity based on competition over a cultural ideal of physical beauty no real girl can attain leads nowhere; it's the relational equivalent of quicksand. It is, in fact, as Nichter says, the basis of "a politics of separation among girls. . . . They reach consensus about her limitations and thereby neutralize the threat she poses. By identifying and naming the flaws and by talking loudly about them, girls strengthen their sense of self-worth in opposition to that of others in a world marked by competition."[38]

For white middle-class girls, the competition is over the feminine ideal, of course, the perfect girl—the perfect body, face, personality all rolled into one package. This is the girl who is chosen—to be loved by the ideal boy, to be looked at and envied by other girls. But once a girl has attained anything near perfection, she opens herself to the envy and attacks of other girls who scrutinize her for any noticeable flaw. "And if somebody notices somebody else's flaws," Pam explains, "they're gonna tell a lot of other people about that, and then people are gonna know that person for whatever is bad about them."

Ironically, I think that for white girls the dream of perfection is also a dream of moving beyond the shame of not matching up to securing a place outside the relentless competition and relational treachery, a place where they can be genuinely and comfortably themselves. When Liza, upper-middle class, conventionally beautiful and so perfectly put together, asks longingly if "there's such a thing as a person who has everything together all the time. . . . Not *appears* to be, but just does," one feels both her hope and her exhaustion.[39] In the absence of a satisfying answer, the race is on.

The struggle is often deeply painful all the way around, because girls know that fitting in means sacrificing not only yourself but your friends. "If they're really my friends," thirteen-year-old Sonja explains, "I shouldn't care what kind of clothes they have and what they look like. . . . [My friend] has braces and she's really fat, but you really like her but you don't want to be seen with her." Girls this age witness every day what happens to "fat" girls and it is terrorizing. As boys are contaminated by femininity, girls risk being contaminated by weight. Kirsten and her friends talk about a "really nice" girl who is teased relentlessly in their junior high school:

> I mean a lot of times the people who aren't popular are a lot
> nicer than those people who are. I mean, just because they're
> not as pretty. There's this one girl, um, I really like her. I'm
> not really her friend, because I don't know her that well.
> She's really nice, but people make fun of her really bad because she's like huge. And um, all the boys are always like
> . . . What are some of the things they say to her?
> JANE: "I love you, Joanne" [in teasing voice].
> THERESA: Or they write on the board someone likes Joanne.
> LYDIA: They call her um, Misty II and Misty Joanne.[40]
> LYN: Does anybody speak up?
> LYDIA: It's so hard, I mean it's hard to stick up for people because you don't want to turn into how that person is being
> treated, so you have to be careful what you say.
> KATHY: A lot of times it does turn on you. It happens to me all
> the time.

These girls are onto something. They know what they can expect if they stand up for girls who threaten the beauty ideal and so they adjust their voices and visions. "The worst thing about being a girl," Natalie, white and working class, laments, is that "you get put down about your size or your body or your feelings." Indeed, for girls this age, body and heart are inextricably connected. Given this, it is devastating that peers and friends are the worst perpetrators of appearance teasing and early adolescence is when such criticism is most likely to occur.[41] Such teasing is a kind of "negative verbal commentary" or what Maritza's teacher calls "verbal vandalism"—"like you spray-painted them, in their face or something."

But the emotional effects can be even more powerful than any physical harm; they can have both immediate and long-term deleterious consequences for a girl's sense of self. Such teasing is related to depression, levels of eating disturbance, and self-esteem.[42] The shame and sadness such comments inflict are so deep that the perpetrator is often immediately aware of her power—a power derived from and reinforced by cultural prejudice. Lydia explains the way she sees such prejudice operating:

> We live in a society where I think thin is pretty, and it's kind of hard to say, "Well, so what if they're fat." It's just that . . . I think the way standards have been set, it's just, it's kind of stuck. Like, um, Mr. Webber was telling us in seventh grade that he grew up, or somebody told us, in the south, and they were, I mean, they were taught to not like black people. And it's just, that's just the way they were grown up, the kind of environment they were brought up in, so if you have nothing else, then what are you going to believe, you know?

This reference to racism is important because underlying all the relentless policing around physical beauty is a thinly veiled allusion to white ideals of feminine beauty. As psychologist Janie Ward reminds us, "the identification of beauty as defined by white America has always been an assault on the personhood of black women."[43] And just as white girls police each other, so do girls of color. A white standard of beauty is nurtured by the media, especially by advertisers who, as Susan Bordo explains,

> continuously play upon and perpetuate consumers' feelings of adequacy and insecurity over the racial characteristics of their bodies. They insist that in order to be beautiful, hair must be straightened and eyes lightened; they almost always employ models with fair skin, Anglo-Saxon features, and "hair that moves," insuring association of their products with fantasies of becoming what the white culture most prizes and rewards.[44]

Speaking of African American women, Ward explains, "We can be very cruel to one another when it comes to color consciousness in childhood and adolescence. . . . Judging each other by a false standard of beauty, black teens—particularly black girls—can create a climate in which they or their friends end up internalizing these negative feelings about their looks."[45]

Thus, such gossip about other girls, their bodies, hair, skin color, and clothes does more than establish the parameters of a girl's peer group, does more than send the message that if you go too far and refuse to follow group rules, you risk being voted off the island. Such talk maintains a hierarchy of beauty, acceptability, purity—in short, it supports and even reproduces racist, classist, and homophobic attitudes, values, and ideals. As a result, resisting it is dangerous and difficult.

"I'm so fat," Nichter tells us, is in the end a code for "out of control," for feeling bad all over.[46] It is, then, encoded commentary about a girl's struggle to feel good about herself in a world swirling with contradictions and mixed messages and signs that she is excessive and bad if she is real and true to herself. Putting herself down neutralizes her friends' anxiety. So it also becomes a way of connecting to others, of suggesting she is no better than anyone else.[47] But how does one stay connected to oneself when to do so is so hazardous to one's sense of security and short-term happiness? How does one feel good under constant pressure to profess unhappiness so others won't feel bad?

The Bitch

As we've heard in earlier chapters, for the youngest children bossiness is a gendered insult; it's a name that boys and girls alike give to girls who are considered controlling, mean, or aggressive, but also just too full of themselves. It is a term heavily laden with judgment and moral value. Girl is to woman as bossy is to bitch. "Nice girls," especially nice white girls, don't want this label. Being thought of as bossy or bitchy by her friends is a way in which highly ambitious or assertive girls are socialized into disguising their competence.[48] Maritza is one of those highly ambitious girls.

Maritza attends a private coed school. She refers to her cultural background as "pretty mixed up." In her family there are Jews and Catholics; at weddings or bat mitzvahs she's as likely to hear Yiddish and Spanish as English. At eleven, Maritza is a brown belt in karate, a talented writer, and a girl who is aware that those who appear "all terrific and everything" often harbor deep fears and anxieties. She knows that girls who are fake are dangerous and girls who are bossy or "snobby" are not liked, and so she and her friends monitor each other and themselves. Their fights, in fact, like many girls' fights, serve as reminders to muffle their ambitions and contain their attitudes: "It's usually something like, 'You're just a stuck-up, um, selfish dadadada.'" "Stuck-up means that they consider themselves above other people and selfish means that they only think about themselves. Neither are very good qualities."

A year later, at twelve, Maritza is ever more conscious of appearing too terrific herself. She's in a new, more culturally diverse public school and she finds that "it's nice finding out how good my friends are . . . and it's nice having a niche and a reputation." But, she says, "I try not to be too ambitious because I know what happened to Caesar." Maritza, who describes herself as "clever" and a "nerd," has to be careful. She is being "insulted" and "teased" by other girls and her friend is not supporting her. She knows that there is a "network of spies finding out everything" and it pays to be vigilant. "I want to be at least fairly famous," she admits. "But I don't know. People are jealous of famous people." Maritza is perceptive, she knows from looking around at her peers that "it's easier to go along with the flow."

At thirteen, now in the eighth grade, Maritza is a black belt in karate and is taking an advanced creative writing course at a nearby college, earned as a result of high scores on the SAT. "I had a best friend for a couple of years, but now I don't anymore," she says. This year she's "started to keep a diary for the first time . . . because it's not going to judge me." She no longer likes school, "partly because the kids don't like me too much . . . 'cause I'm too smart. They call me a nerd. They think I'm different." "It's pretty bad," she says, "when it's someone who I think was my friend, and they turn around and start insulting me. I had one girl who sat next to me in class and insulted me for thirty minutes straight. . . . They don't like the way I talk. They think my vocabulary is weird and my grammar is too good. . . . There are some kids who are my friends, but a lot of them would be very happy to see me fail."

Maritza chooses to ignore the insults, to be "nice" so she won't "get in trouble" with teachers and as a means of protection from other girls. "Well, nobody's ever tried to beat me up or anything yet. But they might do that, or they might just gang up against me verbally." Her black belt seems useful, but only as a way to "at least keep myself from being as badly hurt as I would be if I didn't know karate. . . . You know, it really depends on how many kids are there."

So Maritza, who describes herself as "sensitive to injustice" and "pretty outspoken," lies low and this takes its toll on her and her family. "Even if I can contain myself and be nice while I'm at school, then when I go home I get upset and I argue with my mother and my father and my brother, because there's only so much of that you can take." Given her experiences, she wonders about girls and "what 'friend' means to someone."

> Because there are a lot of people I know, and their friends don't seem to act really like friends. . . . Friends just gossip about each other or aren't really nice to each other or jealous of each other. Not ordinary jealous, but really jealous. . . . So jealous that you couldn't be their friend anymore. . . . I would like to know what a friend means to them, because I don't think anyone thinks of themselves as bad or as unfriendly or as unfaithful.

Maritza carefully guards her achievements and capabilities and her strong feelings because they threaten to bring her down—"nerd" can become obnoxious, arrogant, and bitch in no time and the threat of verbal or physical violence means Maritza has to go it alone.

There are other common forms of bitchy behavior, though. Perhaps not surprising, in the context of so much sexual and physical surveillance, is the "back-stabbing," "two-faced" bitch. She could be your best friend, she could be the girl who sits beside you in math class, or she could be someone you don't know. It was bad enough that Adrianna and Marie decided not to vote for their good friend, Lilly, to be class representative and that the less popular girl they supported won by one vote, but then Marie told Lilly it was Adrianna's idea. Lilly was devastated, Adrianna was left with her guilt and outrage, and Marie got what she wanted—an exclusive, inside track to Lilly's friendship. The hope for loyalty—that your friends know that "friends are supposed to stick up for each other," that your friend "will always back you up"—emerges when the fear of betrayal becomes intensified. Who said what about whom behind whose back to get what, or whose friendship, or whose boyfriend is at the back of everyone's mind. If your experience is that "after you leave someone always starts a rumor about you," you learn to be suspicious.

The bitch in this case is an ubiquitous shadow presence in the girls' interviews. She's the natural counterpoint to the perfect girl, and so she exists as an ominous threat, an ever-present phantom representing the possibility of treachery and betrayal. Since some girls discover at one time or another, in one context or another, that "the person that was my better friend wasn't," the likelihood for betrayal exists for everyone and must be carefully guarded against. The "triangles of tension"[49] so common among girls this age, have their roots in such betrayal. Girls often carry out the work of trying to enter or breaking up friendships by talking with third parties.[50]

Well rehearsed in "this pattern of shifting alliances wrapped in skeins of talk,"[51] girls half expect other girls to lie or let them down, and so arguments can get heated pretty fast. Patricia, a Latina, talks about a fight she had with one of her best friends, Brenda, "because of another girl" who started spreading rumors that Brenda and another good friend, Kenya, were gossiping about each other. This girl was "saying stuff that was not true and then we started fighting and then we didn't believe each other and then the girl finally admitted she was lying . . . because a lot of people threatened her." This girl was saying that Patricia and Kenya were calling each other bitches and "a lot of swears" and "saying that I had said Kenya was hanging with boys and that . . . me and Brenda was jealous of her and all this." Patricia regrets the fight because her first impulse was to believe the girl who had lied. "I should have, we both knew afterwards that we should have trusted each other to know that we wouldn't say that stuff." The girl who lied, it turned out, was herself jealous because a boy she liked was interested in Kenya. She was a girl who was well known in the school "for talking a lot of stuff about people." She was the bitch.

A bitch, according to girls this age, is a girl who can be motivated by self-interest, desire, or fear of her own rejection and hurt. In some cases she hides her fear by professing to be tough and invulnerable. In other cases being bitchy gives her the power and visibility she craves, as it does for Tina, who's white and working class. Tina proclaims her bitchiness with pride. "I can be a real bitch. . . . I'm happy . . . just to be a bitch. I'm a bitch and proud of it!" More often a bitch is a back-stabber or two-faced. This form of bitchiness is more endemic to white middle-class girls, perhaps because, in their desire to be chosen as romantic partners by white boys, their forms of girlfighting (which involve conflict, not at all appealing to those in power) tend to be more covert and indirect. Of course for these girls the irony is clear. The prohibition against saying mean things, which seems to include any strong feelings or direct expression of opinion, means that most things are taken underground or out of relationship—or said behind others' backs. Does it hurt worse "when your friends say they don't like you and they are just pretending to like you," or when they "say something behind my back, then act nice?" Neither, of course. Girls who cannot express the complexity and range of their feelings and expect to be understood typically play both ends against the middle and hope against hope that they don't get caught.

In the case of the back-stabber, it's the secrecy that makes for treachery, the secrecy that makes twelve-year-old Neeti observe that "everybody is friendly in our class" but there "are always people who have hurt feelings." In the absence of direct expressions of anger and confusion, girls' relationships begin to look like they are governed by what Hannah Arendt calls "the rule by nobody"—there is no source, no one to blame for the pain.

The need for a friend to "have your back," and the fear and anger at betrayal crosses racial and class lines. The betrayals girls enact on each other derive largely from the rejection of their marginal place in the social order and their desire to have power—to be visible and taken seriously. As girls come up against the dominant culture, as they receive messages about how girls ought to look and behave in order to fit in and be accepted, they also come to know from experience that this assimilation to the ideal of white femininity will ensure their subordination. When girls call each other bitches (or even when they embrace their "bitchiness"), they are appropriating misogynistic language used to control and constrain girls and women; they are using the tools of patriarchy against other girls.

MY BEST FRIENDS ARE GUYS

In her first-year interview, at eleven years old, Maritza says a curious thing—for her at least, since she rarely mentions boys in her interview: "I think boys are a good change from girls, because sometimes girls can be really soft and really giggly and really stupid, so sometimes I switch over to boys and play with them. And most of the boys accept me."

The refrain "most of my friends are guys" emerges at early adolescence and gains momentum throughout the middle school years, just as girls are pressed to be more narrowly feminine and surveillance and scrutiny of other girls intensify. I don't think this is a coincidence. Listening to girls explain why they look to boys for friends tells us a whole lot about what they hope to escape and what they desire and hope to gain.

Signs of increasing control and constraint among girls and their friends are fully evident. Sondra, white and middle class, talks about how her wish to know another girl is thwarted by that girl's friend. "It's sort of like she possessed her or something," she explains. "She was like, Margaret is mine, you know, and you can't touch her." As Bea, also white and middle class, says, girls are "picky about who their friends hang out with, they want to control who their friends hang out with." Girls "try to change" their friends, "choose friends for you," pressure you "to dress like them." Control is a big thing for girls this age, especially white middle-class girls. As Lauren explains her fights with her best friend, "she likes to have complete control and so do I."

People overcontrol when they themselves feel threatened and controlled, when they are uncertain, when the environment is unpredictable and unsafe, as it is so often among girls. It's at this developmental moment that many girls simply opt out of relationships with girls and shift their allegiance to boys. As fourteen-year-old Liza, white and upper-middle class, says:

> Girls are not always the best friends to have. I would rather have a guy friend. Girl friends are really picky, the slightest thing you do wrong . . . guys are more accepting as friends. Girls are more critical of you. You have to be careful about what you do and say or else [girls] will think you are really weird. Guys are more accepting. I think they're more like a true friend relationship rather than something else.

Amber, white and working class, agrees. She hangs with guys because "girls are so picky. I'm not picky like most girls are. If you have a hair out of place, they'll tell you about it." They act "like they're better than other people." And "guys are easier to talk to," agrees her friend Emily. "Girls are worried about their reputations and keeping friends with the most popular girl, stuff like that. Most guys don't care. It's not important for [guys] to blab their secrets around." "When I'm with my friends that are girls it's more gossipy," says Susan, also white and working class. "We gossip wicked bad; with a guy you just talk. . . . I don't like to talk about people behind their backs. . . . Girls are harder on girls than guys are on guys." Thirteen-year-old Faith agrees, "You have to watch what you say with girls."

According to these girls, boys are less "picky," less "stuck up," less "cliquey," they tend to "stick up for each other," they "get along with each other," and "they'd never say anything behind my back." Guys "have more confidence in themselves than girls usually do." If you were a guy, Tammy says, you wouldn't "have to worry about people making fun of you, or worry about people telling you the way you should or shouldn't dress; you don't have to worry about other people's opinions or attitudes toward you." Looking out on the rocky landscape of girls' friendships, it looks pretty "happy-go-lucky" for guys.[52]

Girls say they want this simplicity; they want to escape from the intensity of girls' judgment, they want the relief that comes from "not caring." But they also want power—the power not "to have to worry," the power that promises freedom from constraint, from control, from regulation. It's important to underscore that this constraint comes not just from other girls, of course. It comes from parents and teachers and other guardians of the culture anxious that girls fit in. ("Don't you want to be liked?" they are asked. "Don't you want a boyfriend?") And it is experienced, increasingly so, within romantic relationships with boys. Alecia's guy friend became "weird" when she began to date him, for example. "Me and Jon were really good friends and then he asked me out," she explains. "And after that conversations ended. We started talking about, 'How was your day?' And I was like, 'Fine.' It was weird." Fourteen-year-old Tanya, who's white and middle class, struggled with her boyfriend's jealousy when she hung out with a guy friend. "He got really mad and upset and didn't want me going out with him. . . . I decided to stay home."

But while the constraint seems to come from everywhere, girls take their feelings and frustrations out primarily on other girls; they blame and turn away from girls as the source of their problems. The power that girls gain comes at the expense of other girls (and ultimately, themselves) because it draws on and thus perpetuates stereotypically gendered arguments. Girls negate other girls for being so typically and frustratingly girly. Girls join boys by rejecting and denigrating other girls or by hiding or rejecting any evidence of those parts of themselves that could be called conventionally feminine.

But is this possible? There is almost nothing in our cultural stories or imagery that supports egalitarian friendships between boys and girls. In fact, we assume it can't be done or at least sustained. The movie *When Harry Met Sally* is based on this generally accepted view. When girls do become friends with boys they typically do boy things like sports, or hang out, or "we pick on each other, throw each other in snow banks, kick each other around," and "talk about boy girl things, not girl girl things." Even though they reject the emotionality associated with being a girl, in their friendships with boys girls tend to take over the relational realm, naming and carrying boys' feelings for them. Girls know that "guys keep emotion in," that they are "expected to be macho all the time" and "keep everything inside and not share it," and so they offer this service, which sometimes includes talking to girlfriends or asking girls out for their guy friends.

At the same time, the rewards for rejecting other girls and being an honorary "guy" are real. Both boys and girls this age tend to think it is better to be a boy in this culture. Girls are more likely to consider their own sex role as a liability, a source of limitations,[53] and boys agree. When Myra and David Sadker asked junior high students to write about how they would feel if they woke up the next morning in the body of the opposite sex, boys found the idea horrifying. For many, death was better, and they wrote elaborate stories of escape and suicide. The girls, on the other hand, articulated a range of benefits and freedoms they would gain. Not surprisingly in a culture that values it, masculinity significantly predicts self-esteem for early adolescent girls and seems to correlate with a sense of self-worth, romantic appeal, close friendship, and social and scholastic competency.[54] Being a girl or being associated with femininity just doesn't get you very far in school or in society. The girl who is girl-identified or not yet into boys, the girl who likes both boys and girls as friends, the girl who wants to be accepted and known on her own terms, is faced with a truly monumental challenge—she is up against what Carol Gilligan terms the wall of Western culture.[55] And why hit your head against the wall when you can benefit from applying the mortar?

"When the times are a crucible, when the air is full of crisis, those who are most themselves are the real victims." Girls who show they feel good about themselves, who are overweight and dare to eat normally or wear skimpy clothing; girls who are simply satisfied with themselves, regardless of size; girls who tenaciously call out in class or genuinely and publicly take pride in their achievements; girls who are individuals, who stand up for themselves or for someone who's hurt or treated badly, who hold to their complicated selves in the face of relentless pressure to be one thing or the other, risk being called stuck-up, braggarts, bitches, sluts, or other girl-slurs used to keep them in their proper place. In their refusal to comply or to placate narrow ideals of femininity, they remind other girls of what they have given up in doing so. Refusing to bow to pressure, they raise anxiety and uncertainty in other girls because they expose Hannah Arendt's "rule by nobody" as a rule by somebody with a vested interest in maintaining the current order of things.

The need to sort out what it means to be acceptably feminine is heightened at this developmental moment, pressed by media images, the demands of boys, and the competitive relations between girls. Is a girl a girl or a wannabe boy? Is she a boy's girlfriend or a girl's girlfriend? She moves between these options and pressures, and the tension rises. Because she cannot take out her anxiety and frustration on those who are more powerful—in part because it's dangerous to do so, in part because she cannot yet fully know how this power moves through the social body to shape her—she takes it out on a safe target, other girls. There is a cultural language of denigration and subordination and victimization readily available to her and every good reason to either embrace or disconnect from those qualities that make one traditionally feminine, conventionally a girl.

 Unlike those who see this age as simply and inevitably the height of girls' meanness and cruelty to other girls, a kind of relational wasteland of sorts, I see it as an opening rich with possibilities. So much is happening at early adolescence because girls are arguing about, contesting, negotiating femininity and their relationship to it. The concept is up for grabs and that's why there is such anxiety and such a need to control others; that's why all the talk, the gossip, the fighting, and justifying. There is pressure to line up with or decontaminate from cultural views of femininity and girlhood, to be sure, but girls bring a range of voices and experiences to this moment. In relation to the narrow cultural ideal of beauty and femininity, all girls to some degree experience their failure to match up; all girls feel excessive, outside the lines. They are too smart, too plain, too short, too fat, too loud, too silly, too . . . something.

That's what makes this developmental period a site of radical possibility, a potential site of resistance.[56] The times are a crucible. The air is full of crisis and everyone's decentered. Girls are fighting with such intensity because nothing is certain or safe. Whatever pathway they choose must be vehemently protected and constantly justified. A deep and visceral awareness of the fragility of "reality" and the insecurity of the center accounts for the lateral or horizontal forms of aggression. But it's the carrot dangling before the girl who best mirrors and supports the cultural notions of femininity that accounts for the ferocity of girls' attacks on one another. Fighting is not endemic to adolescent girls, but the anxiety of change is. This anxiety and the energy that fuels girl-fighting can be directed in far more constructive ways than the typical forms of horizontal violence we see among girls. But whether because we deny its existence, fear it, see it as trivial and temporary, or dismiss it as a natural part of growing up female, most adults fail to engage girls in any consistently meaningful and genuine conversation about these issues.

Maritza begins her eighth-grade interview with a description of a story she's writing. It's a telling story, given the voices of girls in this chapter and also her particular journey. "It's about a princess who isn't beautiful. . . . Well, she, um, has a real hard time. . . . Tradition has it that . . . anyone who wants to court her has to announce his intentions on her eighteenth birthday. But no one steps forward. So this is the ultimate humiliation." The princess runs away, meets a peasant turned noble-man "who hated being a noble," and they fall in love. But the princess "decides not to marry this true love of hers." She returns to her duties as queen "and things got better for her, and she had a good time. . . . She had more freedom as she got older. . . . It was no longer scandalous not to be beautiful." Her only nemesis, "her biggest enemy, who she was jealous of," a very beautiful duchess who "had everything she wanted"—like "a secretary to do her fan mail—was put out of commission by a very unfortunate accident" that "involved a doctor, a barber, and a lot of chocolate cake." The queen thus lived a contented life "and she was able to do things, like, um, [start] a noble-peasant exchange group."

Maritza's story reminds us of the rewards and disappointments girls face in the present culture and also of what lies beyond cultural ideals of beauty, romance, and femininity; how these ideals nurture jealousies between women that choke out possibilities for real social change. When girls take out their anxieties and fears on other girls, rather than on an oppressive culture that serves up their self-hate on a silver platter, then things can go on uninterrupted. But when girls refuse the tug of convention and move beyond or disrupt old jealousies and rivalries, they change the usual order of things, they invest their energy in serious matters, and the world breaks open.

5

Patrolling the Borders

High School

Me and a bunch of friends went to the beach. We looked for guys, tried to get a tan, and made fun of people. The better you look and better you think you look, the more confident you are. But as soon as you see someone prettier or skinnier, then your confidence is shot to hell, and that's basically what high school is. One girl we don't like—she's real popular, but we were saying, "At least she doesn't look good in a bathing suit." I wish I could be more carefree, but I get self-conscious. I think about my behind. That day, I wanted to wear shorts.

—Reagan, 16

One of the main reasons girls are mean to each other is the competition between them. We grow up doing this, and adult women do the same thing.

—Meagan, 16

I'M SITTING ON WOOD BLEACHERS watching a women's college basketball game. My daughter and her friend Lara, both five years old at the time, have eaten their fill of popcorn and candy and are now climbing up and down the bleachers at the far end of the gym. As I watch them laugh and chase one another, two separate conversations edge themselves into my consciousness. In front of me is a group of male students. They are loudly commenting on a player they have labeled "Big Red." "Marry me!" one yells. I don't hear much more than their snickering and groaning and something about boxing out with that big butt of hers, but the message comes through. Then to my upper right, I hear three women students talking about a girl they all know. "It's the way she walks into a room," they smirk. "You should see her."

She has too much "attitude." I can hear their self-justified disdain and also their pleasure. This is a fun conversation. Both ends against the middle, I think to myself. Between a rock and a hard place. Can't win for losing. Girls get it from both sides, which means all sides. I glance at my daughter and her friend—five years old, loud and full of themselves, bigger than Big Red and with loads of attitude, and I feel an immense sadness.

Adolescence is the time when girls feel the big squeeze, between the gaze of boys and other girls' judgments. Not surprisingly, then, girls' friendships are many things: sources of intense pleasure and support, ingenious covers for forbidden feelings of anger, aggression, and sexual desire, and sites of struggle and resistance to increasing social and parental control. They can also be the cause of confusion and pain.

A lot changes between eighth grade, and, say, ninth and tenth—in part because of social and cognitive development, in part because of the way adults have set up schools. Most kids go from smaller K-8 elementary, middle schools, or junior highs to larger regional or comprehensive high schools. This means that at the very time when kids are struggling to understand what it means to fit in, to be connected and in relationship with each other, adults have structured a series of separations—from friends, from familiar learning and social environments, and also from past reputations, pressures, and expectations. Some girls find the move to high school difficult and alienating, while others find it a huge relief. I'll venture to guess that the way a girl experiences this shift has a lot to do with her social standing and relational experiences in middle school. High school can be tough or it can be a new beginning—it presents a broader canvas, gives the sense of wide-open possibilities, so many new faces, and so many more options.

But even here appearances can be deceiving. That intense social cauldron of girls' friendships that defined early adolescence may be gone, but in its place is a more rigidly enforced set of rules for success. Middle school was about searching, scrambling to figure things out, and fit in—everything was destabilized, in an uproar. High school is about knowing, or pretending you know, what you are about. Hall passes, tracking, police officers at the door, and desks in straight rows announce the seriousness of the goings-on. Girls in junior high worry and fret and talk incessantly about cliques and in-groups. Girls in high school more or less just live in them, hiding through cool demeanors just how deeply invested they really are. Popularity for a girl has everything to do with her appearance, the way she speaks, the friends she has, the boys she attracts, and how smart she is or chooses to reveal she is. She has to be the complete package—beautiful in a light-skinned, slender white middle-class way, athletic, nice, desirable but not openly desiring, smart but not arrogantly so. This ideal, as we have seen, is a setup for girlfighting—made worse by the fact that so few admit the fraudulence, the impossibility, of it all.

The split between girls who buy into this "Reality" and those who don't is now mature, as deep in girls' psyches as it is in the culture. For many the seeds of distrust have flowered into full-blown competition and animosity, even as they manifest themselves in ever more subtle ways. While differences were visible and choices and possibilities up in the air just a few years before, things have settled in. Differences are now part and parcel of everyday life, but they don't necessarily enhance relationships the way they did for the younger girls. More likely they are now excuses for fighting and judging and separating from other girls. Divisions along class or racial lines or along lines of sexual identity now seem almost "natural" and "normal."

A girl is likely to be "popular" if she unquestioningly adopts and voices the "heterosexual script."[1] As we've seen, at the heart of this script are traditional views of male-female romantic relationships in which boys desire and girls are desired, boys are subjects and girls are objects, boys look and girls are looked at, boys are central and girls are marginal. Within this script sexually active girls are sluts and worrying about one's reputation and appearance is a full-time job. Boys, on the other hand, are "players"—the goal is to be with as many girls as possible and not get caught. Boys brag among themselves. Girls fight other girls over reputation and slights and blame girls for their boyfriends' betrayals. The script is built on the lie that who and what a girl is, distinct from a boy and from male desire, can never be enough. It's only within this script that the usual forms of competition between girls make sense: who looks the best, who is most popular, who gets the guy.

New levels of intimacy with and loyalty to boys have a deep effect on girls' friendships at this age, and much of this chapter focuses on the consequences of this shift. As we have seen, there is an early and powerful coalition between the heterosexual script, its relationship to cultural stories of romance, and girls' intense desire to be seen as normal, to fit in, to belong. At the heart of potential exclusion are fear and anxiety about not being loved or chosen.

Journalist and researcher Sharon Thompson listens to girls blame "other" girls—girls who are not like them—for their boyfriends' unfaithfulness as they fight for boys' attention, and she hears them split from other girls as they fixate the need for love on a particular boy or man.[2] Listening to girls in their early teens, I also hear their gossip about "other" girls whom they describe as "two-faced" and untrustworthy. They complain in voices full of anger and disgust that these are the same girls who are "stuck on themselves," and who "strut around" all "stuck-up," with "an attitude problem." These other girls will do "anything" for attention—lie, tease boys, or steal other girls' boyfriends. "Other" girls are obsessed with appearing physically beautiful, they are false and superficial; they act and speak in ways that openly garner male attention. Other girls are "mindless airheads" or they are "whiners" and "complainers." They are sluts, out of control; they wear tight, provocative clothes, make gross comments, or throw themselves at boys. Other girls speak too much or too loudly, they are obnoxious in-your-face types, who bully, push, or intimidate other girls. Other girls are aggressive and brag about their accomplishments.[3]

By high school, many girls have become practiced in voicing these misogynistic cultural stereotypes of girls and women and ascribing them to other girls. It's as though girls become voluntary spokespersons for the status quo, missionaries for the heterosexual script when they claim that "other" girls are "hos" and "bitches." "Other" girls are those held up to and judged through a male gaze, against male standards of behavior and beauty, cast in those now familiar derogatory roles: good girls or bad, Madonnas or whores. Cultural messages and childhood patterns of girlfighting have become crystallized for adolescent girls; they have become social reality.

THE MISSIONARY POSITION

In the first segment of the PBS documentary series, *American High*, we meet Sarah, pretty, long thick red hair, brown eyes, in love with Robbie. The show begins with a camera shot of Sarah's backside as she moves toward her classroom in a crowded hallway. We hear Robbie's voice-over and realize he is holding the camera. He zooms in: "Look at that ass! Whose ass *is* that?" And then we see a close-up of Sarah later, alone, talking to the camera:

I was practically, like, this flat like thing of clay, okay? And Robbie like basically molded me into the person that I am. I didn't feel anything and Robbie taught me that life was like this wonderful thing and . . . I'm scared for myself. Like I'm a kid still, you know, I just turned seventeen and I already found the love of my life. I mean Robbie's . . . going off to college, it's so hard for me. He's like my life; it's so scary.

In this era of "grrl power," we don't want to think that there are many Sarahs in the world. Her story sounds like a 1950s throwback, something from the *Donna Reed Show*. But if most girls wouldn't say so in such explicit terms, living for and fighting for the love of a boy is still a pretty common experience in high school. Sarah, we imagine, has classes to study for, sports to play, girlfriends to hang with, but all these pale in comparison to Robbie. Robbie, on the other hand, is a free spirit hanging with "his boys," playing basketball, flirting with other girls, and while he seems to love Sarah, we get the clear sense that when he goes off to college next year he's not looking back.

In this depiction of adolescent reality, in fact, there's no actual mention of Sarah's girlfriends. And in the interviews with girls this age, I hear over and over again how groups of friends and close girlfriends are breaking apart. Girls describe this as a "mature" shift, a sign of newfound "independence," and also as an awakening to the "selfish" nature of girlfriends they once knew and trusted. Mimi, white and middle class, talks about the changes she's experienced with her friends, how her "group" who once "used to get in fights with each other but at the same time . . . were best friends" now "have gone our separate ways and the group has disintegrated and everyone is more themselves than they were before." Recasting the group of once close friends now as "obnoxious in a way" and talking about how "people have changed" for the better "since the group has disintegrated," Mimi is joining in the cultural celebration of individualism and separation as signs of maturity and psychological health. And yet, in this view, there is no public space to mourn the loss she's experienced.

Girls in middle and later adolescence are "finding themselves" and their individual voices, true, and sometimes this means separating from peer pressure and their past reliance on cliques—a good thing. It's good, for instance, that fifteen-year-old Natalie, white and middle class, has changed from someone who "just kind of went along with what they did" to someone who is able to say, "You can do that to yourself,

I'm going this way." But what's curious is how often this newfound "maturity" is entwined with derogatory judgments about being feminine and with the negation of particular other girls as immature, needy, or untrustworthy. It's almost as if girls can't explain their personal growth without dissing other girls in some way. This shift comes at a time when girls are actually in more physical danger from *boys* than ever before, when young women in their high school years are nearly three times more vulnerable to an attack by a boyfriend or former partner than women in other age groups.[4] Ironically, then, a move away from other girls may be connected to an attempt to move toward protection. Pleasing and appeasing boys might ensure safety, while being the kind of girl who lives outside the lines, who rocks the patriarchal boat by hanging tight with other girls or being too strong, bold, or aggressive, invites danger.

Not surprisingly, in a culture that obsessively promotes heterosexual romance and values male independence, assertiveness, and protection, the disintegration of girls' groups and the tensions and fighting between close friends are most often associated with finding and keeping boyfriends. Lanie, who's white and attends a private girls' school, sums up a lot of what I hear from girls this age when she complains about her best friend since third grade, who "just kind of drifted off; she met a boy and that was the end of our relationship and the end of our friendship." While Lanie partly blames herself for "holding on too strong" and for getting "superjealous," of the boyfriend, and saying finally to her shocked friend, "I don't want to be friends with you," she was upset that no one else seemed to understand her point of view. "Everyone was coming up to me, 'How can you do this to Renee? How can you do this to Renee?' when they didn't see what was happening to me, and how many times I had been let down by her."

Lanie's experience points to the general cultural assumption, one that white girls in particular tend to internalize, that girls will and should privilege romantic relationships with boys over girlfriends, even the closest, long-term friendships on which they've come to rely for emotional and psychological support. In the midst of such expectations, the deep sense of loss, jealousy, and anger girls feel when their friends privilege relationships with boyfriends are considered irrational and selfish, immature, and even unnatural. Mary, also white and middle class, telling the story of a girl who lost her best friend, is shocked at the girl's emotional reaction:

I guess she thought of her . . . as her best friend, you know, and oh my god, I can't live without this girl, how am I going to make it through the rest of my high school years. . . . So this girl was like in tears. It just seemed so unnatural, you know, I mean we sat there and we were looking at this girl cry, you know, over this friend and we're like she's just *a girl*, you know, it's not *a guy*, it's not your *boyfriend*, it's not your life, you know, life goes on.

This reference to "unnatural" is more than an observation; it's also meant as a warning. Being too close with another girl raises eyebrows and this girl's emotional reaction to the loss of her girlfriend is cause for suspicion and scrutiny. This was also the case with Alicia and her friend Pam, both white students at a private boarding school. "We are pretty physical," Alicia says, and "one night I was upset . . . and she was hugging me and Nina came in and she interpreted it as something different; she interpreted it as something sexual." Nina then "talked to anyone and everyone, anyone who had an ear." So Alicia confronted her: "I said, 'How do you interpret our friendship, what do you see?' She said, "I feel there is something sexual about it,' and I said, 'Nina, I am going to clear that right away out of the air right now. There isn't and all I can see in that is that you really don't know either one of us." Nina eventually apologized for "really hurting" her friends, but the damage had been done. Alicia explains:

The next day Pam was in my room and I was painting and . . . and she is sitting way over here and I am sitting way over here and we weren't talking and it was really awkward and I felt like we couldn't sit on the bed together anymore, and . . . Pam started crying and it was terrible because I didn't feel like I could go over there and hug her, it was awful, I hated it . . . we talked about it and then we hugged and it was getting back the same way it used to be, but . . . I think it is going to take a long time to have things go back the way they were before and I don't know if they ever will. . . . She made it seem like there was something wrong, she used words like it is unhealthy, and things like that, and that is really bothering me because I never thought of it that way, I didn't know how anyone else could.

Pam and Alicia have what psychologist Lisa Diamond and her colleagues call a "passionate friendship," an intense, deeply intimate, nonsexual bond that offers them emotional support and a sense of being understood and accepted. "Similar to lovers," Diamond reports, passionate girlfriends "may affectionately stroke, hold, or cuddle each other" and experience feelings of anxiety when they are separated.[5] "Nina's judgment did just what it was supposed to—warn Alicia and Pam that they had crossed a line by raising the specter of lesbianism. This story shows not only how girls' expressions of closeness and intimacy with girlfriends are hampered by strict codes of sexual and gender "normalcy,"[6] but how girls benefit socially by policing or separating from transgressors and reporting their behavior to other girls.

Reporting "to everyone and anyone" on what she had seen allowed Nina the opportunity to announce her own heterosexuality and her own compliance with what's considered "normal" or "natural" between girls. In this way, Nina supports a heterosexual script that makes suspect, even pathologizes, intimate connections—sexual or asexual—between women. In effect, the word comes down—if you want real intimacy, be normal, find a boy.

Girls calling each other dyke or lesbian have particular force because they are names applied by girls to each other. "More specifically the power of the word 'lesbian' to control girls is secured precisely because girls do experience their relations with each other as passionate."[7] Nina's actions, in effect, control Pam and Alicia's freedom to express their trust in and love for one another in ways that are most comfortable and supportive.

Clearly friendships at this age can contain the emotional intensity of romantic relationships[8] and a deep sense of sadness is a natural response to lost love. "What hurts me?" Mimi explains, "I guess not being as good friends with some people as I used to be, that hurts. I see them sort of fading away and just not being close to people." As Lanie recalls during the troubled stretch with her childhood friend, "I can remember many times walking down the road and just running up to her after not seeing her. And things like that I miss because I never really had it with anybody else and it was such a letdown when we weren't as close, because it was like a part of me." And yet now Lanie wonders if what she thought was a true and deep connection was even real for her friend. Now she says, all her anger and confusion again rising to the surface, "I hate her, but I don't. And I hate hating her!"

Like Lanie, other white girls talk a lot about friends they once loved and trusted who now "just swim in and out" of their lives, depending on boyfriends or shifts in popularity. Girls in the ninth grade, new to the pushes and pulls of the high school scene, express the greatest ambivalence and uncertainty about these separations. Being so intimate with their best friends in junior high now threatens their individuality and independence, and yet these girlfriends are the people who affirm and reflect their innermost selves. "For me it is important to have a sense of independence, from even a best friend," Dawn, who's white, explains:

> Your best friend is someone you can tell a lot of things to, but still if you don't keep sort of an independent state of mind from her, if you let things get too crossed . . . you can sometimes get mixed up as to who you are. You can sort of lose your individual self. . . . Like when you are best friends you share a lot of things like you share your secrets and you share your terminology, like little words that people will say . . . and you know something is wrong when you say something that you know she would say. It is not really that good to be that dependent on someone else—to be completely the same.

This desire to be an "individual" voices-over Dawn's experience of intimacy and adds new pressure to separate from her best friend. The affirmation that comes from sharing secrets and being validated threatens the wish to be, and to be seen as, independent and self-sufficient. Rather than work this out with her friend, though, separation seems the only avenue out of confusion and dependence. Ironically, this criticism of girlfriends is rarely applied to boyfriends, regardless of how controlling the boys are or how dependent the girls are on them.

Girls—and again this was something I heard primarily from white middle-class girls—move into high school distancing themselves from their old friends. It would be easy enough to explain this change in relationship by saying they've developed into different people with different interests, but they don't. They justify the shift by denigrating their old friends who, they now determine, were "on popularity highs," or "were smart, but they just didn't try," or who "sort of act like they have a chip on their shoulders . . . and they act sometimes more mature than they are," or who were just plain "snobby." The denigration often picks up on cultural stereotypes of girls and women. Rejected friends might be girls who gossiped, would "stab each other in the back," or who "acted really meanly," or were "rich and spoiled" and would sit there "talking about herself and how she was so great."

As white girls move through high school, this separation from girl-friends—whatever its motivation—increases and becomes more "natural." "I really don't like it and it amazes me, that happens a lot with friends," Taylor says trying to explain what happened with her and her friend. "I grow up a lot and realize I don't like them." Trying to explain why she and her best friend "just kind of drifted apart" in the summer before their junior year, Alice first wonders whether "it was just me es-tranging myself from all my old friends, but then I take a step back and I realize that it's like that for everyone and everyone is struggling through the same thing." Indeed, it appears that her whole class "is be-ginning to split up . . . and it seems like now it's impossible for every-one to be friends with everyone. It's just, everyone's going their sepa-rate ways. . . . Everyone's already losing the closeness that we all used to have." This relational shape-shifting is an odd feeling for Alice, be-cause "it's not like we're mad at each other or anything." It's just that "a lot of people resent the fact we all have guys to go out with."

Indeed, the world seems filled with untrustworthy and "self-cen-tered" girls, girls who "complain and whine" and "worry and think about the same things," "the kind of girls that would shake your hand and stab you in the back at the same time," girls who are "perfection-ists," who "criticize and criticize." Distrust and betrayal are in the air. Sometimes when I read these interviews I feel like I'm in the middle of an *Ally McBeal* episode. I can almost hear the low jealous tiger growl that Lucy Liu's character emits whenever a potential female rival or an-tagonist walks by. As Teresa, white and seventeen, explains,

> I got the boy and she didn't and our relationship was really strained until we broke up. . . . I think it is a competition, you always want what you think is the best and I don't think, a lot of people don't want to, but they do settle for something less in what they would consider the perfect male or something like that. And if two people want something very much and one person gets it, that makes the other person feel jeal-ous and bitter that she didn't get it.

So, once gain, it's almost always about the boys, at least on the sur-face. On this issue, girls of color and white girls agree. Janelle, who's African American and middle class, has no problem justifying her deci-sion to go after a boy her friend liked. Her friend was "constantly going around complaining about her problems" and her reluctance to approach this boy. Finally she asked Janelle to talk to him for her. One night at a party the boy, who only had the description a friend gave him—that "a short black girl . . . was interested"—mistook Janelle for her friend and asked her to give him a call. "I took the initiative," argues Janelle.

> I mean everybody knows that she likes this guy . . . but she just, she wants someone to do it for her . . . what she can do herself. And by my way of thinking was, I can take the initiative and give this guy a call myself. Why should I do all this work for her when she has a better chance? I mean really, she looks better than me. If I can do it, why can't she? Everybody would be like, "You knew she liked him, how could you do that?" But they don't understand. Liking isn't everything. I mean if you like somebody and you don't take the initiative to do something, then your liking doesn't mean anything.

Girls have been preparing for these separations for a long time. Cultural and media messages and sometimes parental hopes and dreams collude to remind girls that other girls are not trustworthy and that, like Cinderella and Snow White, they must excise other (deceitful, "snobby," selfish) girls and women from their lives and turn to a prince of a boy for "real" loyalty, intimacy, and security. The heart of the gender status quo, heterosexual romance, depends on this relational missionary position—boys on top, girls on the bottom.

Janelle taps into and finds justification in the heterosexual script which privileges romance with boys over friendships with girls, and which places girls in competition for boys, and sets them up against other girls. "This mess-up in the friendship started this summer," Julie, white and in the eleventh grade, explains, "because she had a boyfriend and she was spending so much time with him and I felt really left out." Fiona's sixteen-year-old friendship suddenly changed in her junior year of high school "because she was dating this guy really serious." "He's a jerk," Fiona, white and middle class, says, "and he was like jealous of me because I was her best friend and we were together all the time and then I don't know, she like let him take her over and there was no way I could even get her and so I avoided her, not because of her, but because of her boyfriend, which I did not like at all, and he didn't like me."

Girls, especially in the latter two years of high school, complain bitterly that for their once dear friends, "boyfriends always come #1."

Even girls who really value their female friends feel pressure to privilege their relationships with boys. "I am thinking about my friends that I have had for so long and that have meant so much to me and have helped me through so much." Kris explains. "And I really hate it when a girl just picks up and drops all her friends when a boy comes along, you know, and I don't want to fall into that category." But, she adds somberly, "I can feel myself slipping farther and farther because . . . my boyfriend . . . is really, really dependent on me, which is really hard. I feel that pressure all the time."

Even when the boy is long gone, wounds can remain and fester. Sixteen-year-old Lillian, who's white and working class, voices her anger and pain at the dissolution of her best friendship—a friendship that had begun in fourth grade and survived profound changes. "I'm godmother of her baby," Lillian explains, "I was there when she found out she was pregnant, for the nine months of pregnancy. . . . When she had him, I was in the room. . . . I'd do anything for that kid. . . . He was like my son. That's how close I felt to him." By the time the baby arrived, the father was long gone, having cheated on Lillian's friend with another girl. When Lillian went out one night with a friend who "hangs with" the father, everything changed "in a day . . . like that." Now separated from both her friend and her beloved godchild, Lillian is devastated. "If she said it to you, if one of your best friends in the whole wide world didn't trust you or thought that you were a liar . . . that hurts more than if she stuck her hand in your chest and ripped out your heart." The two girls have lost each other. Meanwhile, the father is living with another girl, out of the picture, and off the hook.

"THE PROBLEMS ARE BETWEEN GIRLS"

Ana, Latina and working class, explains:

> It's like they can't stand another girl that dresses nice or with a nice looking boy because they start talking about those girls or something, or they start trouble with those girls, or they probably used to go out with those boys before and they start trouble with the girls. But with the boys, there's hardly any trouble with the boys. The girls, maybe because they're jealous, you know, and I think it's more with the girls be-

cause you hear, you see fights, girls, girls. And it all has to do with boys, jealousy and you know, the way they dress. She got new clothes and all that.

It's fights over boys and jealousies between girls, Julie who's white says, that explain why at her all-girls' private school, "you see at least three people cry in a day."

Oliva, a Latina sixteen-year-old, agrees and she rejects girls who make boys "number one on their list." "They make it sound like boys are everything; they need boys to live. And it's not like that. You need yourself to live. . . . They say, 'I like him but he doesn't like me, Oh, I have such a big problem.' You know, they don't feel good about themselves, but they'll try to do everything to make everybody happy, except [make] themselves happy." But Oliva has had her own boyfriend-girlfriend problems. Her close girlfriend betrayed her when "she started talking about me. . . . She would say I did it with this guy and I go out with that guy and I still see that one . . . 'cause she was jealous of me." When "somebody" called Oliva's house and told her mother she was pregnant, her mother, fearing that "trouble is starting," sent her out of the country to live with relatives for the summer. Her former friend then began "having relations" with Oliva's boyfriend.

When she returned home, Oliva's boyfriend came back to her and her former friend "told him she was pregnant by him." It wasn't true, Oliva explained. It "was just revenge" and a feeble attempt to get the boy back. While Oliva now refuses to see her former boyfriend—"I don't want to have leftovers"—the blame for his betrayal is placed firmly on the other girl. Her boyfriend was the innocent victim of a manipulative, jealous, and hateful young woman.

Oliva, like other girls who blame girls for their boyfriends' betrayals, is "working off prevailing understandings that boys are not responsible for their sexual activity because they are hormonally programmed to want sex, unlike girls, whose job it is, therefore, to make sure that boys do not get aroused."[9] Good girls keep boys' arousal in check; girls who don't are sluts. If they get in trouble, if they get hurt, it's their fault.

Even when girls remain friends, relationships with boys threaten all kinds of rifts. Alice struggled for the longest time over whether to tell her best friend that she knew her boyfriend had cheated on her. Sworn to secrecy by the male friend who told her, she steps back from the scene—"I'm kind of a bystander who sees what's going on." While there is no "right" answer here, the dilemma creates a distance between her and her friend. Telling would burst her friend's bubble, create "a hole in a big circle, because what [she] thought was real wouldn't be real anymore." "There's no question in my mind," Alice says, that "I would want to know" in that situation, but she finally chooses to stand back and to privilege the romantic relationship—"it's theirs, not mine"—over the closeness and trustworthiness of the friendship.

The common assumption that girls and women are naturally competitive and jealous and back-stabbing undermines girls' relationships. Girls shouldn't have to weigh the truth—and their love for their friends—against suspicions about their friends' "real" motives. But they do. Tamara, white and middle class, struggled with whether or not to tell her friend "her boyfriend was hitting on me a lot, coming on to me." Tamara "didn't like this kid at all," and thought her friend should know "she was dealing with such slime here," but she decided not to tell. "She wouldn't have believed me because she was so wrapped up in him and she would have said it was me, making something up." Gina wonders what to do when "an old boyfriend says something that my best friend . . . should really know . . . it has negative connotations about her." She decides to say nothing because to talk with her friend might be interpreted by others as "very catty." "It's narrow-minded to do things like that, it's too gossipy for me to handle, it's too complex; he said it, she said it." The conflict remains, though, because when her friend found out, she felt betrayed. "She got more hurt by not knowing something. . . . You know, 'Why didn't you tell me?' Well, 'I didn't want to.'" What makes such decisions "a little sticky," Tamara explains, is the fact that when it comes to boys, girls' motives cannot be trusted. "If you do tell, then . . . sometimes the friends will sort of connect you to that statement, you know, she was the one who told me and how mean of her to tell me this, it can't be true. She's lying, she wants to go out with him or, you know."

Girls against girls. It now seems to have everything to do with heterosexual romance, with boys. Even allusions to popularity and to how other girls dress and act ultimately come down to choosing boys' desire and approval over close friendships with other girls. But this privileging of romance and desire for boys' love and attention depends on swallowing whole negative stereotypes of girls and women and calling them reality. It depends on girls separating from passionate friendships and love for girls in order to be seen as normal and natural. It depends on girls' insecurity and mistrust of other girls. It depends on self-editing and performing a certain kind of girl. It depends on girls like Kailie, white and middle class, feeling "really insecure, because I started thinking you know, what are people saying about me? What am I doing that's so wrong?" Even girls who resist, who assert their strength and confidence and love for one another, often find themselves in the impossible situation of claiming their voices and their sense of self against, and at the expense of, other girls.

BOYZ IN THE HEAD

Boys don't actually have to be present to explain the emerging separations between girls. Such divisions can take place when "the only boys in sight are those in the head."[10] Girls draw on readily available sexist stereotypes of girls and women as excuses to separate from other girls, to join boys, or privilege their relationships with boys. Girls, they say, are complainers, too sensitive, too picky, too selfish, demanding, emotional, irrational; they are back-stabbers, bitches, weaklings, and wusses, and this justifies leaving them for relationships with boys, who by comparison are the opposite of all this. When girls speak in these ways about other girls, they "indicate the persuasive power of the male gaze to seek out even those spaces which by their very definition are girl only."[11]

This form of targeting or scapegoating of people in your same subjugated group is familiar to those who study the psychology of oppression. When girls enact horizontal violence by using negative stereotypes about femininity against other girls, they do so to distance themselves and thus to avoid being victimized by those stereotypes in turn. By joining those with the power to define and enforce such stereotypes, however, they also affirm them as "Reality" and ensure that these stereotypes live to control and denigrate another generation of girls. In other words, girls become handmaidens to insidious forms of sexism.

Such negative views of girls as untrustworthy, fickle, or bitchy are readily available explanations for other girls' actions. At her school, Mimi admits, there's "a big problem here about trust between the girls, and a lot of people here are very two-faced and people always talk behind other people's backs and that is kind of painful sometimes." In this context, Mimi continues, "I mean your best friend can sometimes turn around on you very easily and then you wonder if they are your best friend or not. . . . They say things behind your back and they call you names and they sometimes just say things that aren't true, so other people will get mad at you. I don't know why. It is sort of strange." Mimi notices how "girls seem to be the ones who do that," while "boys don't care. . . . I think girls are a pain in the neck that way. I think girls worry too much about what other people think." Mimi admits to being one of those girls who worry too much and she hates this about herself. She knows at some level that her fear of what others think does what it's supposed to—it keeps her in line. "I always wonder if people are calling me bitch behind my back and I always wonder what they say about the way I look. Sometimes the way I look or the way I dress, or the way I act about certain things, if I do things like drugs, I always wonder what they say about me. It's just about everything I guess. It's strange."

Yolanda, Latina and working class, describes a time when she was out drinking with a bunch of friends and said no to a boy who wanted to have sex. Her biggest concern was not whether she really wanted to have sex, but her reputation and the harsh judgments of other girls:

> I don't want to be known as some girl who's going to sleep with every guy she meets and I know girls who are like that and I don't like girls who are like that. I mean, I usually don't like girls to begin with, I don't know why. I always get along better with guys and I find that girls are very cruel and that's just something that I have always felt and so I don't like girls a lot to begin with, and I especially don't like girls who are easy and sleep around with guys and I see how guys treat those kinds of girls and they get no respect at all. And I didn't want to be known as a girl who didn't get respect from guys and who's treated like a slut.

Yolanda's personal experiences justify her opinion of girls as cruel and judgmental. Girls made fun of her name and she "saw the way girls treated each other, stabbing each other in the back, talking about each other so much, being really cruel, being mean to each other, just you know, stealing boyfriends and just not being nice." On the other hand,

"I saw the way guys got along and if they get mad at each other they deal with it immediately, you know, physical, let's get it out, and I don't, with my friends now that are guys, I don't see them talking about each other and being really mean and I still see girls doing that now." Her boyfriend's friends, she says,

> give me so much respect and I go out with them and I guess I am treated like one of the guys, but that doesn't bother me because I have my boyfriend who sees me as very feminine. . . . I just find that girls are very cruel and they treat each other terribly, and they're back-stabbing, and I just don't like that, so I guess I've always gotten along better with guys, because I don't see them doing that and I don't like that, so I guess that's why I tend to stick around guys more.

Although fifteen-year-old Susannah, African American and middle class, admits that it's a "man's world" and women have to work "twice as hard," she agrees with Yolanda.

> Girls are bitchy. I mean they will stab you in the back, if they see a cute guy come along and they think he will look at you, they will stab you in the back. So guys are usually better friends. Guys are usually truer friends. They will stick by you through thick and thin, whereas girls forget it, a cute guy comes along, that's it. . . . Girls sort of look through you, they don't look at you. They look at the way you dress, the way you act and then decide if you can be a friend, where a guy will look at the way you are first, he may not look at that. Like when he is looking for a girlfriend, he may look at the way she looks and stuff first, but usually as friends, they do make better friends.

When she's asked what it means to be a woman, Caryn, also fifteen, says, "girls fight with each other like you would not believe. They are always so jealous of each other." Caryn, her blonde bangs nearly covering her eyes, regrets going to a private all-girls' school because she can't have "boys as friends . . . because some of my best friends are boys and they are just much easier to relate to, I think. It's so much easier to talk to boys because they don't gossip and they don't get into running around, saying, 'Oh guess what so and so did last night.' I mean, let's face it, we all do it." And girls "have a tendency to always be more competing between another girl or whatever," Lena says.

> You know, girls compete with other girls . . . more often than a guy would compete with another guy . . . and when you're surrounded by a whole bunch of girls it's something you've really got to get used to, you feel like you get more put down, and you're being in competition constantly. . . . They are all trying to get a compliment from the other, so much worrying about how much better this other person looks than they do, rather than what is good about them.

Guys, it would seem, are just more important—their opinions matter more; they are more real, less competitive and jealous. It's no wonder that Britt was so shocked when her teammates praised her for scoring two goals in a soccer game. As she explains, "a lot of times girls, you know, want to put each other down more than up and, not that they're mean, you know, but . . . a lot of girls, you know, don't compliment you on little things. . . . I think they probably even consciously don't do that just because it puts them down a step or something. There's always that sort of competition there."

Naomi, an African American sixteen-year-old who attends a private girls' school, also likes boys "a lot better than girls" and has "a lot more guys as friends than I do girls" because the boys "are really nice, they are cool people, I like them." On the other hand:

> Girls, I can't stand girls, because they are, first of all, either they are your good, good friends or they are jealous of you and I don't know, they're just so stupid, they are stupid. . . . They worry about such stupid little things, like guys don't worry about little things, but girls worry about makeup or hair. . . . They make it, it is disgusting and like, "Oh god, I hope he likes me." If he likes me he likes me and if he doesn't, he doesn't, you know what I mean? They make such big deals out of stupid little things. And guys, you know, they treat me, guys are more down-to-earth than girls, they are. And they are just a lot more fun to be with and, like, guys are so much closer to each other than girls are to each other.

Patricia, Latina, echoes Naomi's views. In spite of the fact that she has a history of close girlfriends—one girl, in fact, "I've known since she was six or seven, and we've always been best friends"—now, she says, "I don't even bother with girls." Instead she has a male best friend, Rashad.

Girls, they start too much, they're . . . like hypocrites and if you do something, they're so nosy and gossip and everything, they're all in your face, "Oh, yah, you know, that looks nice and ahahaha," and then you turn around and they're like, "Look at her, look what she has on, she looks so stupid." I think boys, boys don't really, don't go into gossip and . . . they aren't worry warts, gossiping and jealousy and, I don't know, they're not so feminine [laughs]. . . . [Girls] like here, they can't get sweaty. I like to play basketball, so I always play with the boys and um, I'm like, "Do you want to play?" "Oh no, I don't want to get all sweaty and this and that." . . . But with a boy best friend you can tell him things . . . and he cares about it, but he doesn't care about it so much that he'll go around and tell someone. . . . To me, boys understand you more, like if I have a boy problem, then I'll say, "Rashad, this happened," and he's like, "Why did you do that? You know, boys don't like when you do that." . . . But if I tell a girl, she would like, "and he got mad because of that?" because, you know, girls don't know. But boys do and he's like, "It's easy to talk to you because you understand me more."

Finally, someone says directly what's implied in so many of the girls' comments. Girls are simply too, well, "feminine." As we've seen with younger girls, being feminine is associated with weakness, with gossip and jealousy and back-stabbing behavior, with dishonesty and complaint and refusal to get sweaty. Girls who don't want to be associated with these qualities necessarily distance themselves—decontaminate themselves—and align with the opposite; that is, with boys. But we can see the trap and the pathway toward self-hatred. Brought up from day one to be girls, initially to enjoy girlness, to have close girlfriends and to be like mom, it dawns on them gradually that this pathway will invite denigration and disparagement in the public world. These are not the terms typically associated with success, not the qualities that will gain you respect.

On the other hand, boys have qualities that others admire and write about, their qualities have built a nation, changed the course of history, fought terrorism, made things happen. We believe this in part because our history books have left out women's contributions and stories of courage and because our present culture needs to believe in male protection. Where, for example, did anyone mention the brave women firefighters, police officers, or soldiers after the tragedies of September 11,

2001? We are led to believe that boys and men have knowledge and power and that befriending them, being chosen by them, will offer power by association. Seventeen-year-old Dakota, white and middle class, knows this well. When she's asked to talk about a time she felt really good about herself, she talks about a boy she has recently become friends with, who says he likes her because she gives him "a different perspective," and because "he was looking for someone like me." Dakota is most pleased that this boy chose her and not her best friend who is, by comparison, "snobby" and "high class." Her new male friend "keeps telling [Dakota] the difference" between her and her girlfriend. "He always compares the way we do things and why he would rather be friends with me than with her." Dakota believes, then, that "I'm doing the right things" and her girlfriend, her "best" girlfriend, in fact, "doesn't have morals."

One begins to wonder what's going on here, when feeling special and having morals means separating oneself from other girls, even one's closest friends. But can we blame Dakota for making the choice to go with what buys her the most, casts her in the best light? Being chosen by boys, being the token girl who isn't a "girly girl," isn't a "wuss," or a "snob"—in short, isn't typically feminine—means gaining power, casting off marginal status, and moving to the center.

But of course, the center holds because it has the persuasive power to reassert itself by repeatedly defining so clearly what it is not—not of color, not gay or lesbian, not differently abled, not poor, not female. What's so ironic is that girls can sit together, have fun, enjoy each other and themselves as they build their sense of self-esteem, even their sense of collective loyalty, by denigrating other girls. Aiesha and her friends sit in a circle at their inner-city public school in the Midwest and chat with Sandy, a volunteer and friend who comes to the school to work with them and support them. This is not a place or a group of girls we would typically associate with the center of power and privilege. All the girls in this group are African American and Sandy is Latina. This is, however, a particularly strong group of girls, who proclaim themselves "the most loudest freshman ever!" at their high school and who exclaim, "We *know* we got power!"

Still, it's the other girls they go after as the problem in their school—the power to be who they are arises, in part, from who they are most definitely not. "Girls," Melissa begins, "will back-stab you over stupid stuff. Over boys, over what somebody said, over popularity. Be in the right crowd, the popular crowd. They do all this stuff, just out of, I guess, attention." "Or they jealous of what you got," Tatiana agrees, "or they just never liked you . . . from the get go." "I agree with them, Angela says. "They're just jealous of us, you know. Because girls, they're jealous. And boys I think, they don't care, they just don't care. I mean if their friend do somethin' like that it's like, oh well, I got more friends. But if a girl do somethin' like that they feel they got betrayed in a way." "Some are, some ain't [back-stabbers]," Aiesha adds, "You gotta watch who you hang with."

These girls cover a lot of territory in their conversation—they talk about who's popular and why, about the different groups in their school, about the male basketball players who are so full of themselves and, as Angela says, "think they be runnin' something and they ain't. We have to let them know now and then that they ain't runnin' as much as they think they is." They know that "men" have the power in this country. "Look at the President," Aiesha says indignantly. "We ain't never had a woman president, never!" And yet while they proclaim that "women are the backbone; we hold [men] up," when asked about cliques in their school, it's a group of other girls—the girls they are not—that best help them define themselves as defiant, bold, and strong.

SANDY: How about the other groups and cliques?

AIESHA: We got the clueless girls.

MELISSA: Yeah, the bubbly headed girls that just act like they don't know where they at.

TATIANA: You know, they act like they from California and things, like it's summer all year long.

AIESHA: And then it's snow outside and you got little sandals on inside the building.

ANGELA: No, no, you don't do that.

MELISSA: You just don't do that.

SANDY: Are these all one-race girls?

AIESHA: No! They just airheads! In general, black, white, Puerto Rican . . .

TATIANA: They just the clueless ones. We got 'em all. [laughter]

Boys in their school, they complain, especially the sports stars, are privileged—"they say whatever they want to and don't get in trouble."

Certain racial groups—the whites and Puerto Ricans, they claim—are given unfair, unearned advantages in the classroom. Angela explains:

> If you're Puerto Rican, some teachers . . . they'll read the statistics on the Puerto Rican race and what's the dropout rate . . . and they'll say, I want you to do better, therefore I'm giving you the extra chance because I believe you can do that. . . . A white person, I know you can do better than this, I know your mind, I saw your family. You're nice. . . . I'm gonna give you another chance. Black people, it's like puttin' up with it, I know how *you* are. . . . I know your type, therefore you're not in my class.

In spite of their experience of sexism and racism, it's the "clueless" girls of all races that this group of girls goes after—and they have fun doing it. Such girls are an uncomplicated easy target, one that has the disdain of the wider culture and the disdain of this entire group—all can agree that the most feminine, the "bubbly headed . . . clueless ones" deserve it.

This is a conversation I have witnessed in a variety of settings, with girls from a range of class and racial locations. Girls name the unfairness they experience—the unearned advantages boys receive or the privileges offered the upper class, the smart kids, or certain other racial groups—but it's the other girls they fight with. They blame the other girls for treating them badly, stealing their boys, dragging them down, looking dumb, acting like dupes. They deserve it. The attacks are often deeply personal, petty, and aggressive beyond reason. Here again is the horizontal violence. By attacking the "bubbly headed ones," "airheads," or those who "hee, hee, hee," girls are reacting to, living with, and spreading the stereotypes and negative images ascribed to girls. These accusations about girls worry them, make them anxious, and so to prove they are not what others expect of girls, they collude in the misogyny, participate in the denigration.[12]

Moreover, such fighting takes place both between and within racial or class groupings; black girls going after black girls, white going after white. When there is a scarcity of resources or institutionally based privileges or rewards, jealousies focused on other girls serve to separate and divide. At Julia's urban high school, there's a rift between the Portuguese girls who speak Portuguese and those who speak English. The English-speaking girls are perceived as conceited by the girls who speak Portuguese, in part because the teachers treat the girls who speak English better. Clarissa, African American, found herself caught between two groups of friends after she began attending a predominantly white private school. Her black friends from home became angry with her. "Old friends say, well you are going to this white school, you want to be white, or stuff like that. So the outside pressure is trying to remain black." This isn't rage at institutions or at economic or cultural factors that perpetuate such divisions, the actual cause of one's pain or exclusion; this is rage at people in pretty much the same situation doing the best they can. Fighting other girls doesn't change much, but it's safer and it gives a short-term sense of power and control.

So, what moves high school girls to fight? Clearly a lot of things, most of which arise out of a desire for control, power, and visibility—jealousy over boys or over how other girls look or dress or act, competition for attention and approval, betrayal and back-stabbing behavior, gossip and spreading rumors, disrespect of any kind. What form does their fighting take? It depends on the context, it depends on the issue, and it depends on the girl or girls. There are contexts that pull for more subtle, relational forms of aggression—in school, for example, when adults are present and watching. There are contexts that pull for direct and sometimes physical aggression—for instance, in a crowded school hallway when a girl accidentally-on-purpose pushes or bumps another girl or looks at her the wrong way. In privileged contexts where there is a good deal of social control and surveillance around ideals of femininity, feelings of anger and aggression tend to go underground. In contexts where poverty, violence, and racism entwine to create high levels of distrust, girls learn to protect themselves and signs of their determination, toughness, and invulnerability are more public and in the service of survival.[13] Is this a threat, a dare, are respect or integrity at stake, is something or someone valuable on the line, is this safe or dangerous? A girl reads the social scene, sometimes checks with others, and makes her decision about how to respond.

GIRL TALK

One way to deal with frustration and anger too risky to express directly is to talk about other girls, to gossip. As well as releasing pent-up feelings, gossip has the added benefit, if done strategically, of keeping other girls in check. Recalling a difficult past year, Gail, seventeen and white, says, "It was like a soap opera, there was this one girl who was telling things this other girl was saying about me and that other girl things that I was saying about her and it was just such a soap opera I couldn't believe it, it was terrible and it didn't do any good to anyone except bring misery and I would never go through that year again."

But gossip isn't always a bad thing. It's been given a bad name and trivialized because it is associated with something threatening—girls and women getting together and talking, knowing things, naming things. "Everybody likes to hear gossip," Anita, who's African American and working class, exclaims. "Whether you are the bearer of the tale or not, everybody likes to hear gossip." "True," her friend Tatiana replies. "Gossip, that's like the gossip capital right there. Everything gossip, that's just like the gossip place. Hair salon. Wherever hair is being done, that's like gossip. In your kitchen, in your basement, in the salon, in your car, wherever, it is a gossip thing." "I wouldn't call it gossip," Janet, another friend, interjects. "We just exchanging news." And the girls laugh. Gossip can be a way for girls to resist and subvert unfairness and abuses of power; it can provide girls with a safe space, a sense of intimacy and belonging, a protective collectivity. The more closely girls are watched, the more restricted their behavior, the more likely they will take their thoughts and feelings underground and "gossip."[14]

But gossip can also be used to undermine that same sense of safety, to create a kind of relational minefield. Gail's metaphor of a soap opera is telling—soap operas depend on secrecy and gossip to create intimacy with their audience, to develop villains, and create a sense of impending danger. Plots are hatched behind closed doors and rumors are planted strategically, only to emerge at moments and in places where one doesn't expect them. This way the originator is protected by distance and time; this is a strategy employed by those who are, at some level, uncertain and afraid. Pauline, Haitian American, explains that while she can't always trust boys because they can "bring it too far," she distrusts girls for a different reason:

> They'll play around with you, but the next thing you know, you come to school and you'll hear that you did this, and you did that. . . . You never know what they're pulling. They just want madly to have that mouth to start rumors. I just don't like them. . . . They do cruel things

to each other sometimes. . . . You hear so many stories, like you can hear one story that you just did something and then you hear another story that you just did something else at the same time. How can you do two things at the same time? It's like, all the stories in the school just need to stop. . . . Sometimes it's about hairstyles, sometimes it's about clothing, sometimes it's like girls having sex with another boy. . . . Stories are flying all over the joint.

The cruel part of gossip in the form of spreading rumors is that it often originates with someone you thought you knew and trusted. This happened to Patricia:

I had a fight with my friend and people were coming up to me telling me that she was saying stuff like, she was talking shit, so I felt bad because they were telling me she always thought you were this, she always thought you were that. And then we fought . . . so when we got back to friends, this girl, she was instigating, she was going back and telling, back and forth. . . . It wasn't true but the way she was telling me, I believed her because I figured she wouldn't do something like that, but she did do it. . . . When you are with them, you trust them and they are the last person you think will think something bad about you. If they don't like something you do, they are like, "Oh, I don't like the way you do this," and . . . "Oh, you look so nice,'" and then when you turn around, "Oh, she looks ugly," you know.

So why do girls gossip if it's such an affront, such an offense, such a painful reality? Because "they are insecure, and it's funny," Tanya, who's white, admits. "Some of it is funny. Like you have to admit, if you heard that so and so was sneaking out of the campus last night or that so and so was off with this guy that you really think is queer, you're going to tell everybody." "Everyone likes good gossip," Lema agrees. Even though she thinks gossip is disrespectful and belongs to a litany of other "bad" things kids do to other kids like "put them down, pick on them, talk about them behind their back," she also admits that "everyone wants to get gossip and you want to know." "I like listening and just keeping my mouth shut. . . . I just mind my own business," she says, but laughs as she admits, "you just kind of contradict yourself if you like listening."

Gossip is fun, in part because "you don't get the whole facts about everything." It's a mystery, a puzzle; it captivates and entices and it provides information unavailable through more public channels. For this reason it offers a feeling of intimacy and connection and a sense of being inside and exclusive. As Lema, Latina and working class, says, "It's like did you hear about what this person did or is going to do or has done . . . and it's usually about the people that you never expected, a 'nice' kid who 'does good in school' who turns out be an alcoholic. . . . It 'could be sex, alcohol, drugs,' anything surprising." Gossip takes attention away from one's own failures and faults and allows girls to feel safe and justified for the moment.

But beyond being just fun and mysterious, gossip has enormous power to move girls to the social margin and so it is often directed at girls who are threatening in some way—too popular, too much attitude, too outspoken. Cheyanne, white and middle class, explains that "a lot of terrible rumors and nicknames" were spread about her good friend because this friend "thought she was sort of above everyone and thought that all her problems were the most important thing." Cheyanne wants to help her friend make her way back to the center and so she tells her what's going on. "She's improving," a pleased Cheyanne says. As Ruby, an outspoken African American girl, explains, "I used to be friends with this girl and me and her stopped being friends so she went around telling everybody rumors about me and just like everybody started to turn against me, but that's about all I knew. I mean they are the same people she talked about, and now she's friends with them, I don't get it. She's really confused, I don't know."

Moreover, as Patricia explains, girls gossip for more deliberate reasons: "to break up friends and relationships." Especially in her public urban school, she says, "if you are going out with someone, they want it to break up. They just, I don't know why. They just don't like seeing people together and they start talking trash." To make her school better, Patricia says,

I'd stop rumors if I could. And I wouldn't have all these like bunchy bunchy friends that's one little crowd and I would have everyone mix together. . . . Because kids hang in crowds, and if one crowd doesn't like the other, or one person in the crowd, then the whole crowd dislikes them and . . . you say oh man, I can't stand her. . . . My friend says

I can't stand her, and I get to dislike the person, but I don't even know the person. So if you mix together you'd say what, I'm cool, I like her. I mean, each person should have their individual taste of another person.

Moriah, a white seventeen-year-old, agrees that girls use gossip to separate other girls and that the impact on relationships is devastating: "The major fights that we have gotten in have been because of other people who have told me things or told her things that turn out not to be true; I regretted them because it was like just because I listened to other people and not to her, you know, we wasted our time being mad at each other." Chandra, African American and in the eleventh grade, struggles to stay close to her friend when other girls tell her not to. "I would start hearing stories about how she is a slut or she is this and that, and I can't believe you are with her because you two are completely different and I'm like, I didn't see anything wrong with her, I thought she was the coolest person on earth and I just never believed she was as loose as they claimed she was, so I always put that out of my mind." When her mother started hearing the stories and pressuring her to end the friendship, a resistant Chandra insisted, "I am going to stay with her, this is my good friend."

As in Chandra's case, it's the unsubstantiated nature of the information that makes gossip so powerful. Because gossip is associated with demeaning stereotypes of femininity—emotionality, irrationality, deceitfulness—it's a loaded, untrustworthy source of information from the get go and often leaves girls feeling anxious and uncertain about where they stand. Diedre, who is white and in the twelfth grade, talks about the ever-present ghost of other girls' opinions.

I have a good time and I look at it, if you can't go out and have a good time and not think about what other people think, meanwhile deep down inside I am saying, "What does she think about me?" you know, and sometimes I wonder if that is just an act . . . the insecurity generated: insecurity I guess I have with myself. Look at that girl, she is so pretty, she is so this. . . . She could be the biggest airhead, but she is so skinny. I say skinny is kind of a goddess, it means the world. If you are skinny you are going to get everything, which is a totally wrong attitude, but . . .

Fear of others' gossip hovers over girls' relationships. Tracey, also white and in the twelfth grade, finds herself reluctant to reveal herself, fearing what others might think or say. "I tried to be very nice, but I didn't want anybody to know me very well. I was afraid that if they found out too much about me, they wouldn't like me, or they would make judgments too early or something and so I didn't want anybody to get to know me really." As a result, Tracey says she acted "kind of superficial and kind of vague. . . . I didn't show my real feelings and I was too smiling and nice." Smiling all the time, especially for middle-class girls, becomes a form of self-protection, a kind of noncommittal "polish," not unlike the protective strategy Katie, sixteen, uses: "I just try to stay, try to stay out of it and play, like if one side says something to me, I won't relay it to her and I won't act like I know anything about either side. I'll just try to stay in the middle."

The specter of rumors and the use of gossip to control and police other girls, to ensure that certain norms of behavior are upheld, certain codes of conduct adhered to, takes a toll. Girls become wary and untrusting of other girls. Oliva, Latina, explains how such relational dynamics have affected her.

> Well, real, real friends, like friends that you can confide in, I don't have many. I really don't have many. Because you can't really trust anybody. . . . The majority won't do anything for anybody else. For anybody else, you know . . . like a little group and then one of them will break rank and they will go to another one and then somebody will say something about another group, and they'll go back and tell the person they were talking about them. Instead of just keeping quiet to themselves, they'll start trouble between those people. So you really can't confide in anybody. You have to really know the person for a long time to know how they are. Before you can say something really confident.

It takes a certain amount of trust and confidence in others to support solidarity and collective action and this tendency to sell each other out, to "break rank," to "start trouble" with other girls makes me suspicious. If girls have to be constantly vigilant among other girls, if they are made anxious about relationships and intimacy, if the relational and social ground is constantly shifting, they will seek out the solid ground of the familiar status quo. Gossip, because it's underground and intimate, holds the potential for achieving solidarity and fostering a strong, supportive, resilient community—one that can contest the usual goings-on. But more often this potential is unfulfilled and even co-opted. Gossip becomes a tool of sexism, a way for girls to keep other girls in line or excluded altogether.

Some girls, like Ana, struggle with the uneasy alliance between their personal truths and pressures from their friends to sell themselves or other girls out. For Ana, a Latina American who attends an urban public school, the struggle comes from "feeling different," like "I don't feel like I fit into the group. . . . I feel so much different because they act very crazy, they do." It's not only her friends' swearing that makes Ana uncomfortable, but the way they hurt other people. "I don't like to see other people hurt. I'm very sentimental. If I see somebody and some people are making fun of them, I won't laugh because I feel bad, you know." Because she doesn't swear or talk about people, or "like doing stuff they do," Ana wonders "if they wonder themselves why is this girl not saying nothing." "I don't know," she confesses, "I just don't feel happy. I feel like I know that somebody must have talked about me today. . . . It's this feeling I have inside myself. . . . I don't know why I have this feeling." This feeling keeps Ana on guard, partly because betrayal is in the air; she never quite sees or hears the other girls. "I think it happens. I'm not saying I know it's happening because I don't know what people are saying, I don't know if I am thinking wrong, but it's a feeling that . . . Oh today it's going to go off because somebody did this or somebody did that."

Ana knows what it's like to be on uneven ground. She describes a time when her best friend's former boyfriend came onto her one day at school. He asked to talk with her, then hugged and kissed her in front of other boys "he hangs with." She's adamant that "I did not kiss him at all," and suspects he did this in front of his friends to make his former girlfriend jealous. In any case, retribution was swift—

> everybody was looking at me with a different view, no more the same smiley faces. . . . It wasn't a half hour before they told her . . . and I felt so bad because the next day everybody came up to me, "Why did you have to go kiss [him]? Why did you have to go betray your girl?" It was so bad. I felt like dying. . . . Everybody was so against me; people didn't believe that . . . he's the one who came on. I didn't do anything.

She finally convinced her girlfriend, but others continued to avoid her. People got "the wrong idea. The way they look at me, they just are not the same and the next day they're, forget it, I don't exist any more. I don't know. One day they're all, you know, 'Hi. Bye. How are you?' and then the next day it's nothing. So, I wonder, did you hear something?"

Ana got it all—the gossip, the rejection, and finally, the silent treatment—that aggressive act of shunning that girls use so effectively to instill shame and panic and fear. Girls know what some religious orders have known for centuries, that shunning is a most powerful punishment for all kinds of social sins. Kelly, a white girl from a private school, tells a story about "a friend" she was running against for class officer who told other classmates that she was not qualified. This friend, Kelly says,

> came up to me and hugged me and I was just like, I am thinking you are just a bitch, I mean, I didn't say anything and I could tell, I don't know if she could tell, but I just stood there and she is just hugging me and I'm just like, you are hugging me and you have been sitting upstairs talking about me and you know, you are so hypocritical. . . . She was, you know, you will do a good job, and totally lying in my face now.

Kelly says nothing because she knows that her silence is more effective: "This person is really worried. . . . It's really killing her. She's really worried now. And I didn't say anything to her."

Girls learn early how to give the appearance of being nice even when they don't feel like it. We've seen that the youngest girls know how to be relationally aggressive in indirect ways—how to make life miserable for another girl without appearing to do so. High school girls, with years to hone their skills, can be very good at this. Ella, white and middle class, who describes herself as a "quiet" person who "tries hard to get along" with people, talks about her struggle with a girl who was "very rude . . . really malicious." Ella had decided to join the drama club, to work "behind the scenes" when a girl she barely knew began to target her. "I don't know," Ella begins.

> I was trying to be a nice person. She just did things, she stepped on my hand and she threw away some of my books. She spilled my Coca Cola

. . . and she would do it in a way that looked like she didn't do it or I did it myself and . . . sometimes people didn't believe me, because she was known as a really nice person in school and it was strange. I didn't understand it myself. I don't know why she didn't like me, it was revenge.

Revenge for what she can't or doesn't say, but it felt like there must have been something. When Ella's friends, also friends with this girl, confront the girl, she backs off. The others are fooled, but Ella knows the girl is being "fake nice," that her actions toward Ella are all "polish."

Lenore, white and middle class, complains about her friend who, she says, "is so picky and she always sits there and . . . complains. She thinks she is perfect and I would never want to be like her. I'd kill myself if I was like her." Lenore hates it that her friend is always "stuck to what she thinks . . . sees only her point of view . . . thinks she is right about everything," and "it's always me that has to cave in to her." But because, as Lenore says, "I don't want her to hate me" and because "I feel sorry for her. . . . I just have to be nice to her . . . and I am around her all the time and I get so sick of her." Lenore avoids rather than confronts her friend and admits, "I do have to lie to her a lot . . . I feel like I am always covering things up, like . . . if she's not included." Being the kind of "fake nice" that Ella complains about, Lenore seethes inside, perhaps angry at or jealous of her friend for so boldly speaking her mind and being free of the tyranny of nice and kind Lenore finds herself struggling against.

This is the kind of underground conflict that makes girls look irrational. In fact, girls like Lenore and her friend are working their way through a thicket of contradictory cultural messages that wreak havoc with their friendships—messages about perfection and idealized relationships and how to be pleasing, messages about the untrustworthiness and deceitfulness of girls and women. Lenore hates her friend for not playing the game or performing the right kind of nice girl and yet she remains friends with her, which suggests there's something to be gained here. Her friend is arrogant and says what she thinks. Lenore doesn't stand her ground; instead she lies, covers things up, and then she blames her friend for not seeing that what she says is hurtful or off-putting. Lenore invokes the views of other girls who are excluding this friend. The friend may soon be punished soundly for her refusal to play right.

Lori, who is Asian American, has a similar problem and resolves it in a similar fashion. She talks about how hard it is to deal with a long-time friend who is "incredibly bright. . . . She is smarter than me and I can accept that." But she is also "cocky and confident and haughty . . . and I can't see past that, and I can't see past to the good person that she is. She really is a good person. . . . It's just the attitude problem got to me and I couldn't deal with it." As her friend became more "haughty and independent," Lori backed away. "I didn't talk to her for about three months. . . . I couldn't go up to her and tell her, 'You are acting so conceited and so snotty,' you can't tell that to a person." But Lori was "really, really mad at her." Months passed and out of the blue Lori received a letter on her birthday from this girl. In the letter, the friend confessed that "you have taught me more things about myself than you can ever imagine. I know so much more about me than anyone could have told me and you didn't tell me, you just made me think about myself and how I reacted." Unlike in Lenore's story, though, here nothing was said and everything was conveyed.

This is one way girls fight in high school—indirectly, covertly, hoping their gossip and subtle expressions of anger will be picked up, passed on, and interpreted correctly by the target of their strong feelings. Sometimes, as with Lori and her friend, it does. But sometimes it can be a frustrating exercise in futility, leaving the aggressor and the victim feeling misunderstood and unsatisfied. And sometimes the effect is strongest when the target girl *doesn't* get it. Tennessee, for example, never understood why her friend stopped talking to her: "If we had gotten into a fight because I knew that she had done something, or I knew that I had done something that was rude or something like that, then I would have understood if she was angry with me, but I really didn't understand why and there is nothing more annoying than not knowing why somebody is mad at you." That's the point—the real message of this rejection is about who has the raw power to exclude and to confuse without explanation. Regardless of how it all turns out, the risk is worth it—more direct expression of anger can get you labeled bad, a bitch; can get you talked about and rejected, landed in detention or beaten up, either emotionally or physically. And boys typically don't like uppity girls and bitches. This is the kind of fighting that can go on undetected, even by other girls. As Tennessee says, "the thing about fights and friends that I have noticed is that like a lot of times some of my other friends are in fights with some of my other friends, and I never even find out until much later, you know. It doesn't affect you unless you are in it."

"TIRED OF TALKIN'"

Ana finds it's best to do nothing when other girls "talk trash" about her or avoid her. She turns the tables on them and says, "like, forget it," because "they get mad when you ignore them, see." Then there are girls, like Ariel, who confront issues head on. "When I get mad," Ariel says, "that's the end of the other person. I just hit out to anyone around me. . . . I can verbally cut down anyone to the bare bones." Opal, who's seventeen, white, and middle class, shares this quality of verbal toughness. She's proud that she's direct and confrontational. She describes her response to a girl who talked "behind my back and there is nothing that bothers me more as when someone talks behind my back."

> I said, if you have anything to say to me . . . you come to me and nobody else, and she agreed to that. And then she said something about me behind my back but it really wasn't behind my back. I slammed a window in her face, we were talking through the window and I slammed it in her face and I said "Fine!" and I slammed it in her face because she said something that really bothered me and she goes, "I have had it with this shit," and she goes "God damn bitch," and somebody, one of my friends was sitting out there and heard her . . . and my friends came in and said do you know what Eve said behind your back? My friends knew . . . that bothers me, so I went and found Eve, and I bitched her out and yelled at her and she yelled at me and we talked and we got everything all worked out. You have to really talk.

Alexis, fifteen, white and middle class, is also a straight-talker. She describes a conflict with her friend over the phone. "I could hear in the background her saying things like she just moved to [the city] and high-society bitch and I said to the guy on the phone, 'I can hear people calling me names in the background and I don't really appreciate it, ok, goodbye,' and hung up. And later she called up and said why did you do all that stuff, and I said, 'I can't understand how boring your summer must be that you have to call me up and harass me.'"

Indirect or direct, there are girls like Mary, white and working class, who are, as she says, "tired of talkin'. I get into trouble and fights," Mary says, usually over "stupid things, like people spreading rumors, or . . . like they thought I said something or they thought I did something" or sometimes when she "sees two people fighting," and tries "to be a hero . . . going in and breaking it up." While Mary says she "feels bad" when she fights, sometimes she just can't avoid it. "Sometimes if you are walking down the hall and you bump into some girl and say you're sorry and she won't accept your apology, she'll want to fight you." Fighting, for Mary, is about self-respect and it's about honor.

Respect is especially important for girls who feel the daily experience of inequality and the cumulative effect of microaggressions, such as racist remarks, experiences of invisibility or marginality, lowered or heightened expectations based on gender, race, ethnicity, or class. As Patricia, a sixteen-year-old Latina says,

> I'm not a pushy person or anything. I'm not a bully or nothin', but you know, people, I don't know, people respect me, but it's not because I'm a bad girl or whatever, you know what I mean? It's just that, like I tell them, I tell them straight up, I hate it when people lie or people are hypocrites or anything like that, I just let them know that, don't lie . . . because it's not worth it anyway, because I don't like when people lie to me.

"It's just a matter of respect" for Beverly, an African American fifteen-year-old. "Like if it's just a little thing, I can overlook it," she explains. "But don't keep pushin' my buttons." Being respected is about basic survival. In her urban public school, when someone says "those fightin' words" to Beverly, she feels she has to respond. "'Cause you want people to think that you is hard and they can't mess with you. . . . Respect. They gotta respect you." Aiesha, also African American, agrees. "And if that's what you gotta do to get respect, that's what you gotta do. 'Cause if you don't, people gonna walk all over you. . . . You gotta survive in your territory, you gotta claim your territory, survive in it, do what you gotta do; that's how I figure it."

While it's necessary at times, Beverly, Aiesha, and their friends see fighting as a "negative thing." Partly because it feeds a cycle in which they feel trapped. As Janet, an African American, explains, "See, what it is, if girls act like they hard core, and other girls see that, they get jealous or get mad, and then they want to fight you. So you end up fightin' to stay like that. So if you want to stay hard, you gotta fight to stay hard." If you don't, Aiesha agrees, "people pick on you. Like, I seen a girl, she act like she was hard at the beginning of the school year. She fought, she lost, she started gettin' bumped around the hallway, gettin' cussed out, and she wasn't doin' nothin', she didn't stand up for herself from the get go."

"Getting' bumped" is a physical form of indirect aggression practiced a lot by girls. Just as it's up to a girl to "read" another girl's silence or Medusa's stare, it's up to her to "read" the bump she gets in the school hallway. "The girl that fought her," Tatiana explains, "she had bumped her in the hallway and stuff and she didn't do nothing. Me, I would have had to hit you, you bumped me out there." "No," Angela says,

> first you get real loud and say, "I know your momma taught you the word excuse me. I know you just didn't hit me!" If they bump you on purpose, okay, you can tell if somebody bump you on purpose or if they bump you on accident. 'Cause if they do it on accident, most of the time they say, "Excuse me, oh, I'm sorry." And then you can feel like the way they bump, if they bump you real hard, "I know you just didn't do it." They wanted to bump you. That's what I'm sayin'. If they do somethin' like that and they don't say excuse me, and if it hurt, I'm gonna say something!

Clearly, having an attitude or having too much attitude provokes girlfighting. As Aiesha says, "This one senior, she just, she wanted to get hit in the face, man. She took her popularity and just ran with it, you know." When girls get "too high and mighty," Janet says, "then you gotta bring them back down." "I don't like your attitude, so I don't like you," Beverly exclaims. Girls who are snobs, self-centered, and full of themselves, have to be taught a lesson, have to be cut down to size. "When somebody is self-centered it makes me angry," Tamika says. So many girls talk about such "high class snobbery" and the way such girls "look down on other people." "Snobbiness" seems to be a threat to the girls' egalitarian values, or perhaps to the remaining tenuous threads of girls' collectivity. In a social context where girls are suspect anyway, such an attitude of superiority undermines any last sense of group loyalty or trust that girls will have each others' backs. When one girl "breaks rank" and pulls herself out for special attention, it's boys' attention or adult acknowledgment she's usually after and this often suggests betrayal. Pulling rank, standing out, a girl relegates other girls to the mediocrity of the group. But not just any group—a group of girls, which carries all that old negative cultural baggage. Having an attitude, "being too high in the clouds," as Ana calls it, is thus read by many girls as an overt act of betrayal and disrespect.

And girls who blatantly display superiority in any form enrage other girls. Julia, who is Portuguese, talks about a girl with whom she competes for grades:

> We used to be friends and I couldn't stand her now. She's such a ugh.
> . . . She's conceited. She thinks she's it. She's only a freshman and she,
> I wish I was there on the floor killing her, I don't know. It's like the people that interest me, people that try and people that work to get something, but people that are only giving apples to the teachers, do everything for the teacher, and like don't do anything else in class and people that are there working get the lousy grades and the other ones just get like the good grades, like that doesn't work with me.

Debra, who is white and middle class, is furious at her friend for her superior attitude. In her effort to cut her friend down to size, though, she sounds every bit as arrogant and mean as she accuses her friend of being.

> I want to say to her, "Look, I feel like a little itty bitty kid, you treated me like dirt." . . . She is always thinking of herself to be wonderful, taking that stance, and needless to say she has legs like tree stumps, but do I say that? No. I just leave it out of the question. But she is like, "I was the best dancer, and I am going to do the [dance school]," and she is 40 lbs. overweight, and [she says] "I am an actress," and she just does everything wonderful, she is gorgeous, and I noticed this about her and really, you've got to be kidding. You have got to be kidding, you are never going to be a dancer with those legs. I never say it to her, so I am not that rude, but then I met her boyfriend which really blew me away because him and I always sort of liked each other behind her back and he has been going out with her for a while and we tried not to be naughty with each other at parties and she never knew this and I still don't think she knows and we were talking about John and she said,

"John really doesn't like you that much because he thinks you are too young," and I go, don't tell me that, I am going to tell you a couple of stories you will never forget and I didn't say and I said, "Oh really, tell me some more." And she is going on, and I say, "Do you really think that I am immature, most people have told me I am older for my age." She says, "You act like a sixteen-year-old, and that's good because you are sixteen," and I'm like, "Thanks," and I was furious with her.

At the same time, being tough, having an attitude protects girls from other girls and also from boys. More and more girls are "fronting"—covering their vulnerability with a tough exterior[15]—and donning the "tough guise pose" that Jackson Katz attributes to boys in this culture.[16] Girls who don't want to be associated with weakness and vulnerability end up modeling or posing macho toughness and bravado. As Grace, African American and working class, explains,

> Like say one girl you messin' with, she just got the attitude, you know, anybody wants you, anybody look at you in a kinda way, you know, or anybody stare at you like they want you, you just gonna hit her. That's some people's attitudes some people have. And my best friend, her attitude is like well, if she hits me I'm just gonna hit her back because I don't want to just be hit.

Having attitude means dressing the part. "When she got on boot jeans and one of those tight shirts," Aiesha says of her friend, "she look as mean as life." And in these clothes her friend is ready to fight. "Back up, wait a minute, breathe! 'Cause I have seen her mad; I'll be like, breathe! She's like, no, no, he shouldn't have said that or she shouldn't' have said that! And she won't sit down, she just keeps walkin'." Boys get respect this way, why shouldn't they? As Stephanie, African American and middle class, says, "I am a lot meaner than I used to be. . . . I used to never let anything get to me. I used to just brush it aside. Now, forget it, if you say something to me, I jump all over you, it's so funny. I am really mean now."

Having an attitude is a sign of self-respect and broadcasts invulnerability to the words and cruelties of others. As Ruby, an African American girl whose family is on public assistance, says, "I like [having people talk about me], I can walk by with my head up in the air, but it makes them even madder . . . that snob, you know." While her friends tease her and call her "a witch," Julie, an African American fifteen-year-old, says, "I like that kind of stuff. . . . It gives me the leverage to walk down the hall and shake my booty, you know, and then they get all upset about it. That's their fault. I mean, they can walk down the hall all they want and any way they want, I am not going to be intimidated, you know. I don't care." And there's Jane, also African American, attending a private girls' school, who says, "I am egotistical and ambitious." As a result she takes a lot of abuse from other girls. But what she gets—the label "Supergirl"—is ultimately worth it.

Adolescent girls' identities are continually made and remade through the shifts and rifts in their friendships and peer relations. But this is much more than a psychological or even a relational process, although girls may describe and experience it only in these ways. The nature and possibility of their connections and alliances with other girls are deeply affected by societal expectations and messages—about heterosexual normalcy, about white racial constructions of beauty, about appropriate ways to be a girl in any given context, about the reality of scarce resources and limited chances for visibility and power. The possibility of loyalty and coalition building between girls is constantly threatened by the competitiveness, fraudulence, and disconnection necessary for girls to be taken seriously, to be respected, or to be the chosen token girl who gets the guy or reaches the elite social position in her school.

There are certainly psychological and relational consequences to the losses girls experience. So many girls are looking for trust and genuine connection, so many girls echo Harriet when she says, "if there is a conflict with someone who you are really close to that just divides you . . . that is the worst thing that can happen." There's a lot of walking wounded in high school hallways. For Zoe and her two friends—known to all as the Three Musketeers—life is often an "emotional seesaw" because "a lot of times I feel very happy . . . and then . . . the next minute I feel just really taken down and low." In her school, Tatiana sees girls "walkin' down the hall by themselves with their head down," trying to get by, trying not to be noticed, singled out, picked on.

But this sense of the psychological effaces the very real social and political repercussions of internalizing sexist stereotypes and practicing misogyny. In middle school the energy and movement from one story, one fight, one insult, one friendship to the next provides a steady flow of contradictions and exaggerations that give girls a feeling of drama and provide them with space to question and debate. Now in high school there is a tighter logic, a psychology and a linearity that seems to justify itself, squeeze out contradiction, and refuse social critique. In girlfighting, especially, we see how the public is lived through the private.[17] Whether they are pressed to perform nice girls or tough girls in public, much is happening beneath the surface. Jealousies stir the waters. As Naomi says, "you can't cope with the fact that someone has something or looks like something or whatever else, and you just feel like oh, I wish I had that, I hate her because she has that." Private alliances—established through gossiping, whispering, plotting, strategizing—operate as "microtechnologies of power," Valerie Hey says,[18] giving girls a sense that they are important and visible, but often doing so by negating, selling out, rejecting other girls.

Girls are acting just as people in subordinate or less powerful positions are "supposed" to act with each other. They are becoming card-carrying members of a sexist ideology that stereotypes and judges girls and women and denigrates qualities associated with femininity. Why else would girls sell out their girlfriends, privilege their relationships with boys over girls, choose male friends over female, blame girls when boyfriends betrayed them, distance themselves from back-stabbing, wussy, untrustworthy "airheads" or "clueless ones"? If this is the way the public world sees girls, who wants to be one, or at least who wants to be that kind of girl? Better to become an "independent," intelligent "mature" individual who separates herself from other girls to be with a guy or who decontaminates herself from all that girlyness, to aspire to be one of the guys.

Michelle Fine and Pat Macpherson heard this "feminist individualism" in a series of conversations with a small group of girls from different class and racial backgrounds. Feminism was a flight from "other girls" as unworthy and untrustworthy. Their version of feminism was about equal access to being men.[19] "Girls can be good, bad, or—best of all—they can be boys. This version of . . . feminism reflects a retreat from the collective politics of gender . . . and an advance into the embattled scene of gender politics—alone, and against boys, in order to become one of them."[20] In a sexist culture, girls' movement toward individuality and maturity is too often a move away from being a girl or aspiring to be a woman.

Adolescent girls' preoccupation with loyalty and with the "back-stabbing" behavior of other girls, is thus understandable—negotiating such a treacherous social climate depends on finding friends you can trust, and conversely, excluding people who jeopardize your toehold on popularity or threaten your precarious defense against being hurt or treated badly. But some girls know that too much of their valuable time and energy is taken up with fighting other girls. After months of not talking to her friend and actively avoiding her in the hall, Opal, white and middle class, finally tells her friend, "It was so stupid. . . . It seemed like we were wasting all this time. . . . Life is really short, you know, and you're going to waste time being mad at someone?" Carly, also white, thinks much the same thing. Frustrated that her friends were "putting all their energy into hating" another girl, doing "cruel and unnecessary" things like "writing things on bathroom walls," she says to them: "You guys don't have to kiss and make up and be best buddies, but you also don't have to expend all your energy hating each other." "I think that is stupid," Naomi, African American, says of all the ways girls dis one another. "Jealousy is the worst thing on earth. . . . It's a waste of time."

And some girls even move beyond the psychological to see that, aside from being a waste of personal time and relational energy, fighting other girls ensures the stability of the status quo. "Wasting time" is only part of the point, as Maritza made clear in the last chapter and as Lilly mentioned in the chapter before. If girls spend all their time thrashing about in relational quicksand, scrambling to pull themselves out or to throw someone else in, especially that someone who has the courage to challenge the status quo, stand out, or take a leadership role, they have done nothing to change current patterns of sexism and their intimate relationship to racism, homophobia, and other forms of oppression. They are simply living in it and enabling it.

Clearly, girlfighting is not a short-lived phenomena. As we've seen, girls learn from earliest childhood how to disconnect from, control, and fight with other girls. And girlfighting isn't trivial. It's about something much more than clothes and boyfriends and beauty ideals, although these issues become the justification for dismissing such horizontal violence as a kind of inconsequential "girls will be girls" nastiness. This leads us to consider womanhood, both because girlfighting can take on new and more serious dimensions and because women are still primarily the caretakers and teachers in this culture. Women hold the power to perpetuate or to contest girlfighting in their own lives and among the next generation of girls.

6

From Girlfighting to Sisterhood

She may be an angel who spends all winter,
bringing the homeless blankets and dinner,
a regular Nobel Peace Prize Winner.
But I really hate her,
I'll think of a reason later
. . . .
Inside her head may lay all the answers,
for curing diseases from baldness to cancer.
Salt of the earth and a real good dancer.
But I really hate her,
I'll think of a reason later.
> —"I'll Think of a Reason Later," country song

An eye for an eye leads only to more blindness.
> —Margaret Atwood, *Cat's Eye*

IT'S FOUR O'CLOCK on a winter afternoon and I'm sitting in a small conference room talking about girlfighting with three women—an engineer, an activist, and a businesswoman. We have settled around a square table, one woman per side; the sunlight, weak on this frigidly cold January day, provides barely enough light for the geraniums that line the windowsills. They are blooming nonetheless; in ragtag fashion, clusters of red and pink shamelessly compete for the last long rays. Denise, the engineer—tall, slender, intense—is talking about her childhood, the pivotal moment in second grade when her girlfriends dumped her and she knew for certain what she'd suspected all along, that girls didn't play fair and were not worth the effort.

I had a couple of very close, what I thought were girlfriends, one of whom, in school one day—we'd been friends for several years—actively just rejected me. "We're not friends anymore." And this was extremely disturbing to the point where I remember it clearly and I remember feeling extremely upset by this. So I was left as a floating entity for the rest of the school year, because once a girl is rejected, you know, they're out.

Not knowing what happened or why—"maybe I said or did something . . . perhaps I was no longer appealing"—Denise began to hang out with the boys. "I made the decision by the time I was maybe ten to identify with my father," she recalls. Distancing herself from her mother, a homemaker and community activist, she became "an honorary boy": "I rejected this whole notion of girls rejecting me. I was not going to allow myself to be rejected. I was a very, you know those angry young men? Well, I was one but I was a girl." At fourteen, Denise used to say to her incredulous mother, "'What do you need women's liberation for?' Of course I identified with men, I felt I was really liberated."

Men, like her attentive, demanding father, like the more predictable, transparent boys she played ball with, were where it was at for Denise. A life spent learning boys' rules led her to higher level science classes, to college for engineering, to a stint working for the Navy, and eventually to a construction position, working mostly with men and a few recent women graduates like her younger self. "For me, moving out of girls' groups was a way to avoid rejection," Denise admits. "Boys' groups, you can just keep clawing through power in the hierarchy and the structure."

Carol's story begins in graduate school. A single parent with little money, she enrolled in a master's program in economic development with the help of a scholarship and AFDC. One day "a guy in my department dropped this thing on my desk and he said, 'I just read this advertisement, and, you know, it looks like it was written for you.'" The job was to head a new organization, founded by a well-established economic development group hoping to tap into new monies available to support women's business development. The liaisons from the parent organization, two professional women, were looking for someone to work with low-income women. With a history of activism in women's organizations and work with poor communities, Carol was perfect.

Through those first lean years, Carol put her heart and soul into the organization, sometimes working months without pay. The effort paid off.

I went to my first board meeting and they said, "We want to build a grassroots, statewide, membership based, women's business organization that will work with low-income women." And I said, "I'll do my best." When I took over the board of directors there were six or seven women, all local, all upper class. The paid membership was about ten. Two years later we had a board of directors with representation from all over the state; 50 percent of the board was low-income. We had a membership of over two hundred women. And we did this on a $75,000 grant. At the end of eight years we had a membership of over a thousand women. We had eight regional groups across the state. We had a nationally promoted mentoring program. We were one of the only American affiliates of Women's World Banking. The town was going to give us a $300,000 building. We had received economic development grants two years in a row. I was gonna be getting a national award.

It sounds incredible, but at this point the proverbial shit hit the fan. Carol had done what she was asked, but she admits, "I didn't play by the rules." She had created a truly grassroots venture, wrenching her fledgling organization from the grasp of the powerful parent group that had initiated and wanted to control it, and it became clear that she'd gone too far. Making money was at the heart of the initial project, "but that's not what they told me," Carol said. "It was my intention to give *other* people power." The upper-class women who hired Carol hadn't counted on Carol's vision, determination, or her success. "They were really pissed off at me because I succeeded and I didn't play by their rules. For fifteen years . . . they've been good girls, and they've played by the rules, and they've been screwed every which way they go."

What was most confusing and terrifying for Carol was how personal it all became. Through a series of accusations and calculated moves designed to make her look unprofessional and incompetent, the women set out to undermine her and take back control of the organization. She was "not acting like an executive director," they said; she hadn't "sufficiently matured," did not have "the management skills to represent the organization with the big power players"; they needed "a different image," they needed to move the group to the city "to be a bigger player, i.e., in the man's world." Eroding her base of support through gossip and threats and a thinly veiled classism, they made sure Carol spent her time putting out small fires. In the end, Carol said, "It wasn't the women with the power that did me in. . . . They used my own people to do it. . . . They knew what they were doing."

"If that had been a male board of directors," a friend said to Carol when it was all over, "they would have stopped before destroying the organization." It's clear to Carol that he was right. "These women did not care that they were going to lose the whole ball game," she said, "as long as they got me."

Joan's story resonates with Carol's on many levels. In her former position as coordinator of a regional family planning program, Joan too was enormously successful. Her efforts to develop programs that gave a high quality of care to those most in need ran counter to the agency overseeing their operation. When Reagan came into power and funding became tight, Joan laments, "a lot of things started to happen."

> We did not have enough medical staffing to keep up with the client load. We had a very interesting staff there; I mean we had a lot of politically minded people there. And the women were just coming in the doors like you wouldn't believe. You know, you go up the chain of command and you get less and less support for family planning, so they were really concerned about alienating the funding sources. And they saw me leading the charge basically, as being counter to their interests, which was to keep the money coming into the agency.

Like Carol, Joan spoke truth to power. "I was saying, if we don't pay attention to what's going on with this client load, the quality of care is going to go down." She resisted efforts to cut back, to make people wait six weeks for appointments, to abandon the community trust she and her staff had worked hard to build. And so *she* became the problem: "They were making this big case that I was creating problems in the organization and I was disruptive in ways that were counterproductive." In a classic divide and conquer move, management sent Joan home, with pay:

> I was really isolated. I was home, I was not allowed in the office, you know, and [my staff] was interviewed by a consultant basically to col-

lect information about why I was a problem to the organization.
. . .There was this absolute ban or gag rule on me. . . . And the only way
I could keep my salary was to obey the rules. And I was the sole support. Aaron was home with our son and we had no money. . . . And
everybody stayed away from me. . . . So they divided the medical staff
and kept them out of it and said, you know, we don't have problems
with this program. The problem we have is Joan. And we'll negotiate
with you on resolving this as long as she doesn't come back.

As with Carol, Joan's female staff was co-opted—some feared losing their jobs if they did not comply, others saw an opportunity to advance up the ladder, and still others saw, in Joan's words:

a kind of opportunity to cause some pain to a woman they felt was
way too uppity, you know, that was way beyond herself, that was
doing things. I could sort out, I could see those women that were lin-
ing up to testify against me out of self-preservation or of feeling like,
well that makes sense because Joan's always been a bit beyond the
pale. And these women saw that as an opportunity. An opportunity to,
you know, get my job, be mean, put me in my place, to prove to me that
I couldn't just dream as big as I was dreaming, that I couldn't kind of
pull it off.

As our conversation progresses, the invisible threads connecting
the women's stories emerge. Carol and Joan wonder at the great lengths
to which other women went to bring them down, the personal and
often indirect nature of the attacks, the ways women's fears, economic
realities, desire for power, and institutional protection were used as ammunition against them, the way promises of status and privilege divided the women in their organizations. And Denise, who finds herself
in midlife reconnecting with her mother, realizes at this moment that "I
was identified with those same women who undermined you," speaking now to Carol and Joan; those women "clawing through power in the
hierarchy." She finds herself thinking a lot about the newly hired female
engineers, fresh from school, who assert, like she did at fourteen, that
they are liberated even as they struggle under the weight of daily indignities. She wonders, "How can I help myself, essentially make my
life less constrained? I don't mean constrained like what people are
doing to me. I mean what I'm doing to me."

Men kill their weak, the saying goes, and women kill their strong. Is this true? Does it have to be so? Denise and Carol and Joan, all feminists, sit in a room, each with radically different ideologies, histories, and experiences and each talking about girlfighting and its painful impact—a little girl is rejected in ways that reverberate a lifetime, women "going after" other women for power and opportunities, betrayal heaped upon betrayal. These stories resonate with the stories girls have shared throughout this book; with Sara, for example, who targeted the one girl in her group who could threaten her position as most popular because she had "the goodness and the ability to reveal to the others the type of person I was." They resonate with the group of fifth-grade girls who marked their hands with red Xs and met on Saturdays to draw mean pictures to tape on the lockers of girls they chose to exclude, with the eighth-grade girls who engaged in "verbal vandalism," and with a group of high school girls who threw a "We hope Erin doesn't win party" for their "friend" who was competing in the Miss Teen USA pageant. Girls like Denise who "play by the rules" that promise them power, success, and security in the culture are learning how to become the women Carol and Joan confront. Internalizing a culture that centers male authority and trivializes femininity, they are learning how to strip away other girls' support and to depose other girls who threaten their positions of power—who, because they question the usual way things go, are too full of themselves, too popular, too ambitious, need to be taken out or cut down to size.

These stories from three accomplished women echo cruelties endured by multitudes of girls at different ages who, for whatever reason, either don't know how or choose not to play by the rules—girls who ask the "wrong" questions, know or want too much, act too sexual, speak too loud, like themselves too much, dream too big—all actions that threaten to take too much space, claim visibility and power. These girls can be brought down because they are, after all, "asking for it." Girls who refuse to play the nice girl game, which includes pleasing those in power, threaten to reveal the status quo as deeply sexist, and maintaining it, not as a choice but a mandate. They reveal a pleasing type of femininity as a performance for the right people—boys, adults, other girls who have power and are worth impressing.[1] The difference, of course, is that when women like Carol and Joan don't comply, they are punished in ways that go beyond the relational and the psychological. Their transgressions cost them their jobs, their economic security, and cost the people they served a range of support systems that could have made a difference in their lives. Girls' inhumanity to girls—the exclusions, gossip, teasing, and fighting—prepares the ground for more costly and high stakes social and political disconnections among women.

GOOD GIRLS AND BAD: FIGHTING TO BE SOMEBODY

As we've seen, girls learn early from the media, from school, and from family and friends, just what little girls are made of. From earliest childhood their experiences are voiced-over with familiar platitudes like "be nice" and "don't say that" and they're guided by gendered expectations they can repeat like a mantra. They learn not to trust other girls, take other girls seriously, or value girl things. At the same time, they witness an increase in media images of girls as beautiful and desirable and also nasty, deceitful, physically tough, fearless, and strong. It looks like a new image of girlhood—more girl power—but it isn't really. Sure, girls can be tough—they can don boxing gloves, do martial arts, kick box the hell out of evil—but only as long as they are pleasing to boys and men; as long as there is a comforting romantic subplot to justify their actions, as long as they have a Britney Spears-like body. They can be bold and dominant in some circumstances as long as they are demure, discreet, and subordinate to men in others. This is not a new kind of girl, just the old stereotype with a "tough guise" twist.

Popular girls, the girls we are led to believe guys like, the cheerleaders and the prom queens, have made their choices. But if other girls dismiss them as cultural dupes they have bought into a classic case of divide and conquer. The same goes when those prom queens reject and label other girls who fight or who don't match up to the feminine ideal as deviant or unredeemable social outcasts. Indeed, as educator Natalie Adams reveals, cheerleaders and fighters want the same things— power and visibility and respect. Listening to girls from *both* groups, she hears them talk about "confidence, fearlessness, dominance, independence, and the need to prove they are not another face in the crowd."[2] The social contexts the girls live in—the particular forms of invisibility that threaten them and the avenues to power available to them—simply structure the different choices they make. They are all girls, after all, doing the best they can to create opportunities for self-respect and self-determination. But since they fall out on opposing sides of a preexisting dichotomy—good girls and bad—they are cast against each other, encouraged from day one to see the other as weak or stupid in some way; a sellout, a cast-out.

In *Cat's Eye*, her powerful novel about the complexities of girls' friendships, snippets from which we've seen throughout this book, Margaret Atwood tells the story of successful artist Elaine Risley's life-long struggle to resolve the childhood trauma caused by her friend and nemesis, Cordelia. When eight-year-old Elaine moves to town, Cordelia befriends her. Elaine has spent her early childhood following the migrant rhythms of the natural world with her research scientist father, unconventional mother, and her smart older brother and she is now desperate for girl friends. Cordelia, it appears, is perfect. She is beautiful and "has beautiful manners"; she has older sisters and knows about girl things and proper behavior and Elaine is delighted to be chosen. But Cordelia's nice girl behavior is a cover for a deep sense of failure and imperfection and over time Elaine suffers all the variations of Cordelia's wrath. Elaine must pay penance for her inadequacies, her unpracticed voice, her lack of knowledge—exclusions, derision, public humiliations. "What do you have to say for yourself?" Cordelia asks Elaine, mimicking her own father's demanding question. "And I have nothing to say."

As Atwood follows Elaine through the years, we understand that in this childhood relationship are the seeds of Elaine's sharp tongue and "mean mouth" toward other girls in high school, her resentfulness toward her mother, her alliance with men and their power, her general mistrust of women and her distance from herself. Over time we also see that Cordelia, feeling the weight of her father's expectations, the shame of not matching up, and unable to openly protest to anyone who would listen, acts out her frustration on Elaine. Through their changing relationship, Atwood maps the intricate and subtle nature of internalized oppression as it happens at the hands not of the oppressors—that would be so easy to track—but of other subordinates. She alludes to the need of those without power to enact on each other what they themselves endure on a daily basis and thus, unconsciously, to secure at a very early age, through anger, pain, and loss, their proper place in the patriarchal order.

The real tragedy, Atwood implies in her novel, is that Elaine and Cordelia will never really know each other, that they will feel so totally separate that they will be unable to see the common threads that tie them. What makes Elaine's and Cordelia's stories seem distinct and unrelated, as if they have different causes, is that they are locked in a culturally sanctioned battle against one another—the aggressor and the victim, the bad girl and the good, the mean and the nice. The interdependence of this battle is so obscured that they remain shadows, ghosts to one another. In fact they are, as Atwood says, "reflections" of each other; like "the twins in old fables, each of whom has been given half a key."[3]

So much of girlfighting is between the Elaines and the Cordelias of the world. Between the girls the world has deemed outcasts for whatever reason—personal experience and choice, class, race, or sexual orientation—and those invited in, but on certain conditions—that they please and perform the right kind of femininity. The real culprit is the cultural ideal and the accompanying lie that either attaining it or rejecting it in absolute terms will change anything. It won't, because success in either direction depends on belittling and decontaminating oneself from the girls who took the other path. It's a setup.

These are the choices, the cultural stories, made available to girls and women because each in its own way preserves the status quo. Each offers a kind of power—enough power to keep girls invested in the fiction—and each is desirable in a culture that overromanticizes heterosexual relationships with men and overvalues male approval. Girls and woman know both kinds of power and feel intensely the inner conflicts they create, but in a world that pits them against one another, each is pressed to choose her priority. And if choosing one means seeing the other as a bad choice, as a choice that will contaminate her in some way, the stage for girlfighting and women's rivalry is set, the train is in motion.

The desire for power, of course, is basic and human. Power is just as pleasurable and intoxicating for women as it is for men. If the usual channels are blocked, other pathways are created. In *The Secret Lives of Girls*, Sharon Lamb talks about the social forces that prevent girls and women from owning their aggression, that "source of energy and creativity" that moves girls to express themselves and claim their lives on their own terms.[4] Girls' aggression is "reined in physically" as mothers of young children "increasingly punish girls for their aggressive behavior and decreasingly punish boys." Their aggression is further reigned in socially as "American culture . . . indicts girls for their so-called sneaky aggression, the way they use social exclusions, gossip, and cattiness to punish and hurt." Some girls, more often middle-class white girls, then "turn aggression against themselves: through eating disorders, self-mutilation, hyper-criticism about their talents and bodies, and depression." Those who resist—those who don't pin their hopes or their survival on assimilating to white feminine ideals—often find themselves in trouble and on the outs. While they may have an edge, a creative potential, they may not "have the means always to turn the aggression into a socially important act of standing up against injustice."[5]

Blocking these channels to feeling and expressing power means finding other, safer, more acceptable and sometimes hidden, sometimes destructive pathways. Taking frustrations and anger out on other girls is a perfect alternative. Finding another girl, weaker or vulnerable in some way, or even another girl who is a true equal and thus a real adversary can give girls that exhilarating feeling of being powerful, that pleasure, that "exuberance and joy" that "anyone would feel when they, even for a moment, have control, are mastering a situation" or feel in control of another's fate.[6]

The problem is that such horizontal violence not only doesn't change the power imbalances for girls and women in this culture, but it perpetuates and reproduces them. Our sense of superiority, our fears, our jealousies and competitive longings are repeatedly and compulsively channeled along certain routes; they follow the fault lines in what appears on the surface to be a seamless reality. They are in the fairy tales, stories, rhymes, and jump rope songs we were taught, the dumb blonde jokes we've heard, the commercial, video, TV, and movie images of girls as bimbos (think of Comedy Central's *The Man Show*) or victims or eroticized girlfighters, the messages conveyed in parents' postures, facial expressions, actions, and words when girls aggress or act out or nicely comply. In time, these divisive messages take on a sense of taken-for-granted reality because they are grounded in our earliest memories and understandings of what it means to be a girl or woman.

We can see the slow but clear development of such fault lines as we listen to the girls in this book—the interest and delight in difference and in one another the younger girls express gradually turns to suspicion, fear, competition, and judgment directed at other girls. Much of what girls in early adolescence talk about on the surface refers to differences in appearance and behavior, but this is often simply a cover or code for something much weightier—that is, the pressure they feel to assimilate to ideals of middle-class femininity and the consequences for those who don't or won't match up. Fault lines begin to shift the relational ground in more predictable ways. Girls of color feel pressure to "act white" if they are to excel in school,[7] working-class girls, taught by their families to fight for their survival, find themselves at odds with teachers who support feminine passivity and compliance;[8] girls who are too close and passionate in their friendships with other girls are suspect, and girls who are lesbian or bisexual face ridicule and ostracism.[9]

Girls are on the lookout for "bad" girls by the time they reach pre-school and they are reporting bad girls to adult authorities throughout childhood and then to other girls at adolescence—telling on or gossiping about girls who are not nice or girls who are too bossy, soon they judge girls as too sexual, too bitchy, too tough. Throughout childhood, complaints about other girls are laced with the derogatory—girls are too, well, girly, too feminine, too wussy, weak, deceitful, catty, critical. These are not words girls come into the world with—they are, after all girls themselves. It would seem counterproductive to denigrate the very group they are naturally a part of. But ironically, if they want to "make it" this is exactly what they have to do. This is about having power and to have power and to be taken seriously, girls are encouraged not to like or want to be "those" kinds of girls.

Belonging gives girls the power to exclude all those "others" who don't fit—and, as we've seen, belonging has much to do with race, class, sexual identity, physical ability and appearance. Our culture defines similarity and difference in such social and physical terms. Within these parameters, girlfriends can be quite individual and unique, and so adolescent girls can claim that their decision to hang with these friends rather than those friends is more mature and freely chosen. In fact, their choices have been subtly guided for some time. The psychological sophistication that comes with age just means a more nuanced form of "othering." Pretty consistently white girls choose white girls, black girls choose black, popular choose popular. What's so free about that?

If girls' and women's choices weren't laden with years of accumulated information and subtle pressure, naming and confronting differences and separations between women wouldn't be such hard work. But it is and we can and should do the work of excavating and exposing the cultural roots of girlfighting and, in response, work to develop alternative voices and realities that, in political philosopher Hannah Arendt's words, "move beyond the horizon of everyday life."[10]

We hear from girls of all ages, as we hear from the women above, that there are promises of status and privilege, real tangible benefits to be had for those who sell out other girls or women. But are betrayal and girlfighting the only reality? Or even the primary reality? Is there something at stake for those who uncritically believe in and pass down this "Reality" of girlfighting to girls? Who benefits from assumptions that girls and women are, by nature, back-stabbing, manipulative, and deceitful? While it's absolutely vital to understand that girls and women are capable of deeply felt anger and aggressive acts, both relational and physical, it's equally important to appreciate how girls' and women's anger and aggression have been controlled and manipulated. The problem is not that girls are angry or aggressive—given the social realities of violence, sexual assault and rape, unequal pay, harassment, and so forth, their anger is more than understandable. The problem is that girls' legitimate anger has been co-opted as either erotic, trivial, or pathological, and separated from its real source.

This separation takes a long time and doesn't happen without struggle and resistance. Documenting how girls fight at different ages, what they say and do to each other, what they want and need from each other, does more than provide some kind of voyeuristic pleasure or affirmation of girls' mean nature. It provides vital information not only about how public stories regaling the "nature" of women (or of any other subordinate group) get internalized and enacted through their relationships with other girls (or other members of the subordinate group), but about resistance to this process and how such resistance can be nurtured or squelched.

For each age group there is potential for resistance experienced in the tensions between developmental changes and cultural messages. For the younger girls it's a sense of entitlement and boldness grounded in the concrete reality of their lives. Girls at six and seven may offer up the party line about gender if they think that's what adults want to hear, but they are also quite clear that their lives are more nuanced and complicated. Here in this space is possibility for questioning and critique. Likewise, girls in later childhood wonder aloud about the pressure they feel to disconnect from their thoughts and feelings in order to be accepted. Another opening. Girls at early adolescence experiment with different voices and try on a range of identities. These are all moments of possibility, "sites of radical openness," to use bell hooks's phrase.[11] If adults choose to really engage girls at these developmental junctures, rather than to collude with the usual order of things, we can help to raise girls who are questioning, wide awake to the cultural scripts they confront, prepared to respond as fighters in the very best sense. Even if the risks are high and girls choose less than direct paths to safety, we need to provide them with critical tools, with knowledge, and with "dangerous memories of suffering and freedom from which they can draw."[12]

THE RETURN OF THE OPPRESSED

The problem is that these moments of radical possibility for girls can be felt as moments of danger for women. These developmental junctures tear at the inseam of a fabric that feels familiar and safe. These are the moments when girls are likely to express their pain and anger and when they are most likely to question us about our compromises and the range of issues, behaviors, messages to which we have spent a lifetime accommodating. In their push toward conflict they raise the specter of abandonment or punishment—the things that happen when we have pushed the envelope, caused trouble.

In recent years, when I have talked about girls' friendships and girlfighting at conferences and other public settings, women respond, filled with the ghosts of their girlhoods. They examine old scars from relational triangles and cliques, relive betrayals and losses in the most vivid terms, speak to the girls who hurt them as if they were in the room, e-mail me with long and detailed stories of betrayal. These are successful, sometimes openly political women connecting with the wounds of the past that haunt their present lives and friendships. It is a mystery they are still unraveling; it preoccupies them when their daughters are hurt and also when their own friendships strain under the weight of personal conflicts, family obligations, workplace pressures, or political disagreements. Old fears and confusions atrophy their present interactions and stymie the possibilities available to them.

That such conflicts are experienced and remain in the psychological and relational realm, cut off from their wider social and political underpinnings makes sense, of course. But it ensures that nothing really changes. The relational scar tissue too often prevents us from seeing the big picture, from putting two and two together. Too often we choose familiar patterns, reproduce the status quo that has us scrambling for scarce resources, and blaming each other because we rarely look up from the personal struggle to wonder why we see the same basic scenario repeated all around us. As Inga Muscio explains, the problem is not in us, it's in

> the *standard* of how we perceive community, and the ways we judge women based on very negative thought patterns we've adopted in order to survive in this society's environment of out-and-out destructive tendencies. As it stands, American women have no frame of reference for relying on each other—cultivating trust, love, standards of beauty and sexuality, economic power and sisterhood. . . . Women choose to be catty, cruel, prejudiced, competitive or jealous of each other partly because we grow up learning that negative behavior towards women is perfectly acceptable, and partly because it is a difficult *task* to see ourselves in our perceptions. Seeing ourselves requires effort and commitment. . . . It is less *directly* painful to *ourselves* to respond negatively to women than to honestly figure out what other women represent inside of us that we either dislike, fear, wish we "possessed," or are afraid to love.[13]

Fighting is painful, but dwelling in the personal does more than raise your blood pressure. There's something beyond us to be appreciated if we want to have any real impact on girlfighting. How and why girls fight varies because their relationship to the cultural ideal varies, the avenues to personal and political power vary, our cultural stories and scripts about femininity vary, and thus what other women represent inside of us that we fear and are afraid to love varies. Renee, the mother of Domonique, whose voice has been sprinkled throughout this book, understands something about this. "It's really unfortunate that as girls of color, women of color, we keep shooting each other in the foot and we need to get past that and get over that," she says. "I mean I had these frustrations as a girl, as a teenager and I'm still having them as an adult. And here I'm watching my daughter and I'm like, oh my gosh, it still continues." Renee connects her daughter's personal struggles to a social history when she talks about the historical split between black women who were "brought inside the house" and those who "stayed outside." And although "there was nothing that could be done"—no one to blame but those in power, "it did foster animosity between us" that has been passed down through the years, an animosity based on skin color and special privileges. Renee worries about how the "infighting amongst our own race . . . filters down into the children" so that girls of color fall into the trap of fighting each other instead of the unfair system they grow up in. "Within the black culture, I see little girls are angry at each other," she says.

> This one has more than that one. They're talking about class issues. . . . This one's prettier than I am. This one's hair looks better than mine. This one's smarter than I am. They have it on so many levels. And by the time you get them all together they are so angry that they can't even express themselves. . . . It's worse when they're in the situation with white people and everybody looking on; they just see another black girl fighting. And they don't understand the dynamics of what's behind it.

It's so important that we address this wider social and historical perspective—this struggle, as educator Maxine Greene says, to both care for children and "to connect to the undertaking of education . . . to the making and remaking of a public space . . . of dialogue and possibility."[14] Moving beyond the personal, the relational, allows us to be "conscious of the normative"—to refuse, as Hannah Arendt says, to be taken in by the surface of things, and to appreciate, as Renee says, "the dynamics of what's behind it." We need to do this before we can imagine the possible or "what *might* be in an always open world."[15]

UNVEILING THE "PLAIN WHOPPING LIE" AND CONSIDERING "WHAT MIGHT BE"

Carol Gilligan invokes an essay by Cynthia Ozick in which Ozick refers to the "purposeful excision," the systematic omission of women as contributors to culture and tradition, as "the plain whopping lie." In the absence "of the available minds of half the population," Gilligan explains, patriarchy has been read as "nature" and girls' and women's voices have been "distorted by the sound-system of the world."[16] In this distortion girls have been fed a public reality profoundly out of relation to their experiences, one that has fed them a version of femininity laced with betrayal and distrust, complaint and deceit.

It is very curious that just as girls are feeling more powerful than ever, as their voices, their talents, knowledge, and capabilities are entering the public world like never before, we become consumed with their "meanness" and their inappropriate aggression. They're making us nervous. They could organize. Things could change. Indeed, as Adrienne Rich once professed, "connections between and among women are the most feared, the most problematic and the most potentially transformative force on the planet."[17] If girls and women gain entry and power, if they speak their wide range of truths publicly and clearly, things *will* change. We should be suspicious of attempts to quiet them, tame them, or label them bad because this might just be the reassertion of the status quo, an attempt to manage and control with the same old lie.

Psychologist Mark Tappan writes that the key aspects of internalized oppression—self-deprecation (taking anger and frustration out on oneself) and horizontal violence (taking it out on people like oneself) are not immutable or permanent psychological qualities. They are the result of becoming skilled at, making our own, and unwittingly passing on through our relationships those negative and oppressive stories, images, and voices we've experienced in our daily lives.[18] We can interrupt this process by using the same cultural means. This effort entails working with girls and women to "unveil the world of oppression," rejecting the negative images with which they are presented in our culture, and replacing old myths and images with new, more positive ones.[19] By providing girls with what Tappan refers to as "critical capital"—the cultural tools that enable them to challenge and critique the status quo and move toward true freedom and liberation, we can work against girlfighting, not by blaming, policing, or fixing girls, but by offering different stories about what it means to be female and providing experiences of affirmation and power.

Nancy Fraser explains that these new stories, and the spaces and possibilities they open up "are formed, ironically, out of the very exclusionary practices of the public sphere."[20] But such counterrealities, such possibilities can only occur when women and girls come together, learn from each other, question what we've been told, and come to know that we are not alone. Let me provide one example of the unveiling of oppression and the creation of a counterreality that was truly transformative for the women who experienced it.

When Mary Belenky and Lynn Bond began their project "Listening Partners," they had in mind the simple idea that bringing together poor white women, isolated from one another in the Green Mountains of rural Vermont, would empower them, give them hope and friendship, and affect how they thought about themselves and their children. They got this and a lot more. After meeting with the women for two years in a local women's center, the researchers saw firsthand how this public show of support—emotional, structural, and economic—transformed the women's lives. "Powerful images of agency flooded the final interviews of the Listening Partners participants," the researchers write.[21] The women began to form a community and to take themselves, their minds and voices, seriously. Some went back to school, others worked toward their GEDs, some secured jobs or began volunteering in community organizations and their children's schools; some left abusive partners. Others did the smallest things that made a world of difference—they got driver's licenses; one woman got herself a pair of glasses. They began to believe they had something important to say in their homes, to their husbands, and they began to listen to their children.

In time, these women came to tell different stories about themselves and began to experience and create a different reality than the lie they had been sold. They created what Fraser calls "counterpublics," where they openly opposed stereotypes of themselves as stupid and at the mercy of social service agencies and asserted new identities, interests, and needs.[22]

Unveiling the world of oppression in relation to girlfighting means refuting the prevailing notion that "girls will be (mean, nasty, backstabbing) girls." It means arguing that girlfighting is not the only, or even the most central, aspect of most girls' relationships with girls or women's relationship with women. It's revealing the wide-screen view of girlfighting and understanding that the flip side of such fighting is, in fact, a desire for close female friendships. This is not coincidental. We live in a culture that requires a woman to decontaminate herself from femininity in order to be taken seriously, but which also requires her to act like a woman in order to be protected or chosen by most men. Women need other women who understand the difficulty of this untenable position. They need to confide in friends, work things out, talk about their frustration, confusion, and anger, and find courage to rethink things. They need support to challenge the way things usually go.

But women also need and want to be visible, which means competing for the scarcity of resources available—the attention, the top grades, the boyfriend or husband—and the scarcity of direct and transparent avenues to power. And this means that the relational world is ripe for betrayal. The media play on feelings of suspicion, anxiety, and competition; there is a readily available social language of feminine deceit and betrayal any woman can use for her own benefit. We saw it in the ads girls see in magazines—using gossip and jealousy to sell shoes or hair products. Girls' and women's intimate friendships with other women often arise out of this treacherous climate and serve as protections against such possible betrayals and deceits. To understand this intimacy is to appreciate the forces that undermine and threaten it.

As long as the relational missionary position remains in place, the same old competitions and jealousies for the attention of men will remain in full operation. As long as girls accept and come to believe the messages that boys are better, as long as they take men more seriously, idealize the qualities associated with maleness and want them for themselves, girlfighting will continue. If women's efforts to be taken seriously, to reach the top of their professions, to be the best, are measured by the degree to which they are unlike most other women, women will continue to sell each other out.

In her provocative book, *Woman's Inhumanity to Woman*, Phyllis Chesler documents the visible and invisible ways women undermine and hurt one another. Chesler gives an impressive range of examples— personal, cultural, historical—of women's violence and betrayal toward women. There are degrees of cruelty, to be sure, but at the heart of most of them is the desire to have power or to be taken care of, protected, supported, or loved by those in power positions, typically men. Whether we are talking about girls in the United States who call other girls sluts and hos or Cambodian women who throw acid in the faces of their husbands' lovers, "these are battles among the oppressed, the harsh intersection of mutual tragedies—woman against woman."[23] As Susan Griffin reminds us, "It is always easier for a woman [or girl] to take out her rage over her silence and her powerlessness on another woman than on that culture itself."[24]

Unveiling misogynistic forms of girlfighting and the ways they support the status quo is one thing. Equally important is providing reality checks and counterpublic stories of what girls and women can achieve together and in coalition. As I documented the various forms girlfighting can take, I kept recalling the end of the Cambridge Documentary Film *The Strength to Resist: Beyond Killing Us Softly*. Sociologist

Gail Dines is speaking to a room full of young women and men about advertising and its damaging messages about gender. She points to the picture of a woman in an all-too-familiar magazine ad projected on the wide screen behind her and reads the copy aloud: "Don't hate me because I'm beautiful." She then alerts the audience to the reality this ad effaces:

> I want to say that we don't hate each other. Women in fact love each other. We love her so much that we created a movement that gave her battered women's centers, rape crisis centers, that fought for equal pay, that fought for reproductive rights. We don't hate each other. We, in fact, love each other enough to fight for the rights of each other. . . . Remember, men never gave us the vote. Women got the vote because they organized and fought for it, just like African Americans got civil rights because they fought and they organized. Not because the whites had an attack of conscience. It doesn't work like that. And it is a lie to suggest, in any way, that women are so mean and so simple-minded and so bitchy that all we have to see is a nice head of hair and we hate her. So I want to say we truly love her and we are the ones who've made a difference in this woman's life.

Society works through the subtle and the not-so-subtle barrage of images, ideas, and voices to create a fiction of seamless and objective reality, so that after a time we are no longer aware and no longer name the things that influence us, but take them as commonplace or natural.[25] It's just the way things are, we begin to think. Girls will be girls, boys will be boys. In fact, notions about what it means to be female and male encroach slowly and it's the constant repetition that finally gets us, not any one thing. As adults we barely notice or register what, as children, surprised us; no longer call into question what we once, in our childhood "naiveté," protested vociferously. "No fair" is a child's cry; "life is unfair" is an adult's response.

When we listen to young girls, we soon learn how rootless such seemingly natural assumptions about gender or race or sexual identity are. They remind us with their questions and resistance that the social "Reality" we have unconsciously accepted, what Hannah Arendt called "the rule of nobody,"[26] is actually a litany of voices and images repeated by individuals and groups of somebodies. Perhaps because girls, at least up to the time they reach adolescence, are allowed more freedom to cross gender lines, they remind us daily of our own limitations and preconceived notions about what's possible; they catch us in our contradictions. By their natural desire to be curious and to explore and experience the range of options, girls point out the degree to which we have internalized narrow social stereotypes, and remind us of our own supporting role in a system that promotes such stereotypes in myriad ways.

The nature of evil, Arendt says, is thoughtlessness and inattention. "We resist evil," she explains, "by not being swept away by the surface of things, by stopping ourselves and beginning to think, that is, by reaching another dimension than the horizon of everyday life."[27] An indication of such superficiality is the thoughtless use of cliches, stock phrases, and social stereotypes. The way we talk about gender in this culture—the way we dichotomize it and separate it from its relationship to race, ethnicity, class, sexual identity, ability and disability, from history and social context—is often evil in its superficiality and banality. While we may have no active or intentional desire to hurt or limit people—our children especially—our prevailing assumptions about what makes for a good girl or a real boy, can cause untold pain and suffering.

Unveiling oppression means understanding how the different social and cultural worlds in which girls develop into women affect the choices available to them, guide their behavior, structure their possible fields of action.[28] It's not by chance that girls' denigration, their anger and aggression are directed at other girls. The available avenues to power—being chosen by a boy or being as tough and entitled as any boy—set girls against other girls. Offering counterpublic realities and alternative voices and vision means creating ways for girls and women to feel powerful that don't center male power and don't sell out other girls and women.

This leads me to the opposite of girlfighting—to sisterhood. By sisterhood I mean something both personal and political. Sisterhood means having compassion for, openness to, and generosity toward those girls and women who are different from us, whether in the ways our culture tends to obsess about—such as race, class, or sexual orientation—or because they make different personal or political choices. It means being a witness in the defense of those who are treated badly, being brave enough to speak up, to act up. And it means working toward forming collectives of women or girls not to experience the benefits of personal friendship and support, but to work for wider social and political change. As Bernice Johnson Reagon argues, coalitions are not our homes and we don't have to like each other or be friends to work together against injustice.[29]

It might seem that by invoking sisterhood I'm coming dangerously close to professing a return to women's nature—the very move I've been arguing against in this book—that I'm suggesting that if girls and women could unveil and overthrow the shackles of oppression, we would all agree with each other, come to see that beneath it all we're really all the same, and the world would change for the better. I'm not saying this. I'm acknowledging, in fact, the deep and very real social, cultural, political, and psychological differences between women, while at the same time recognizing that there are structural and systemic forces that work against collective action or coalition building among women, preventing women from allying themselves with one another. These forces are tied to gender and interlocked with race, class, and sexual orientation. One can see them at work whenever women or those from other subordinate groups do come together to dismantle or speak out against oppression.

A few years ago a colleague, Sandy Grande, and I tried to do just that, and the mixed results of our efforts speak to the complexity and difficulty of such work.[30] Sandy is Native American, I am white, and we are both from working-class backgrounds. We brought together nine women students, hoping to explore the barriers they (and we) experienced to developing friendships and alliances across color lines. Five of the students were women of color—three were African American, two were Latina. Two of these women of color were working class, all were heterosexual. Four of the students identified as white—two of these students were Jewish, one was working class, two were lesbian.

Playfully dubbed "Chick Flicks" by Marianne, one of the African American women, our group planned to watch movies and use them as a starting place for honest conversation. To begin, we chose *Girls' Town* and *Mi Vida Loca*—two films about tough, outspoken young women who hang together to confront oppressive circumstances. We sat on couches, chairs, on the floor, eating popcorn and candy, laughing together, whispering, chatting. After each movie, we crowded together around microphones placed carefully in the center of a coffee table, our bodies positioned in a horseshoe, allowing the video camera to frame us as a group. It was a promising start, but after just the two film discussions, it became clear something was not working.

At least it was clear to the women of color. After the second gathering, they asked to meet in racially segregated groups because, they said, the conversation "wasn't going anywhere." They needed some space and time together to think things through. The white women felt just the opposite—they thought that after a rough start they were just reaching a certain "comfort level" and that things were becoming more "informal" and real.

The difference arose, in part, because the white women and the women of color had come to the group with different assumptions, assumptions deeply connected to race. The white women assumed the women of color all knew each other and that they were a group, an alliance. This wasn't, in fact, true. There were differences in race, ethnicity, and class among these five women of color and some of these differences created tensions that would be important to air in the conversations. But the white women saw only color and initially this made them feel left out of something secret and personal. Instead of turning to the other white women, though, they stood alone, feeling separate and unsupported.

The women of color assumed we would have a conversation about gender and race in which "we just were gonna say it." They hoped to move beyond the usual polite conversations about race that happened in this predominantly white private college; they expected to talk about differences and they expected conflict: "I thought when we knew we were gonna be there we weren't going to be scared of conflicts," Shana, who is African American, said. The white women, on the other hand, expected to bond by talking about what they had in common—gender. "I felt like the reason we were having this discussion was to talk about gender," Trish said. "But then it was turned into, like, race . . . but that doesn't have anything to do with being a woman, so I just don't see, I mean all this discussion about race here. . . . Wasn't the focus supposed to be about commonalities among women?"

The white women and the women of color began in radically different places. They defined womanhood and femininity differently; they spoke differently about fear, conflict, vulnerability, learning, anger. Distrust built as things went unsaid. It seemed impossible to stay open. If we couldn't talk here in this relatively safe space, how could we ever drop down to that place where the real fault lines between us began or explore the trace disturbances in the land between "us" and "them"? Over many years we had participated in different cultural realities, defined ourselves by being "not them," and when we came together to talk about what we might share in common, we choked on the sedimentations of cliché.[31]

We did struggle, but the best part of the struggle did not happen together. As the white women's guilt and need for reassurance from the women of color directed the group attention toward their insecurities, the women of color called it quits. We discovered things, had insights, but we had them within our segregated groups and so the overall landscape remained the same. The white women began to see how their privilege, their internalized domination, allowed them not to think about race, to see gender in homogeneous terms, and to center their psychological needs.[32] They began to appreciate how their fear of conflict shut down discussion and made them feel safe. But when Anna, who is white, says, "I think white women deal with their anger privately," and names her fear of women of color's anger, the women of color are not present to hear and respond. When the women of color speak about their "hope" for such conversations—that the white women might really understand the structured nature of their privilege and might listen and say things like "I never thought of it that way," or "Really? Wow, I never knew that"—there are no white women to hear and understand.

Women of color have written extensively about how knowledge and radical possibility can arise from their collective experience in the margins.[33] White women, so close to the center of power, seeking the love and protection and promise of shared power with white men, have more often known individual competition. "White women, whether adolescents or adults, are the most silent/silenced group with which we have worked," Weis and Carbonell-Medina write, "speaking softly about the horrors of their lives only in one-to-one interviews, never in a group context."[34] This has been my experience as well. When I've brought white girls or women together in groups, they have held so tightly to their private lives, believed so strongly in their unique individual experiences that they are shocked to discover other girls and women have similar experiences, questions, doubts, revelations, and fears. As Weis and Carbonell-Medina say, we have to help young women weave a collective strength that moves beyond the individual; we need to provide them with a set of lenses through which they can do social critique and open up the possibility of a gender collectivity that works across traditionally antagonistic (race, class, gender) lines.[35]

But as the voices of the girls in this book attest, it would be simplistic to draw the lines too starkly between white women and women of color. In spite of the difficulties we felt in our "Chick Flick" meetings, there were moments of genuine connection, understanding, and goodwill. We all knew that we were not supposed to have this conversation. We had little past experience, we were not well prepared by our educational systems, we carried historical baggage, and we carried the weight of a culture that has fed us healthy doses of fear and cynicism. Most important, we had been actively taught to distrust each other because we are women. It's not surprising that Sharon Thompson finds in her study of a diverse group of over four hundred girls that "othering" girls is what young women do—whether they are white or of color—and they do so by speaking through the divisions deeply embedded in the culture, moving along a hierarchy of good and bad: "Good girls treat other girls bad; bad girls derogate girls who have a different vice or more stigmatized identity: drugs instead of sex, lesbianism instead of promiscuity; bisexuality instead of lesbianism. Or, other girls are traitors to their gender—two-faces and backstabbers. You have to keep your eye on them all the time."[36]

The voice of girls and women in this book reveal the plain whopping lie, the cover-up, the misogyny that feeds girlfighting. After the unveiling, after the realization that coalition building is difficult, threatening, and also very powerful, what next? How do we support counterpublic realities, provide alternative voices, experiences, and possibilities? How do we support girls who ask more of us?

7

This Book Is an Action

I would like women to treat each other in good ways.
— Phyllis Chesler, *Woman's Inhumanity to Woman*

IN MY HOMETOWN of Waterville, Maine, there's a lot of concern about school-based bullying. Recently a principal invited me to talk about my work on girlfighting at an in-service day for fourth- and fifth-grade teachers. I was eager to share what I'd been hearing from girls and also to understand how this school was grappling with the issues. I arrived at the school along with the teachers at about 7:45 in the morning, and after coffee and muffins we positioned ourselves at the low round reading tables at one end of the library. I spoke about the ways girls talked about fighting, about how their stories expand and refute our usual understandings of who bullies, how, and why, and then I sat back to listen. The school had recently begun a plan to reduce incidents of bullying, based largely on the work of Dan Olweus.[1] Olweus, considered the "founding father of research on bully/victim problems" is a Norwegian psychologist who has done extensive research on the topic in Sweden and Norway. Together we watched a video of a local practitioner-consultant who advocates Olweus's views and methods, and then I listened to the teachers discuss how best to address and, in time, to eradicate bullying in their school.

Olweus declares that "it all boils down to a matter of will and involvement on the part of adults in deciding how much bullying should take place in our schools."[2] Ah, if it were only that simple. His approach depends on adults actually seeing, interpreting, and then consistently responding to what's going on between kids. The reality is that teachers aren't always very good at identifying bullies. "Unfortunately, adults within the school environment dramatically overestimate their effectiveness in identifying and intervening in bullying situations," researcher Susan Swearer concludes.[3] And as we've heard in story after story, girlfighting in particular—whether direct or indirect, physical or relational—usually occurs out of adults' view.

Not surprisingly, then, Olweus's research findings are in direct contradiction to what the girls in this and other studies of girlfighting report and what nearly every parent and teacher concerned about the issue tells me. He finds that bullying behavior decreases with age, bottoming out in middle school for girls as well as boys. Yet all evidence I've seen points to middle school as the apex of girlfighting behavior.[4] If, as Olweus suggests, the success of his bullying prevention program is all about adults' responses to what they see, and if they see virtually nothing in middle school, programs based on his work would have minimal impact on girls' behavior.

Olweus, in fact, doesn't deal much with gender or with development. If he did, he might consider that the younger girls are simply likelier to recognize and report bullying because it tends to be more open and they tend to be more vocal about felt hurt and perceived unfairness. As girls get older they learn to hide their anger and aggression from view and they also take in the broader cultural message that full-fledged bullying is a boy thing; it doesn't include things like rumor spreading, note passing, gossip, or exclusion. The combination of hiding or masking their conflict and aggressive behavior and relabeling it as the culture does—unimportant, just what girls do—means that by sixth and seventh grades girls are unlikely both to reveal their conflicts and to label their behavior as bullying.

I like, however, the fact that Olweus is so clear that bullying is about the imbalance and abuse of power. Yet he doesn't account for the convoluted ways power is experienced, desired, expressed, and channeled in a sexist, racist, homophobic society—he doesn't address the subterfuge of girl-to-girl or other forms of horizontal violence. After an elementary school was praised in our local paper for the success of its Olweus-based antibullying program, a man wrote a letter expressing his outrage. His niece, he said, never benefited from the curriculum.

> She is constantly picked on and ostracized at that school—my heart breaks for her whenever she tells me about the other girls in her class and the cruel way they treat her. Recently, one girl invited all the kids in her class—except my niece—to her birthday party. . . . My niece is a

delightful child. Her only problem is that she cannot afford to dress like the other kids.[5]

What is clear from this story and the others we have seen in this book is that to address negative forms of girlfighting, we need different approaches than what Olweus-based programs are offering. At a time when schools across the country are mandating bullying prevention and intervention programs—primarily in response to the spate of school shootings by boys—it's important not to lose sight of the impact cultural norms and assumptions about gender, race, class, or sexual identity play in children's interactions.

Even if we could detect and respond to the largely invisible dynamics of girls' relationships I doubt this would come close to solving everything. Micromanaging will only make girls more adept at covering their tracks and protecting what power they have. Indeed, the already too close surveillance of girls' bodies, relationships, and sexuality is a big part of why we aren't privy to what's really going on among them. The answer is less about the will of adults or the control over kids than about appreciating girls' need to have control in their lives, to feel important, to be visible, to be taken seriously, to have an effect. Right now girls are put in the untenable situation of receiving social power for acting in ways that objectify them, render them less significant, less visible, and less in control. Again, what we need to do to fight girlfighting is to tackle culturally mediated forms of oppression: to unveil the dynamics at play, provide ways of understanding the limiting and damaging constructions of gender, race, class, and sexual identity, and work to replace them with alternative realities, new cultural stories, critical tools, words, and ideals that interrupt the way things usually go and open up possibilities for girls and women to act together for social change.

PRACTICING SISTERHOOD

Before considering ways to support girls and women, I want to underscore the hard work involved in going against the grain and questioning the status quo: that prevailing assumption that girls will be girls, that they will naturally betray, reject, and undermine one another. As Phyllis Chesler reminds us, "sisterhood must be practiced daily, not merely invoked apocalyptically. Like the practice of friendship, the practice of sisterhood is an ongoing, complex commitment. Such commitment requires the courage of perseverance."[6] Whenever I feel overwhelmed or frustrated at my partial or ineffective attempts to stay on my own side or to raise a daughter who stays on hers, I remember what Buddhist nun Pema Chödrön says: "Every act counts. Every thought and emotion counts too. This is all the path we have."[7]

I have, in my own life, many stories of girlfighting and very few memories of practicing sisterhood. Since my research is explicitly about girls' and women's psychological health and development—especially as it relates to anger and other forms of resistance—the irony is not lost on me. Many personal stories from girlhood are about same gender or social class-related exclusions, triangles, and rejections. I have other stories too, of course. I had wonderful friends and loyal allies, but I did not learn to be a sister and an ally in the way I learned the benefits of selling out other girls. I did not have opportunities to talk about why being an ally is even an important thing to know and practice. This is the point. We have few public stories or images of sisterhood, of loyal friendship between girls and women, of women fighting and organizing for real and lasting social change. Not on TV, not in books or fairy tales, not in teen and women's magazines. Quite the contrary. From earliest childhood, we are fed the jealousy of the wicked queen and the cruelty of the evil stepmother. With very few exceptions, the media images of women's friendship we do have are drenched in the objectification of women and infused with the complexities of romance and heterosexual desire.

I learned early from the world around me that if I was to be taken seriously I needed to gender pass, to distance myself, decontaminate myself from girls and women who were, well, too feminine—too passive, soft, uncertain, deceitful, fearful, accommodating, weak. This was the misogynistic language I was offered to talk about girls and women and I used it to my benefit. I had to prove I was smart and athletic, that I could laugh, play, and hang with the boys. And yet, once in a certain kind of relationship with these same boys, I had to do the relational work, make them feel safe, assure them they were more clever, more athletic, in control, powerful. Until I went to graduate school and took my first course in the Psychology of Women, I would have denied that any of this was imposed on me or that there was anything remotely contradictory about my behavior.

Girls today live no less contradictory lives. The range of acceptable behavior for girls and young women has widened. The category "girl" or "woman" is contested territory in ways it was not for me growing up. There are more visible realities and counterrealities, more awareness and talk about race and class and alternative sexualities, and an understanding of global forces I could never have conceived of as a girl.

What does it mean to practice sisterhood in this current climate? It means creating or nurturing those places where banal social stereotypes can be questioned, where taken-for-granted reality can be challenged, and where together girls can critique the images and ideas they see daily in the media and popular culture.[8] It means encouraging girls and women to widen the definition of what it means to be female by "working against the grain, offering alternative voices to the deafening victim mentality."[9] It means doing the hard work of examining and expanding our own limited realities—our racism, classism, heterosexism, able-bodism, agism; doing our own homework and not relying on others' summaries of the world. This means questioning our active assimilation to "the world according to him," and seeing the value of entering imaginatively into what others take to be real and true—especially those who are different from us.[10]

BUILDING GIRL ALLIES

How does all this translate into practical terms? What can parents, teachers, and counselors do to work against negative and destructive forms of girlfighting?

Girlfighting is often about power and finding ways to feel powerful. Unfortunately, as we have seen, girls gain power by using the tools of sexism on each other in ways that "maintain the broader patriarchal landscape," such as using the language of sexual objectification—calling other girls hos, sluts, and bitches—linked to male privilege, or judging other girls and women against homogenizing images of beauty linked to white privilege.[11] Interrupting girlfighting means advocating for gender diversity—for many ways to be girls of substance—and offering girls opportunities to try on different identities, to experience more visible avenues to power, to challenge sexist, racist, homophobic arrangements, to feel in control and to create environments that feel good to them. This won't get rid of all girlfighting and shouldn't—girls should be encouraged to feel angry and fight in constructive ways about the things that really matter to them. But I believe it will work to reduce the misogynistic forms of girlfighting we have seen the girls in this book talk about.

One warning. This is not your usual bully prevention approach. Girlfighting includes bullying behavior, but as the girls in this book attest it's rooted in a much wider problem of distrust and betrayal among girls and women. Any systematic attempt to reduce bullying must deal with the fact that our cultural stories and media images about gender, and particularly about girls' and women's relationships, cultivate girlfighting behavior. As a result, learning how to unpack and critically examine these assumptions, or as my friend Dot Foote calls it, "culture bust" is vital. The following suggestions are designed to challenge these assumptions and to bring girls and women into different relationship to themselves, to each other, to boys and men, and to challenge dominant power relations. I think we need more than classroom rules, serious talks with bullies, and consistent consequences, although I have nothing against any of these things. But without a shift in consciousness, these efforts have limited effect. We need to unveil the damaging messages girls receive about their "natures" and provide new messages, stories, and opportunities that will galvanize them to take more control over their lives and make changes that interrupt the usual order of things.

DO YOUR OWN WORK

Why are parents made anxious by girls' anger and aggression? Why are they likely to shut it down or see it as a sign of psychological trouble? Why are mothers in particular so bewildered and confused about the girlfighting their daughters report or engage in? Why do teachers cast aside or dismiss girls' whispering, teasing, gossip-filled notes as "little bits of garbage"? In *Cat's Eye* Margaret Atwood implicitly warns women of the dangers of unconsciously passing onto girls what we, ourselves, have suffered at the hands of patriarchy. She alludes to the complicated reasons that adults turn away from girls. Fathers do not fully see, cannot easily decipher the messages encoded in girls' relationships. Theirs is a blindness inherited from power and privilege. Mothers, too, may not see, may not hear, not because they cannot read the signs, but because girls' relationships bring to light the unresolved pain of their own childhoods, the tenuous compromises made for the sake of sanity and survival—the times when they spoke and were not heard, felt betrayed, excluded, all alone. Girls' voices interrupt and disrupt the precarious balance of women's lives and threaten to reveal to women what we once knew but have since forgotten. Girls' struggles and resistance, their anger and sadness, must not be seen or heard, for in them lie the dangerous memories of suffering and freedom.[12]

Mothers, in particular, care deeply about the relational dramas their daughters endure. I think this is because girls' struggles evoke in them deep anxieties and fears, and these emotions—in some cases, long repressed—affect the messages mothers give to their daughters about negotiating friendships and peer relations. Mothers too often pass on the relational equivalent of "math anxiety" to girls in these moments—hearing not their daughters' concerns or questions, but their own deep and unresolved fears. Women, and here I include teachers and counselors, who have not worked through the messy dynamics of their own girlhood relationships and insecurities, risk planting the seed of girls' betrayal of other girls.

Before "helping" girls, then, women first need to work on our own stuff. We can't help girls see, negotiate, or confront girl bullies; we can't offer them constructive ways to respond to their own and other girls' anger and aggression unless we can see and negotiate these things ourselves. This means exploring the roots of our own anger, disappointment, jealousy. It means refusing to make ourselves feel more secure or look better by engaging in slander and gossip about other women. And it means confronting the fears and anxieties that standing up for ourselves, speaking truth to power, or feeling excluded or talked about invokes. This is hard work; it takes time and courage. It's work we must do alone at times, and yet it's work we shouldn't only do alone. Finding or creating a community in which such realities can be addressed honestly and possibilities can be realized and practiced is crucial.

I focus on women here because women are still, by and large, the ones caring for, teaching, researching and writing about, creating curricular materials and developing programs for girls. And yet the very absence of efforts by men to advocate for girls and women absolutely underscores the need for men to do their own work around these issues. Such work would need to focus on critically examining male privilege and the damage of what Gail Pheterson calls "internalized domination."[13] Fathers especially play an enormously important role in girls' lives. How they interact with and treat women and girls, both inside and outside the family, sends clear messages to girls about healthy or unhealthy relationships, equality or inequality, respect or abuse. Such messages translate into how girls expect to be treated by boys in their lives.[14] There are some important research studies and books to which men who wish to work toward antioppressive parenting and teaching practices can turn.[15]

TAKE ADVANTAGE OF THE OPENINGS

At each developmental juncture girls reveal strengths that adults can either fortify or weaken. The younger girls' sense of entitlement, their boldness and clarity are obvious strengths to be nurtured and reinforced. Supporting girls' realities over a Disney version of girlhood is an important start. Engaging young girls' sense of entitlement to their anger and helping them to name the source of injustice is crucial.

Girls in later childhood, at ten and eleven, do something quite amazing: they talk and struggle openly about unfairness, hypocrisy, and the pressure they feel to disconnect from their thoughts and feelings in order to be accepted, to please others, to fit in.[16] This openness provides a real opportunity for adults to join girls in questioning the status quo, to support girls' courage and anger, and to discuss the costs (or benefits) of compromise. Girls at early adolescence make a cognitive shift toward abstract thinking that can make them vulnerable to accepting societal ideals. The pressures to conform can feel overwhelming, but the fragmented, decentered nature of this developmental moment means that for many girls there is a real struggle to try on and reject, push and pull against dominant cultural views of femininity. This struggle provides another opening, another opportunity for adults to engage girls' realities, to choose their messy and complicated lives over idealized images they are confronted with in magazines or on TV.

We can support these struggles, but not without a willingness to take part in conflict—both with girls and with a dominant culture that depends on girls' compliance and conformity for its smooth continuance. These developmental junctures are critical because the questions girls ask invite new ways of seeing, both for them and for the adults in their lives. Their questions are often disruptive of the usual order of things, which is why they can make us anxious. And even worse, the questions are often directed at us—holding us accountable, accusing us of compromising, of not walking our talk. I think adult women especially need to listen to the anxiety these moments raise for us and our desire to shut down or cover girls' pressing concerns and provocative insights.

If girls are bringing their anger and most pressing questions to you, consider it a compliment and a gift. I realize it's hard to be too appreciative when your daughter is yelling at you, but the reality is that you have been let in, you have been chosen to help with the hard work of identity development. She is figuring out who she is in your presence, with you and against you all at once. You can't be there for her if you've never been there for yourself; you can't provide the strength of mind and spirit and the healthy psychological boundaries she needs to stay with herself and her friends in stressful circumstances if you haven't developed these qualities. As Oprah might say, consider this permission to take time for yourself.

DON'T "OVERPSYCHOLOGIZE" GIRLFIGHTING

It's important that parents, teachers, counselors, and therapists appreciate the need for a practice that draws from, but moves beyond the personal and the relational. In this culture femininity is still associated with the private and the psychological. An entire self-help enterprise—books, talk shows, magazines—reflects and encourages this. We are meant to overpsychologize girls' anger and their struggles; to see girls' troubles as simply personal, unique to them, something that can be fixed in therapy or something they must suffer through. But in buying into this narrow interpretation without question, we nurture not girls but the patriarchal order that renders them trivial, subordinate, and invisible. In other words, if anger remains personal and relational, we miss the big picture—the ways in which media messages, institutional practices, and schooling perpetuate certain limited understandings of girls that have real consequences for their present and future lives. Anger, in fact, seems a legitimate response to a society that objectifies girls and women and too often offers them empty roles, roles that in effect say "in the real game of power, you don't matter." The answer in these cases is not to fix girls but to help them locate the legitimate sources of their anger and to provide them ways to understand and confront the pressures and limitations imposed on girls who do not comply with feminine ideals.

A key way to help girls understand such limitations is teaching girls how to read what Lisa Delpit refers to as "the culture of power."[17] That is, to help them understand how the system works and to ask who benefits from certain norms and rules. Adults can help girls develop an eye for what educators refer to as "cultural capital"—those culturally influenced ways of dressing, talking, acting, and socializing that benefit some and render others marginal within schools and society.[18] With a little guidance, adolescent girls can understand how a girl's cultural capital can either buy her a lot or a little in school and question why certain forms of femininity are encouraged and rewarded over others. They can see how girls feel pressed in lots of ways to pass as "nice girls"—always compliant and pleasing—and how for some this is an especially painful process. For example, girls of color are encouraged to act white or "raceless" in school, when doing so disconnects them from the support and strengths of their cultural communities and friends.[19] Teachers often mislabel working-class girls' tendencies to be direct and to say what they want as signs of disrespect and even stupidity, rather than appreciate such differences as survival mechanisms or reflecting different cultural definitions of femininity.[20]

In contrast, it may look good for those girls who easily map onto white middle-class notions of nice girlness because they can look, speak, dress, and act in ways that ensure certain kinds of benefits— adult approval, boyfriends, popularity, even better grades. But growing evidence suggests that conventional femininity is bad for these girls too; that it is associated with loss of voice, lowered self-confidence, depression, body image disturbances, and eating disorders.[21] Again, while these are psychological effects, the roots of these problems are social. We do girls a service when we teach them how to question and critique assumptions about how "good" girls should act, look, and feel. And when we offer girls ways of understanding other girls' pain, anger, and resistance, we provide new possibilities and new reasons to work together for social change.

READ THE SCHOOL CULTURE CRITICALLY

As much as we'd like to believe it, school is not neutral territory. It is, by and large, white middle-class territory, and this means that there are typically one or two forms of girlhood rewarded and responded to within schools. Girls who act white, middle class, and heterosexual, and who participate in activities prized by the institution simply have a better chance of succeeding. This lack of gender diversity and the hidden nature of what Penny Eckert calls "school-endorsed power relations,"[22] contributes to girlfighting as much as or more than anything individual girls bring to school with them. Supporting ideal girls—whether because they are athletes, wear the right clothes, speak the right language, or because they are appropriately indirect in their speech and conformist in their actions—invites the anxiety, anger, envy, and competition of other girls who either covet their privileged place or who cry foul at the unfairness of it all.

Thus schools are more than a backdrop to girlfighting. They can contribute in very real though often subtle ways to girls' growing sense of invisibility and to the fighting and betrayals girls experience in their relationships with other girls.[23] Girls receive messages all the time in school about what a "nice" girl should look and act like, and these messages can subtly reinforce practices that encourage stereotyping, hierarchies, cliques, and divisions among students. Helping girls read the school culture and the messages it conveys about power and privilege can give them some critical distance and explanatory power so that they don't take such messages personally. Who gets the teachers' time and energy and the benefit of the doubt? Who occupies central space in a school? Which groups or activities get the most resources, prime time, and space? Sixteen-year-old Raina could see that in her small private New York City high school, there were "like the people who belonged and the people who didn't." She could also see that the school exacerbated rather than worked against the problem. There were certain school-condoned activities that separated the groups—teachers liked the people who played squash, who were preppies, who fit in and reinforced the school's ideas of success. Offbeat people like Raina were "outsiders . . . outcasts." As a result, Raina and her two close friends "talked about people a lot, like we would just rag on them all day long, like among ourselves." Being "always one of the people who sucked," Raina and her friends protected themselves by criticizing other girls.

These are things to consider and talk about with girls, both in school and out. Providing safe spaces for girls to discuss the climate of their schools is important; more important is encouraging them to develop ways to move beyond discussion and give them room and power to initiate change. This allows girls to address injustices and to experience the hard work of social change. In the process, they learn about the nature of school governance, how to effect policy, how to educate, take risks, and how to work together for a cause bigger than any one person or group.

WORK TOWARD INTERNAL CONSISTENCY
IN YOUR SCHOOL

At the same time as a local high school was planning an antiharassment day that would address issues of both male and female bullying, students were also performing the musical *Guys and Dolls*. In their literal presentation of the musical, male actors sold women prostitutes, sang on stage about women's stupidity, triteness, uselessness, and objectification, while the women performers, prostitutes and missionaries— bad girls and good—sang their woes about needing men, giving up what's most important to them for men, their own hysteria, stupidity, and triteness. A trip to pre-revolutionary Havana in one act added a sprinkle of racism to the performance.

There are a lot of things schools can do to foster respect between students with the goal of mitigating harassment and bullying. One thing that seems important to any effort is internal consistency—encouraging such respect throughout the school, in both formal and informal spaces. It's a problem when high school girls are expected to act and dress respectfully (no low-cut tops or bared navels, please) in class but can play fully decked out prostitutes onstage or when boys are punished for sexual remarks in the halls but can "pimp" women in a school play. And it's strangely out of relationship when there's concern about increased girlfighting in school and yet girls enact a physical girlfight onstage to the hoots and hollers of their classmates. It was fun, some of the students in the audience remarked, to see what great "skanks" their female friends made.

I'm not advocating censorship, but why not use the play as a teachable moment or event—a way for students to talk about the historical period or the ways the play does or does not accurately reflect gender roles, or even a way to discuss the role of parody, absurdity, spectacle, or just plain camp in drama? In the absence of any response from the school, the play was condoned as a space where selling "hot, hot, hot" girls for "cheap" was okay, if just for a few nights.

WORK TOWARD INTERNAL CONSISTENCY AT HOME

In homes where there are two parents, children learn an enormous amount about how to compromise, address conflicting needs, and negotiate power relations. Girls are incredibly observant about how adult women voice their thoughts and feelings and how they express their anger and disappointment. They also observe who has the final say, who makes and enforces rules, and who sets the overall emotional climate of the home. To the degree that adult men are present and assume privilege, power, and control in either overt or covert ways, girls also learn patriarchy at home. Thus, parents who want girls to grow up to be compassionate and to expect fair treatment need to provide home lives in which people are loving and treated with respect and justice. Parents who want girls to voice their opinions need to provide models of listening and responsiveness, especially in the face of disagreement. Parents who want girls to take a stand against bad treatment need to provide examples of adults who say what they feel and want directly to one another, risk disagreement, and work toward workable compromises.

Alternative forms of aggression, such as relational aggression, are methods more likely to be used by those who don't have the power to be direct. If power is not shared and women need to be indirect, to manipulate, or to make passive-aggressive comments to express their anger, their needs, or their wants, girls learn who in the family has power and privilege. These are lessons and relational patterns girls take outside the family, to school, and to relationships.

LEAD BY EXAMPLE, EXERCISE YOUR OWN POWER, CHOICE, AND SUBJECTIVITY

If adults want girls to hold onto their strong feelings and to name and speak out against the injustices they endure in school and in society, we have to be willing to do so ourselves. *Guys and Dolls* created a small stir among a few parents who met with or wrote to the principal to express their concern. Renee is willing "to be the villain" so her daughter can get the education and the respect she "is rightly entitled to." We need to be willing to be seen as the villain, the troublemaker, the "here she comes again" woman.

But again this means also being an advocate for ourselves, a witness in our own defense. When my colleague Sharon Barker asked a group of high school girls what they would tell women who wanted to help them, they said, "Lead your own lives; stop trying to live through ours. Stop acting like it's too late for you." By virtue of being on our own sides, adults who lead lives in full, rich ways within the constraints of our different social contexts give more to girls than we could ever imagine.

DON'T BUY INTO CULTURAL STORIES OF GOOD GIRLS AND BAD; MEAN GIRLS AND NICE

When we question the either-or categories of nice and mean, good and bad, virgin and slut, we make room for the in-between. We allow girls who are tough and outspoken and direct to be something other than "mean" or "bad." We open the door for conversations about difference and the ways these terms are used to support limiting notions of femininity and beauty. We make a space for girls who don't map onto or who actively question white middle-class ideals to have status and visibility and power on their own terms.

Don't label or put down "girly girls" or buy into or uncritically repeat adolescents' labels for "other" girls; don't put down girls who want to be like boys or want male power; don't adopt or offer up mean girl–nice girl or good girl–bad girl language to teach, reward, punish, or to justify suffering and pain. As we've seen, these terms are laden with judgment and they serve to divide and control girls. We can help to take the power out of derogatory words like "bitch," "slut," and "ho" by not letting them contain us, by not using them, and by actively refuting them when others do. We can refuse to accept the usual double standard—boys who are sexual are normal; girls who are sexual are sluts—and help girls understand how a word like "slut" can be used to punish and control them.

It's almost impossible not to lapse into these divisive constructions of girlhood. But we can own the "bad" or "mean" parts of ourselves and give girls permission to feel and talk about the range of emotions. We can affirm how we all have the capacity for anger, joy, frustration, and love, how we all want to feel important and how sometimes we'll do things we're not proud of for love and attention. We can also talk about the importance of civility, respect, and compassion rather than or as much as we talk about "niceness." It's never as simple as an us-them thing; it's all of us.

Girls learn the power of these divisive terms very early. I'm hearing about mean girls a lot these days at home; it's a code word for anything another girl says to my daughter that she doesn't like. "Rhonda was mean today," she complains. When I question her, she tells me things like "Rhonda touches my hair," or "Rhonda's too loud," or "Rhonda always wants the same color pencil as me." Rhonda, I think, wants to be included and is having a hard time expressing her desire. My daughter is using the word "mean" because it's a word that has power in the culture; using it justifies her wish to distance herself from Rhonda because there are things about Rhonda she doesn't like. The deeper problem I face as a parent is how to encourage my daughter to articulate her feelings without casting Rhonda into bad girl territory. She doesn't have to like Rhonda or play with her, but she also doesn't have to justify her dislike through name-calling or judging in ways that will make others side with her and exclude Rhonda before they even know her. At the bottom of it all, I think, is not Rhonda's meanness, but my daughter's need to impress me with her niceness even when (or especially when) she's having not nice thoughts and feelings. If she didn't think I wanted nice and kind, she might be able to simply say to me that she doesn't want to play with Rhonda. This leads me to the next point.

ENCOURAGE DISCRIMINATING TASTES IN FRIENDSHIPS

We need to rid ourselves of the fiction that girls should like and be friends with everyone. Girls learn early that "good girls" monitor the relational weather and feel responsible for other people's feelings. It's important to like everybody; as a result the word "friend" gets watered down. Girls adapt by distinguishing best friend from close friend, good friend from okay friend, and so on. It's important to encourage girls to choose people as friends who are affirming. It's okay not to be friends with someone as long as you treat that person respectfully. Most important, mistreatment is *not* a quality of friendship or love. Encourage compassion, but don't emphasize the hurt feelings of others over her own hurt feelings. Encourage girls to be friends with those who listen to them and treat them well. Encourage girls to speak directly about what they need and want from their friends and to know their boundaries and what they are unwilling to give up for the sake of a particular relationship.

ADDRESS GIRLFIGHTING WHEN YOU SEE IT

It's important not to dismiss girlfighting as unimportant or trivial—something we're more likely to do with relational forms of aggression. As researchers and girls tell us, relational aggression has very real consequences and often precedes physical aggression for girls. "By addressing the relational aspect of aggression early and often, practitioners working with youth are in essence conducting overt violence prevention," Scott Okamoto and Meda Chesney-Lind argue.[24] We have all seen, tragically, how teachers and administrators can contribute to school violence by looking the other way when boys bully and tease one another. Girls' forms of violence and aggression are even more likely to go unnoticed and unnamed. Elizabeth Bush, the one female school shooter, gave none of the signs we now identify as precursors to such violence, no indication that she would bring a .22-caliber pistol to school. She didn't boast or brag about "pulling a Columbine," she didn't play violent video games, listen to Marilyn Manson, or make bombs in her garage. She wasn't rejected by a love interest. She wanted to be a nun or a human rights activist. She protected those who were teased and vulnerable. But she regularly endured, unseen and undocumented, the taunts and ridicule of the popular girls she so admired. She was tormented for her appearance, betrayed, exposed, and rejected by girls she confided in. Before transferring to another school, she was even pelted with stones by other girls. At first her sadness turned inward; she became depressed, resorted to self-mutilation. Her invisible misery went unnoticed by her parents and led even her closest friend to believe "she seemed really happy" when they spoke the night before the shooting.[25]

There is little training for teachers and school administrators to spot and understand these near invisible cycles of popularity and isolation among girls.[26] Encourage your school to provide teacher education on alternative forms of aggression and to understand how and why girls and boys are encouraged to express their anger and aggression differently. Moreover, teacher training should not stop at understanding how relational aggression plays out among students; there should be efforts to train staff to respond to relational aggression in productive ways. Freitas and Chesney-Lind write about how hard it is for practitioners to watch girls be "mean" to other girls and boys, as well as how difficult it is for practitioners when they are targets of relational aggression themselves.[27] If a school intends to adopt an antiharassment or bully intervention program, it's essential that the program not only address power imbalances as they play out in peer groups, but encourage critical thinking about the ways in which some such imbalances are normalized and subtly encouraged by schools and other institutions.

SUPPORT "MEAN" GIRLS;
SUPPORT MOTHERS OF "MEAN" GIRLS

I say this for a number of reasons. First of all, if we dismiss or label "mean" or "bad" girls who are too outspoken, angry, direct, tough, determined, or difficult to control, we may miss the leadership potential of such girls. These are the very qualities that can galvanize and enable girls to really make a difference in their schools and communities. Rather than punish or reject girls for their boldness or toughness, we might consider ways to engage them and channel that energy.

Second, we don't know nearly enough about what's going on for "mean" girls or, indeed, for girls who are victims of mean girls. I've had enough conversations with adult women about girlfighting to know that inconsistent and untrustworthy family dynamics, neglect, abuse, and oppressive conditions of many sorts can play out in complicated ways with friends and peers. After an article about my work came out in a local newspaper, a woman e-mailed to tell me about how fear of her tyrannical and brutal father had divided her and her sisters. Her mother could not protect them and so the four girls played out their rage and fear on each other. The survival strategies she learned at home carried into relationships not only with the boys she became involved with, but also with girlfriends. We all need compassion for those struggling to make sense of oppressive conditions. Setting up programs and structures that girls can count on for consistent support and affirmation can help not only girls, but may encourage different conversations and relationships between the girls and their mothers.

Girls can also be "mean" and "tough" because they experience the daily indignities of sexism, classism, and racism. Developing a tough girl exterior is a way for some girls to survive hostile environments or it may be a way for girls to be visible and accounted for. On the other hand, what may look like "toughness" or "meanness" to you or to some girls may be just the way things go for other girls—it may be part of how girls play and tease, how they create space for themselves and their friends or how they initiate other girls into their group. Again, making room for gender diversity and appreciating the power of social and cultural context to determine what's possible or impossible for girls is fundamental to supporting girls.

ENGAGE GIRLS' ANGER AND HONE A SENSE OF FAIRNESS AND JUSTICE

There is a fraught relationship between anger and ideal femininity. Angry girls and women are cast as bitches and rejected by both girls and boys. The pressure on girls to split off their anger is enormous and the rewards are clear. But anger is ultimately about self-respect, a sign that a girl takes herself seriously. That's why philosophers and psychologists alike refer to anger as the "political emotion."[28] Anger used constructively can be a real source of power. We need to work with girls to develop possibilities for social action and constructive channels for their anger and justified rage. Letter writing campaigns, community action projects, organized protests, and opportunities to publicly voice their realities all encourage girls to participate in and to create realities that place them at the center while they do the work of connecting their anger to something bigger than themselves.

Much girlfighting is about displaced anger. Adults can help girls to know and own the real sources of their strong feelings and to make considered choices about how to express them and to whom. Catch a girl in an angry moment and talk with her about ways to express her feelings and be heard. If you can catch her expressing her anger in a clear and constructive way, support her by saying something like, "I admire the way you did that."

Appreciate the power and consistency of the messages to girls that they should not express anger or start conflicts. Appreciate the ways the culture reveals girls' and women's anger as dangerous or trivial ("you're beautiful when you're angry"). It's not enough for teachers to send girls to a room to "work it out," or to expect girls to apologize and make up. Those who have social power will just have license and opportunity in private to prove it. And chances are the girls will perform nice and kind friendships when you're around, while the hurt and fear and anger moves into the active underground. Girls need guidance about how to stay clear and centered in their disagreements and they need support for not giving up their convictions to maintain a false relational harmony. Again, this demands that adult women confront and work through our own fears and anxieties, our own desires to be loved and included at all costs, our desire to raise "nice" daughters or to have schools and classrooms free of messy conflict.

FOSTER SOLIDARITY BETWEEN GIRLS, BETWEEN WOMEN, BETWEEN WOMEN AND GIRLS

As we've seen, deceit, manipulation, and distrust are part and parcel of our cultural definition of femininity. As a result, it's very hard for girls to trust other girls, especially when the stakes are high. Avoid a "girls will be girls" message when what you really mean to say is that all girls are petty, mean, or back-stabbing, or that all girls engage in exclusive cliques and clubs. Instead, affirm girls' relational strengths and the potential for collective action and help girls identify things that they can change to make their environments better places. Model healthy, committed relationships with women. This does not mean covering over the fears and jealousies that can arise in girls' groups or between women; it does mean examining the real sources of such feelings. "A real solidarity can be built through shared anger," Sharon Lamb says. Encourage and help girls "to identify common enemies . . . whether they are 'the media' or 'advertising' or 'the system of inequality' or 'poverty.' If girls fight against these forces together, they can build solidarity while integrating feelings of anger with caring."[29]

Provide real alternatives to fairy-tale images of girls and women, of women being chosen by a man, of girls who are victims and need saving, of girls or women who reject other girls to gain male power, or make themselves over to be accepted or cool. Seek out books and magazines like *Hues* and *Teen Voices* that present a diversity of cultures and body types and interests. Give girls a range of options and some breathing room, and focus on their individual and collective strengths. *New Moon Magazine* is great for younger girls. It's advertisement-free and I especially like their attempt to redefine true beauty as "good works, great hearts, and activism." Read aloud newspaper or magazine articles about girls' and women's accomplishments and bold or courageous actions, like the story of two teenage girls in California who courageously worked together to fight their abductor. Be on the lookout for local girls and women who stand for something, go against the grain, or risk speaking out against injustices. Seek out girl friendly interactive websites like Zoey's Room that provide positive cyberspaces for girls to connect and be creative.[30]

DEVELOP HARDINESS ZONES FOR GIRLS

The nonprofit I helped to create, Hardy Girls Healthy Women, is based on the importance of developing "hardiness" in girls. Hardiness is a concept taken from health psychology to describe people who continue to thrive in stressful circumstances. The stress and distress that so many girls experience can be understood as a loss of control in many areas of their lives, a struggle to create identities and belief systems to which they can wholeheartedly commit, and a sense of isolation in dealing with the challenges that face them. Hardiness begins to define areas of knowledge, skills, and support that an individual can develop to resist and transform stresses.[31] Offering girls opportunities to develop ideas, to take action on issues that really matter to them, to experience the challenge of changing their schools and communities for the better, develop hardiness.[32] This perspective takes the attention off girls and moves it to the social contexts that either help or hinder their healthy development. Through this perspective, the relational and educational contexts, both in schools and other community organizations in which girls find themselves can be assessed in terms of their capacity to facilitate hardiness or to be "hardiness zones."

CREATE SAFE SPACES FOR GIRLS AND FOR WOMEN

One of the best things we can do for girls is to help them stay with the complexity of their realities in the face of simplistic views of what a girl should look like, act like, be like. Many girls use diaries and private writings to hold onto their strong feelings because there are few public spaces for them to go to. We need to provide opportunities for girls to come together to create a counterpublic language and alternative realities. In such safe spaces we can help girls practice their critique of a media rife with damaging stereotypes and negative voices. Such spaces are places "for breathing, relaxing . . . without the constant arrows of stereotypes and social hatred."[33] In these spaces girls can talk, plan, and organize for social change, write poetry, critique the media, and practice sisterhood.

QUESTION THE HETEROSEXUAL
OR TRADITIONAL ROMANCE STORY

There's nothing wrong with romance, although one might wonder why it's sugarcoated in the heterosexual script and spoon-fed to little children before they have a chance to know what it is, why it matters, and who they might want to love. The dominant story of heterosexual romance commonly places girls in subordinate relationship with boys. When you see such stories, question them. Disney's *Beauty and the Beast* is a great movie to discuss with girls and boys because of the tenacity of the romance story in which Belle is the object of male desire, the subject of male violence, and responsible for creating relational harmony out of chaos. You might also want to discuss the contrast between brainy, innocent Belle and the busty dancing barmaids or question why men are cast as uncontrollable animals that lust for power and control over women. There are countless examples in the media of male violence, girls set against girls for the attention of boys, and girls encouraged to change boys or to hold boys' emotional lives. Talk with girls about them when you see them.

Question connections between male desire and violence; refute the line that boys chase, hurt, or kick girls because they like them. Question prevailing assumptions that boys only want sex and girls only want relationships, or that boys are ruled by their hormones and so it's up to girls to control them. Talk with girls about what *they* want. Acknowledge girls' desire and talk with them about sexuality and the choices available to them. Encourage friendships with boys who respect and like girls, and check your anxieties when you see or hear about passionate friendships with other girls.

DEVELOP MEDIA LITERACY

It's curious how we immediately think about the direct impact of the media when we talk about boys' aggression. We think about all the bad messages boys get—the alienation reflected in the likes of Marilyn Manson, the vitriol spewed by Eminem, the gratuitous violence that laces video games, the sexism and violence of the World Wrestling Federation. We have an assumption about how culture operates on or mediates boys' actions in ways that don't quite apply to girls, in part because for boys the connection appears to be so open and direct—violence begets violence.

But of course the same processes apply to girls, though the messages are quite different. It's harder to appreciate the convoluted ways in which white middle-class femininity and homogenizing beauty ideals connect to girls' violence and girlfighting. In part this is because girls are positioned differently in the culture with respect to power—direct channels are blocked, so alternative, more hidden forms of aggression develop. The cultural stories girls are likely to hear about their part in the heterosexual script inscribe competition with other girls for male attention as a primary avenue to power. Girls may feel powerful competing and winning in such relationships, but it is empty power that moves girls from the subject of their own experiences to the object of others' pleasure or admiration or envy.

Developing media literacy—providing girls with the language and tools to be critical of the things they watch and read and hear—can't happen early enough. When my daughter was three and four we were looking through magazines and watching TV with a critical eye for gender and racial stereotypes. At seven she knows that TV wants her to believe that certain colors, activities, toys, or clothes are only for girls or only for boys. I want her to know that her life is richer and more varied and more interesting than the two-dimensional stereotypes with which she's confronted. What I find most difficult is teaching her not to dismiss or judge other girls who do like things she associates with stereotypes—like the color pink or frilly dresses. It's okay to like pink and to enjoy wearing dresses, I remind her; what's not okay is to like these things only because TV or books tell you to. Granted, it's a hard distinction for younger girls, but I try to remember that I'm just planting the seeds.

We need to provide little girls with the tools for critique and trust that they can be agents of change. Recall that when seven-year-old Jeanine began to refuse to be a girl in pretend play because she thought boys got to do all the exciting things, her girlfriends argued with her that girls could do anything too. Their mothers had prepared them for this. They knew about stereotypes. Jeanine's mother also knew this and said so, but it was Jeanine's peers who had the real effect.

Publicly question and scrutinize the relentless repetition of idealized femininity and its relationship to narrow views of beauty and openly contest the commodification of girls' bodies. "The fashion-beauty complex" provides a constant barrage of images of *"what I am not"* to remind girls and women of their failure to match up to beauty ideals and their need to transform and improve themselves with products. This produces in girls and women an estrangement from their bodies.[34] It also feeds competition with and aggression toward other girls and women.

Parents can also e-mail or write to advertisers, complain about images or story lines, and join groups like Media Watch. I like the organization Dads and Daughters for many reasons, but especially because it targets advertisers who denigrate or show unrealistic images of girls. It was their e-mail and letter campaign to "Sun-in" that caused the company to pull the girlfighting message: "Four out of 5 girls you hate ask for it by name. Stop hating them. Start being them."[35]

PROVIDE OPPORTUNITIES FOR HER TO USE HER BODY THROUGH SPORTS AND "FREE FIGHTING"

Those who play sports know that there is something liberating in feeling your body extend to the very limit. But I also think Simone de Beauvoir was onto something when she distinguished mere rule-bound sports with a good free fight. Self-defense classes, boxing, and martial arts can offer girls a chance to exhaust their deepest rage and know their full strength and capabilities. They instill girls with confidence about their place in the world and a full awareness of what their bodies can do. They also encourage girls and women to take up space. Iris Marion Young argues that the messages girls typically receive about femininity "suppress the body potential of women" and provide "a sense that the body is positioned within invisible spatial barriers." (Watch the ways boys and girls sit in a typical classroom and you'll get the picture—boys all spread out; girls folded in on themselves.)

It's important to encourage girls to redefine femininity to include strength and courage and to reimagine "our bodies as strong, active subjects moving out to meet the world's risks and confront the resistances of matter and motion."[36] This awareness of and comfort with their bodies centers girls, connects mind and body. Fully inhabiting our bodies as subjects rather than objects radically alters our relationship to the public world.

TALK BACK

We need to talk back to the culture and name the reality of our lives. As I write this I recall that the last two times I've taken my daughter to the movies, it's been to movies with male lead characters: *Harry Potter* and *Jimmy Neutron: Boy Genius*. Both times we sat through six or more previews of upcoming movies, all with boy leads. I named this for my daughter. She argued with me because all the movies also had girls, although in secondary roles. This opened up a larger conversation about why this is so and what it says about who is watching and who's willing or not willing to watch what. These conversations I have with a seven-year-old are almost always uneven and incomplete and I never feel very certain about them, but they provide a space for both of us. When Renee watches TV with her daughter, she talks back to the screen. "We were watching something and this lady fell in a pond . . . and started yelling for her friend and I said, 'Stop yelling! Save yourself!'"

Talking back, bell hooks argues, expresses a person's movement from object to subject.[37] When we encourage girls to ask questions, to read the culture critically, to say what they think and feel, to pay attention to their own realities, we encourage self-respect and we provide space for truth to emerge and for collective change to happen. Girls need other girls to affirm their reality and so they need to speak out. If all girls dismissed the idea of a "slut," Deborah Tolman says, the word would have no meaning and thus no power to control. "I'm waiting for the day when all the girls will start standing up for themselves so I won't look like such a bitch," Sarah exclaims. If just one group of girls stands up for itself, Sarah will look and sound and feel different.

In her book *The Skin We're In*, the psychologist Janie Victoria Ward offers a four-step model for parents who want to help their children identify, address, and resist the vast range of racist, sexist, or classist issues they face today. This model allows parents to think of conflict as an opportunity to talk with their children and help them understand that even when they feel victimized, "they still have power to psychologically resist, to refuse to buy into the reality being thrust upon them, or to do things differently."

- *Read it*—help your daughter break down racist/sexist/classist experiences by exploring the situation with her. Ask questions about what happened, about her feelings and reality, and about the different perspectives involved, that help her make connections and see larger patterns.
- *Name it*—acknowledge the presence of racism/sexism/class bias "and bring its reality into full consciousness, however painful this might be." Naming is a powerful experience and essential, because only through naming can someone actively confront injustice.
- *Oppose it*—help your daughter consider constructive forms of resistance. "Responsible resistance should be tied to a healthy and

positive sense of oneself and one's moral values and to a sense of where one wants to be in the future."

- *Replace it*—help her put something new and affirming in the place of the feeling, attitude, or behavior that is being opposed. It helps a girl resisting the prevailing ideas about what girls should want/be/care about "to take a stand for fairness and justice, reinforce personal integrity, and instill the confidence and power that result from taking effective, positive action."

Reading, Ward says, is the hardest of the four steps to learn and practice. *Naming,* however, takes the most courage and fortitude.[38]

PRACTICE VOICE, ENCOURAGE ACTIVISM

Provide girls with a lot of different venues and opportunities to voice their thoughts and feelings and practice their debating skills. Drama, debate clubs, discussion groups, book clubs, mentoring programs, can all be places where girls speak and take themselves seriously. There are some wonderful nonprofits that do programming for girls, the goal of which is to offer alternatives to media images and encourage girls to be strong, independent, and confident and to work toward building solidarity with other girls and women. Nationally, organizations like Girls Inc. can be invaluable resources.

To whatever extent possible, encourage girls to move out of their comfort zones, to widen their perspectives by establishing connections with those from different communities and circumstances. Civil rights teams in schools can be great places to expand consciousness, cross race and class boundaries, and work toward justice. In many schools one can also find wise and generous adults who volunteer their time to run groups or do special projects. Dot Foote has such a group here in Maine called the Diversity Coalition, in which she works with high school girls and boys to address not only the personal but also the structural imbalances of power in their school and community. Members express their strong feelings and views through a combination of drama, music, slam poetry, and social action projects. One of the most effective projects the Diversity Coalition has undertaken is their Tales of Harassment in which members talk to middle school students about their experiences of being both persecuted and persecutor, opening the door for girls and boys to address these issues in their own lives.

ACT LOCALLY WITH THE WORLD IN MIND

Encourage girls to take a worldly perspective. Girls who appreciate that the world is bigger than the social dynamics of their school are less likely to be devastated by the vicissitudes of peer rejection. Rather than spend her time playing girl-targeted video games in which she shops, decorates a house, or designs clothes, encourage her to investigate who makes the clothes she wears and what their lives are like. Rather than read magazine articles that encourage dieting or looking perfect, encourage her to consider who "goes without" in her community. Initiate a community garden and organize volunteers to take the harvest to a local food bank or city soup kitchen. Help her explore what life is like for girls and women around the world. Help her to cultivate a healthy criticism of consumerism. Work with her to develop a community-based environmental project or connect her with human rights organizations to find out how she can make the world a better, more caring, and just place.

ALLOW GIRLS SPACE TO PRACTICE AND GROW

Educators Pam Bettis and Natalie Adams encourage teachers and parents to take seriously the "in-between" places that girls create and occupy—both what is said there and what happens there. Peer groups and internet chat rooms, school buses and bathrooms and hallways all matter a lot to adolescent girls. It's important not to micromanage or to disperse what goes on in these places because much of what happens there is in the service of creating identities and negotiating power—something girls need to develop and practice. This doesn't mean abdicating responsibility—we should know how important these places are *and* also be aware that these places can be especially rough on girls who are marginal in some way—because of race, class, weight, disability, and so forth. But our work with girls can only take place effectively if we give them space and opportunity to practice and make mistakes.

TAKE GIRLS, OTHER WOMEN, AND YOURSELF SERIOUSLY

Carol Gilligan writes about how young girls' physical games, as well as their conversations with each other and with adults, reveal a healthy irreverence and resistance to the fundamental unfairness of patriarchy. If taken seriously and supported, this "healthy resistance" has the potential to grow and turn into something political. "Girls' questions about who wants to be with whom are to them among the most important questions and they take sharp notice throughout the day of the answers given to these questions, as revealed through nuance and gesture, voice and glances, seating arrangements, choices of partners, the responses of adult women and men, the attitudes of authorities in the world."[39] Our responses become their touchstones on a journey that can either affirm their experience and knowledge, or lead them to justify a culture that devalues this experience as marginal and unimportant.

We need to see the bigger picture and to understand why, within the usual order of things, girlfighting seems so petty, funny, or erotic. It's supposed to look that way; it's supposed to relegate girls to the margins and to trivialize what's important to them. In fact, girlfighting is a powerful force that mirrors and contributes to wider social divisiveness. It's not by chance that, in the face of the betrayal and relational treachery it fosters, many girls turn toward boys as friends. With boys, girls claim, what you see is what you get; boys say what they want and do what they say. Their fights are open and brief and life goes on—no congested feelings, no emotions distorted from weeks of repression. In fact, girls are giving up a lot in this move and there is no legitimate space to mourn this loss. "The avoidance of grief signifies an avoidance of love," Gilligan argues. "We cannot grieve what we cannot love. To love women, however, means to harbor the suspicion that women's minds would change the traditions, reopening the most basic human questions, including how we experience ourselves, how we know what we know, how we love and what we value."[40]

TELL THE TRUTH

"Truth and peace do not often coexist. Telling the truth offends, startles, endangers, and upsets the status quo."[41] Girls need to hear the truth and they need to be encouraged to tell the truth. They need to hear about both successful and failed attempts at sisterhood and they need to be taught how to practice sisterhood in their own lives so they can imagine a reality that splits the taken-for-granted world open. What happens when women and girls get together to become allied against a common foe? Can they cross racial and class lines? Can they ferret out heterosexism and homophobia? Can they make real changes? The truth is both that it's very hard *and* that it's worth the struggle. The truth is that there are consequences—real dangers—to taking yourself seriously and challenging the status quo. Telling girls the truth means helping them understand their choices and preparing them for the consequences of their actions: people are likely to get annoyed or angry with them, misunderstand them, want to change them, even try to hurt them. They may get in trouble, boys may not like them, other girls may exclude or betray them. The changes they work hard for may not hold. The attention they receive may trigger jealousy and splinter their group, dividing them; they may fall back into the same dichotomies they wanted to avoid—the good girls who are the real radicals, the bad girls who acquiesce too much. Telling the truth means preparing girls for all this and reminding them that conflict and disagreement are healthy and that they don't always have to like and agree with the people they are in coalition with.

In the final analysis, as psychologist Karen Horney understood over half a century ago, we need to be "sensitive to the difference between the creation of a problem and its solution."[42] "If a tree, because of storms, too little sun, or too poor soil, becomes warped and crooked, you would not call this its essential nature."[43] And you would not blame it, ridicule it, denigrate it, or distance yourself from it lest you too become warped, especially if you yourself had narrowly escaped the storms or were lucky enough to be planted in the sunlight. Girls and women enter a culture in which there are certain kinds of pushes and pulls, limits and options, in which there is too little sun or too poor soil and they make do with what they have. Blaming other girls and women, repeating old dichotomies of nice and mean, good and bad just stirs up the dust. Instead we need an awareness that begins with a generosity of spirit and an appreciation of relationships, but which extends beyond the personal to the social and political.

Why shouldn't girls be angry and aggressive? And why shouldn't they take it out on other girls? As Natalie Adams tells us, girls are fighting to be somebody.[44] They want to feel powerful, to be visible, and to be respected. Why wouldn't they go after those "girly girls" they come to see as weak, vapid, and stupid? They make good targets, after all. Our cultural stories about girls and women have ensured that. We need to open up new options, widen the field of action, and offer girls legitimate avenues to power so they don't go down those nasty underhanded or openly hostile roads and so they don't take their legitimate rage out on other girls. Let's stop blocking their paths with the usual slew of sexist, racist, and homophobic messages so they are forced to practice what Janie Ward calls resistance for survival tactics. Instead, let's create together, in sisterhood and across generations, a resistance for liberation.[45] We shouldn't be selling girls out to old stereotypes; we should be joining them in creating a counterpublic discourse about girls, about power, and about possibility.

Appendix

Emma Willard School Study (1981–1984)

Age: 14–18 years old
Sample Size: 97 interviewed the first year, several reinterviewed in
 subsequent years
Race: 90 white, 7 African American
Class: middle/upper-middle class
Information Source: C. Gilligan, N. Lyons, and T. Hanmer (eds.)
 (1990). *Making connections.* Cambridge, MA: Harvard Univer-
 sity Press.

Boys and Girls Club Study (1985)

Age: 11–15 years old
Sample Size: 44 girls
Race: 50 percent white, 50 percent African American
Class: poor and working class from three urban neighborhoods in
 the Northeast
Information Source: B. Bardige, J. Ward, C. Gilligan, J. Taylor, and
 G. Cohen. (1988). Moral concerns and considerations of urban
 youth. In C. Gilligan, J. Ward, and J. Taylor (eds.), *Mapping the
 moral domain.* Cambridge, MA: Harvard University Press.

Urban Neighborhoods Study (1986)

Age: 12–14 years old
Sample Size: 34 girls
Race: white, African American, and Latina
Class: working class
Information Source: J. Ward (1988). Urban adolescents' conceptions of violence. In C. Gilligan, J. Ward, and J. Taylor (eds.), *Mapping the moral domain*. Cambridge, MA: Harvard University Press.

Laurel School Study (1986–1990)

Age: 7–18 years old
Sample Size: 100 girls
Race: 86 white, 14 girls of color
Class: 80 percent middle/upper class, 20 percent working class
Information Source: L. M. Brown and C. Gilligan (1992). *Meeting at the crossroads: Women's psychology and girls' development*. Cambridge, MA: Harvard University Press.

Cambridge School Study (1991–1994)

Age: 13–16 years old
Sample Size: 26 girls
Race: 8 African American/Caribbean, 4 Latina, 8 Portuguese, 6 white (Irish/Italian American)
Class: poor/working class
Information Source: J. Taylor, C. Gilligan, and A. Sullivan. (1995). *Between voice and silence: Women and girls, race and relationship*. Cambridge, MA: Harvard University Press.

Strengthening Healthy Resistance Project (1990–1992)

Age: 9–12
Sample Size: 18 girls
Race: 13 white, 5 of color (Latina/white, Caribbean American, African American, Chinese American, Southeast Asian)
Class: middle and working class

LYN M. BROWN'S STUDIES, ADDITIONAL INTERVIEWS, AND FOCUS GROUPS

Rural Maine K–8 School Study (1995)

Age: 5–14 years old
Sample Size: 45 girls
Race: white
Class: working/lower-middle class

Rural School Study (1995)

Age: 6–7 years old
Sample Size: 6 girls
Race: white
Class: 5 poor/working class, 1 middle class

Working-/Middle-Class Girls from Maine Study (1995–1997)

Age: 11–14 years old
Sample Size: 19 girls
Race: white
Class: 13 poor/working class, 6 middle/upper class
Information Source: L. Brown (1998). *Raising their voices: The politics of girls' anger.* Cambridge, MA: Harvard University Press.

Montessori School Study (2000)

Age: 8–9 years old
Sample Size: 5 girls
Race: 4 white, 1 African American/white
Class: middle/upper class

NYC Girls Study (2000)

Age: 15–16 years old
Sample Size: 4
Race: white
Class: middle/upper-middle class

Cleveland Study (2000)

Age: 14–16 years old
Sample size: 8
Race: African American
Class: working class/poor

Brooklyn School Study (2000)

Age: 12–14 years
Sample Size: 15
Race: white
Class: middle class

Total: 421

Notes

NOTES TO THE INTRODUCTION

1. Talbot, February 24, 2002.
2. Talbot, February 24, p. 26.
3. Maguire, 1995.
4. Lamott, 1994, p. 104.
5. Tavris, July 5, 2002, p. B9.
6. Bettis and Adams, in press.
7. Young, 1980, p. 138.
8. The Emma Willard Project, the Laurel Project, Boys and Girls Club, Urban Neighborhoods, Cambridge School, and the Strengthening Healthy Resistance Project.
9. Individual and group interviews with elementary and junior high girls in central Maine; group interviews with junior high girls from a suburban school in Brooklyn, New York, and high school girls from a comprehensive school in Cleveland, as well as individual interviews with a small number of high school–age girls from New York City. Please see the appendix for more complete information about all these projects.
10. Descriptions of this "voice-centered" method can be found in Brown and Gilligan, 1992; Brown, 1998; Gilligan et al., 2003. Given the large percentage of white girls in many of the studies, I oversampled for girls of color in my analysis.
11. Chesler, 2002.
12. Rich, 1979, p. 187.

NOTES TO CHAPTER I

1. See Kimmel, 2002.
2. Wong and Csikszentmihalyi, 1991.
3. Belle, 1989.
4. Clark and Bittle, 1992.
5. Berndt, 1982; Caldwell and Peplau, 1982; Camarena, Sarigiani, and

Peterson, 1990; Furman and Buhrmester, 1985; Parker and Asher, 1993; Savin-Williams and Berndt, 1990.

6. Brown and Gilligan, 1992.

7. Pipher, 1995.

8. Carlip, 1995; Edut, 1998; Findler, 2001; Shandler, 1999.

9. See, for example, Adams, 1999; Bettis and Adams, 2004; Brown, 1998; Carroll, 1997; Fine and Macpherson, 1992; Hey, 1997; Inness, 1998; Lamb, 2002; McRobbie, 1991; Walkerdine, 1997.

10. Muscio, 1998; Nichter, 2000; Tanenbaum, 2000; Wolf, 1997; Wurtzel, 1998.

11. Inness, 1999.

12. *Utne Reader*, 1994.

13. Avenoso, 1997.

14. Brotman, 1999.

15. White, 2000.

16. Dolan, 2001.

17. Benjamin, 1997, p. 13.

18. Moretti, Holland, and McKay, 2001, report:

Although boys continue to outnumber girls as perpetrators of seriously violent crimes including homicide, recent statistics point to disproportionate increases in other violent crimes by girls. . . . The most notable increase for girls was between 1995 and 1998 when violent crime jumped 10%. In the U.S., arrest rates for violent crimes in girls under 18 . . . increased by 125% between 1985 and 1994 compared to an increase 67% for boys. (P. 2)

Since 1987, according to the FBI, "violent crimes by girls under eighteen climbed 118 percent," more than twice the increase for boys during that time (Ford, 1998, p. 13). Chesney-Lind and Belknap (2002) report that "arrests of girls for serious violent offenses increased by 27.9% between 1991 and 2000; arrests for girls for 'other assaults' increased by even more: 77.9%." They caution against any simplistic reading of these data, however, explaining that dramatic increases for "other assaults" reflect changes in police practices and the relabeling of noncriminal offenses like "runaway" or "family offenses" into violent offenses. In spite of these increases, it's important to remember that boys are still 80 percent of those arrested for serious crimes of violence in the United States (Chesney-Lind, 2002).

19. Books like Wiseman's *Queen Bees and Wannabes* (2002) and Simmons's *Odd Girl Out* (2002) both rely primarily on girls' experiences with relational aggression.

20. Rys and Bear, 1997, p. 89; see also Grotpeter and Crick, 1996; Crick, 1995, 1996.

21. Wiseman, 2002.

22. Talbot, 2002; Meadows, 2002. Nearly all the girls reviewed in these articles are middle class and white. Indeed the only diversity apparent among the girl-types *Newsweek* profiled—alpha, beta, and gamma—was hair color. All the girls were heterosexual, white, and aspired to top-tiered colleges.

23. de Beauvoir, 1952, p. 330.

24. de Beauvoir, 1952, p. 331; thanks to Natalie Adams for referring me to this passage.

25. See Thorne, 1993.

26. Children Now, 2001, pp. 9, 17.

27. *Elliot Moose, Timothy Goes to School, George Shrinks, Corduroy,* and *Marvin the Tap-Dancing Horse.*

28. Although *Dora* is one of few shows that will risk a girl's name in the title, even if, as in *Corduroy* or *Clifford,* a girl is a central character.

29. And boys will not read about girls or books written by girls, as the author of the popular Harry Potter book series, J. K. Rowling, clearly understood.

30. Fisher and Silber, 1998, p. 80.

31. Fisher and Silber, 1998, p. 78.

32. Fisher and Silber, 1998, p. 81.

33. For a closer examination of gender, race, and class in Disney films, I highly recommend the educational documentary, *Mickey Mouse Monopoly: Disney, Childhood, and Corporate Power* by Chyng Sun and Miguel Picker, distributed by Media Education Foundation.

34. Disney didn't help matters much in their remake of *Cinderella.* Casting a diverse group of actors, such as Brandy, Whoopie Goldberg, and Whitney Huston, looked promising. However, the story remained essentially the same, only now the white middle-class ideal is played out with an African American Cinderella and a white evil stepmother.

35. See Tolman et al., 2003; Tolman, 2002.

36. Schoefer, 2000.

37. *Dateline,* NBC, November 2001.

38. Pollitt, 1994, p. 155.

39. Siciliano, 2000.

40. Vivelo, 1992.

41. Children Now, 2001, p. 18.

42. Katherine F. Heintz-Knowles, researcher for Children Now's *Fall Colors* report.

43. Manzano, 2000, p. 10.

44. Ruby, 2000, p. 11.

45. Newsmakers, *Newsweek,* September 23, 2002, p. 79.

46. Inness, 1999, p. 5.

47. Phillips, 2000, pp. 39–40.

48. Debold, Wilson, and Malavé, 1993, p. 57.
49. Jack, 1991, p. 104.
50. Brown, 1998, pp. 112–113.
51. Debold, Wilson, and Malavé, 1993, p. 59.
52. Tanenbaum, 2000, p. 192.
53. I take the term "horizontal violence" from Freire (1970/1993).

NOTES TO CHAPTER 2

1. Sheldon, 1992.
2. McLaughlin, 2000.
3. Walstrom, 2002.
4. See Brown and Gilligan, 1992.
5. Thorne, 1993.
6. "Boy code" is a term William Pollack uses in his book *Real Boys* (1998) to describe all the hidden messages and expectations about masculinity that boys in this country feel pressed to comply with.
7. Gurian, 2002.
8. Annie Rogers, 1993, uses this phrase to describe young girls' "ordinary courage."
9. Voice training was introduced as a process in Brown and Gilligan, 1992.
10. Sheldon, 1997, pp. 234–237.
11. Maltz and Borker, 1982.
12. Lamb, 2002.
13. Sheldon, 1992, pp.7–8.
14. Crick, Casas, and Ku, 1999, p. 376.
15. Parker and Gottman, 1989, p. 111.
16. Crick, Casas, and Ku, 1999, p. 383.
17. Sheldon, 1996, pp. 59–60.
18. Brown and Gilligan, 1992.
19. Brown and Gilligan, 1992.
20. Deborah Tolman, 2002, talks about such cover stories, particularly with respect to muting girls' expressions of desire and sexuality.
21. Sheldon, 1996, p. 59; Ely, Gleason, and McCabe, 1996.
22. Brown and Gilligan, 1992.
23. Brown, 1998.

NOTES TO CHAPTER 3

1. Sullivan, 1953.
2. Apter and Josselson, 1998, p. 20.

3. Apter and Josselson, 1998, p. 23.
4. Ward, 2000, p. 107.
5. Bordo, 1993, p. 264.
6. Jack, 1999, p. 192.
7. I've taken this subtitle from Dana Jack's 1999 book, *Behind the Mask.*
8. Apter and Josselson, 1998, p. 22.
9. Ward, 2000.
10. Goodwin, 1985.
11. Hughes, 1988, p. 679.
12. Hughes, 1993, p. 138.
13. Goodwin, 1985, p. 328.
14. Goodwin, 1995, p. 265.
15. Brown and Gilligan, 1992.
16. Jack, 1999, pp. 213–216.
17. *New Moon Magazine*, on-line voice mail, www.newmoon.org.
18. Freire, 1970/1993, p. 117; Tappan, 2002.
19. Thorne, 1993, p. 95; see also Eder, 1985; Goodwin, 1985.
20. *New Moon Magazine*, on-line voice mail, www.newmoon.org.

NOTES TO CHAPTER 4

1. Lynch, 1991.
2. Galambos et al., 1985.
3. Hey, 1997, p. 75.
4. Hey, 1997, also makes this point.
5. Larson and Richards, 1989.
6. Cash, 1995; Fabian and Thompson, 1989.
7. Newman and Newman, 1997.
8. Erikson, 1950.
9. Gilligan, 1990, 1991.
10. Gilligan, 1997, p. 111.
11. Magner, 2002.
12. Lamb, 2002.
13. Brown, 1998.
14. Hey, 1997, p. 50.
15. Hey, 1997, p. 51.
16. Hey, 1997, p. 59.
17. Hey, 1997, p. 123.
18. Hey, 1997, p. 128.
19. Eder, 1985; Evans and Eder, 1993.
20. Merten, 1997.

21. Thorne, 1993, p. 97.
22. Fox, 1999.
23. Tanenbaum, 2000, p. 160.
24. Tanenbaum, 2000, p. xv.
25. Tanenbaum, 2000, p. 11.
26. Fine, 1988; Tolman, 2002.
27. Tanenbaum, 2000, p. 25.
28. Hey, 1997, p. 63.
29. Nichter, 2000, p. 4.
30. Nichter, 2000, p. 36.
31. Berg, 1992.
32. Eisele, Hertsgaard, and Light, 1986.
33. Young, Sipin, and Row, 1968.
34. Nichter, 2000, p. 16.
35. Nichter, 2000, p. 19.
36. Nichter, 2000, p. 20.
37. Parker et al., 1995; Okazawa-Rey, Robinson, and Ward, 1987.
38. Nichter, 2000, p. 21.
39. Brown and Gilligan, 1992, p. 230.
40. Misty is the name of a horse in a book series popular with girls this age.
41. Cash, 1995.
42. Fabian and Thompson, 1989.
43. Ward, 2000, p. 108.
44. Bordo, 1993, pp. 263–264.
45. Ward, 2000, p. 109.
46. Nichter, 2000, p. 47.
47. Nichter, 2000, p. 47.
48. Hey, 1997, p. 65.
49. Toth, 1981.
50. Thorne, 1993, p. 94.
51. Thorne, 1993, p. 94.
52. Note, of course, that it isn't so great from the boys' point of view. Boys use relational aggression at this age, as well as more physical forms of aggression. But this is how the culture relays girls' relationships and how girls justify their shift in allegiance.
53. Simmons and Blyth, 1987; Wylie, 1979.
54. Lamke, 1982; Mullis and McKinley, 1989; Rose and Montemayer, 1994.
55. Gilligan, 1990, 1991.
56. hooks, 1990.

NOTES TO CHAPTER 5

1. Tolman et al., 2003.
2. Thompson, 1994, p. 245.
3. Brown, 1998.
4. According to the U.S. Department of Justice (1998), young women between the ages of sixteen and twenty-four experience the highest rates of violence by current or former intimate partners. Victimization rates are similar between racial groups, except that black women between twenty and twenty-four years old tend to experience more attacks than white women. A Children Now/Kaiser Permanente poll, December 1995, finds that 40 percent of teenage girls between the ages of fourteen and seventeen report knowing someone their age who has been hit or beaten by a boyfriend.
5. Diamond, Savin-Williams, and Dube, 1999, p. 195.
6. Evans and Eder, 1993.
7. Hey, 1997, p. 114.
8. Diamond, 2000.
9. Weis and Carbonell-Medina, 2000, p. 639.
10. Hey, 1997, p. 128.
11. Hey, 1997, p. 129.
12. See Freire, 1970/1993, as well as Memmi, 1967, and Fanon, 1967, for more detailed elaboration of the mechanisms of internalized oppression and horizontal violence.
13. See Way, 1996.
14. See Thoma, 2000.
15. See Debold, Wilson, and Malavé, 1993.
16. Jackson Katz coined this phrase to explain the tough guy performance (guise) that serves to mask and thus protect from ridicule the emotional vulnerability many boys and men in this culture experience. For those interested in this issue, I highly recommend his video, *Tough Guise: Violence, Media, and the Crisis in Masculinity*, available from the Educational Media Corporation.
17. Hey, 1997, p. 128.
18. Hey, 1997, p. 128.
19. Fine and Macpherson, 1992, p. 176.
20. Fine and Macpherson, 1992, p. 200.

NOTES TO CHAPTER 6

1. Phillips, 2000.
2. Adams, 2001, p. 4.
3. Atwood, 1988, p. 434.

4. Lamb, 2002, p. 143; See also Jack, 1999, for an elaboration of the creative potential of aggression.

5. Lamb, 2002, pp. 142–143.

6. Lamb, 2002, p. 186.

7. Fordham, 1993.

8. Brown, 1998.

9. Diamond, 2000.

10. Arendt, 1963; quoted in Assy, 1998, p. 2.

11. See hooks, 1990.

12. In her book, *Women and Teaching* (1988), Maria Harris talks about such memories as dangerous because they make demands on us; they call us to action against oppression and victimization (p. 35). Harris quotes politician theologian John Baptist Metz, who says such memories "illuminate for a few moments and with a harsh steady light the questionable nature of things we have apparently come to terms with, and show up the banality of our supposed realism."

13. Muscio, 1998, pp. 136–139.

14. Greene, 1988, p. xi.

15. Greene, 1988, p. xi; quoted in Belenky, Bond, and Weinstock, 1997.

16. Gilligan, 1998, pp. ix–x.

17. Rich, 1979.

18. Tappan, 2002.

19. Freire, 1970/1993; also, Robinson and Ward, 1991; Ward, 2000.

20. Fraser, 1993; quoted in Weis and Carbonell-Medina, 2000, p. 627.

21. Beleky, Bond, and Weinstock, 1997, p. 128.

22. Fraser, 1993.

23. Mydans, 2001.

24. Griffin, 1981, p. 207.

25. See Butler, 1991.

26. Arendt, 1971.

27. Arendt, 1963.

28. Davidson, 1997, p. 18.

29. Reagon, 1983.

30. See Brown and Grande, in press, for a full description of this project.

31. Maxine Greene's phrase, 1988.

32. "Internalized domination is the incorporation and acceptance by individuals within a dominant group of prejudices against others," Gail Pheterson explains. "Internalized domination is likely to consist of feelings of superiority, normalcy, and self righteousness, together with guilt, fear, projection, denial of reality, and alienation from one's body and from nature. Internalized domination perpetuates oppression of others and alienation from oneself by either denying or degrading all but a narrow range of human possibilities" (1990, p. 35).

Mark Tappan (2002) argues that internalized domination must *also* be understood as a form of mediated action. As such, it results from the full appropriation (including both "mastery" and "ownership") of cultural tools and resources that transmit dominating/privileged messages and scripts.

33. For example, Anzaldúa, 1987; Collins, 1986; hooks, 1984; Lorde, 1984; Pheterson, 1990.

34. Weis and Carbonell-Medina, 2000, p. 629.

35. Weis and Carbonell-Medina, 2000, p. 637.

36. Thompson, 1994, p. 228.

NOTES TO CHAPTER 7

1. Olweus, 1993.

2. Olweus, 1993, p. 128.

3. See Crawford, October 2002; also, Swearer and Doll, 2001.

4. And boy bullying behavior, for that matter. Recent studies done in the United States reveal that in general bullying behavior occurs most frequently from sixth to eighth grades. See Nansel et al., 2001.

5. *Waterville Morning Sentinel*, December 13, 2001, Opinion page, B5.

6. Chesler, 2002, p. 474.

7. Chödrön, 1997, p. 141.

8. Weis and Carbonell-Medina, 2000, p. 638.

9. Weis and Carbonell-Medina, 2000, p. 641.

10. "The world according to him" is a phrase Sandra Bartky uses to refer to "the ensemble of meanings that reflect a man's more privileged location in the social totality" (1990, p. 112). The "epistemic risk" that women take in being the primary caregivers in heterosexual relationships is an empathic entering of his world and giving over of the world according to her.

11. Jewett, in press.

12. Harris, 1988.

13. Pheterson, 1990, p. 35.

14. See Kelly, 2002.

15. See, for example, Gilligan, 1997; Kimmel, 1996; Pollack, 1998; Stoltenberg, 1993.

16. See Brown and Gilligan, 1992, especially chapter 4, "Approaching the Wall."

17. Delpit, 1995.

18. See Delpit, 1995; McLaren, 1989.

19. Fordham, 1993.

20. Brown, 1998.

21. Brown and Gilligan, 1992; Steiner-Adair, 1986; Tolman, 2002; Tolman and Higgins, 1996; Tolman and Porche, 2000.

22. Eckert, 1989.

23. Eder, 1985; Evans and Eder, 1993; Merten, 1997.

24. Okamoto and Chesney-Lind, 2002.

25. "Girlhoods Interrupted," *Time*, March 19, 2001.

26. Eder, 1985; Evans and Eder, 1993.

27. Freitas and Chesney-Lind, 2001.

28. See, e.g., Gilligan, 1991; Lyman, 1981.

29. Lamb, 2002, p. 303.

30. Zoeysroom.com.

31. Debold et al., 1999. See hardygirlshealthywomen.org for more information.

32. For people who want to engage girls in thinking about and initiating social change, the Ms. Foundation Collaborative Fund for Healthy Girls Healthy Women's publication *The New Girls' Movement: New Assessment Tools for Youth Programs* is essential.

33. Weis and Carbonell-Medina, 2000, p. 627.

34. Bartky, 1990, p. 40.

35. Dadsanddaughters.org.

36. Young, 1979; quoted in Bartky, 1990, p. 35.

37. hooks, 1989.

38. Ward, 2000.

39. Gilligan, 1990, p. 503.

40. Gilligan, 1998, p. x.

41. Chesler, 2002, p. 462.

42. Westkott, 1986, p. 200.

43. Horney, 1952, p. 68; quoted in Westkott, 1986, p. 200.

44. Adams, 1999.

45. Ward, 1996, 2000.

References

Adams, N. (1999). Fighting to be somebody: Resisting erasure and the discursive practices of female adolescent fighting. *Educational Studies*, 30 (2): 115–139.

———. (2001). Girl power: The discursive practices of female fighters and female cheerleaders. Paper presented at the American Educational Research Association annual conference. Seattle, Washington.

Anzaldúa, G. (1987). *Borderlands / La frontera*. San Francisco: Aunt Lute Books.

Apter, T., and R. Josselson. (1998). *Best friends: The pleasures and perils of girls' and women's friendships*. New York: Crown.

Arendt, H. (September 19, 1963). Correspondence between Grafton and Arendt. Hannah Arendt's papers, Manuscript division, Library of Congress.

———. (1971). Thinking and moral considerations: A lecture. *Social Research*, 38 (3): 417–446.

Assy, B. (August 1998). Eichmann, the banality of evil, and thinking in Arendt's thought. Paper presented at the Twentieth World Conference of Philosophy, Boston, MA.

Atwood, M. (1988). *Cat's eye*. New York: Doubleday.

Avenoso, K. (January 19, 1997). Schools see rise in girls' fighting. *Boston Globe*.

Bartky, S. L. (1990). *Femininity and domination*. New York: Routledge.

Belenky, M., L. Bond, and J. Weinstock. (1997). *A tradition that has no name: Nurturing the development of people, families, and communities*. New York: Basic Books.

Belle, D. (ed.). (1989). *Children's social networks and social supports*. New York: Wiley.

Benjamin, B. (September–October 1997). In seventh grade, all girls are mean to other girls. *New Moon Network*, 13.

Berg, F. (July–August 1992). Harmful weight loss practices are widespread among adolescents. *Obesity and Health*, 69–72.

Berndt, T. (1982). The features and effects of friendship in early adolescence. *Child Development*, 53: 1447–1460.

Bettis, P., and N. Adams. (eds.). (in press). *Geographies of girlhood: Identities in-between*. New York: Lawrence Elbaum.

Bordo, S. (1993). *Unbearable weight: Feminism, western culture and the body.* Berkeley: University of California Press.

Brotman, C. (June 16, 1999). Mean streak: The reasons may vary, but many agree: Girls have a knack for cruelty. *Chicago Tribune.*

Brown, L. M. (1998). *Raising their voices: The politics of girls' anger.* Cambridge, MA: Harvard University Press.

Brown, L. M., and C. Gilligan. (1991). Listening for voice in narratives of relationship. In M. Tappan and M. Packer (eds.), *Narrative and storytelling: Implications for understanding moral development* (New Directions for Child Development, No. 54). San Francisco: Jossey-Bass.

———. (1992). *Meeting at the crossroads: Women's psychology and girls' development.* Cambridge, MA: Harvard University Press.

Brown, L. M., and S. M. Grande. (In press). Border crossing—border patrolling: Race, gender, and the politics of sisterhood. In P. Bettis and N. Adams (eds.), *Geographies of girlhood: Identities in-between.* New York: Lawrence Elbaum.

Butler, J. (1991). Imitation and gender insubordination. In D. Fuss (ed.), *Inside/Out: Lesbian theories, gay theories.* New York: Routledge.

Caldwell, M., and L. A. Peplau. (1982). Sex differences in same-sex friendships. *Sex Roles,* 8: 19–32.

Camarena, P., P. Sarigiani, and A. Peterson. (1990). Gender-specific pathways to intimacy in early adolescence. *Journal of Youth and Adolescence,* 19 (1): 19–32.

Carlip, H. (1995). *Girl power: Young women speak out.* New York: Warner.

Carroll, R. (ed.) (1997). *Sugar in the raw: Voices of young black girls in America.* New York: Crown.

Cash, T. F. (1995). Developmental teasing about physical appearance: Retrospective description and relationships with body image. *Social, Behavior, and Personality,* 23: 123–130.

Chesler, P. (2002). *Woman's inhumanity to woman.* New York: Nation Books.

Chesney-Lind, M. (November 2002). The meaning of mean. *Women's Review of Books,* XX, 2: 20–22.

Chesney-Lind, M., and J. Belknap (May 17, 2002). Gender, delinquency, and juvenile justice: What about girls? Paper presented at Aggression, Antisocial Behavior and Violence among Girls: A Developmental Perspective: A Conference. Duke University, North Carolina.

Children Now. (2001). Fall colors: 2000–2001 prime time diversity report. Children Now.

Chödrön, P. (1997). *When things fall apart.* Boston, MA: Shambhala.

Clark, M. L., and M. Bittle. (1992). Friendship expectations and the evaluation of present friendships in middle childhood and early adolescence. *Child Study Journal,* 22 (2): 115–135.

Collins, P. H. (1986). Learning from the outsider within. *Social Problems,* 33: 14–32.

Crawford, N. (October 2002). New ways to stop bullying. *American Psychological Association Monitor,* 33 (9): 64–65.

Crick, N. R. (1995). Relational aggression: The role of intent attributions, feelings of distress, and provocation type. *Development and Psychopathology,* 7: 313–322.

———. (1996). The role of overt aggression, relational aggression, and pro-social behavior in the prediction of children's future social adjustment. *Child Development,* 67: 2317–2327.

Crick, N. R., J. Casas, and H. Ku. (1999). Relational and physical forms of peer victimization in preschool. *Developmental Psychology,* 35 (2): 376–385.

Davidson, A. L. (1997). Marbella Sanchez: On marginalization and silencing. In M. Seller and L. Weis (eds.), *Beyond black and white.* New York: SUNY Press.

de Beauvoir, S. (1952). *The second sex.* New York: Vintage.

Debold, E., L. Brown, S. Weseen, and G. K. Brookins. (1999). Cultivating hardiness zones for adolescent girls: A reconceptualization of resilience in relationships with caring adults. In N. Jonhson, M. Roberts, and J. Worell (eds.), *Beyond appearance: A new look at adolescent girls.* Washington, D.C.: American Psychological Association.

Debold, E., M. Wilson, and I. Malavé. (1993). *Mother-daughter revolution: From betrayal to power.* New York: Addison-Wesley.

Delpit, L. (1995). *Other people's children: Cultural conflict in the classroom.* New York: New Press.

Diamond, L. (2000). Passionate friendships among adolescent sexual minority women. *Journal of Research on Adolescence,* 10 (2): 191–210.

Diamond, L. M., R. C. Savin-Williams, and E. M. Dube. (1999). Sex, dating, passionate frienships, and romance: Intimate peer relations among lesbian, gay, and bisexual adolescents. In W. Furman, C. Feiring, and B. B. Brown (eds.), *Contemporary perspectives on adolescent romantic relationships.* New York: Cambridge University Press.

Dolan, D. (April 8, 2001). How to be popular. *New York Times Magazine:* 44.

Eckert, P. (1989). *Jocks and burnouts: Social identity in the high school.* New York: Teachers College Press.

Eder, D. (1985). The cycle of popularity: Interpersonal relations among female adolescents. *Sociology of Education,* 58: 154–165.

Edut, O. (ed.). (1998). *Adios Barbie: Young women write about body image and identity.* Seattle, WA: Seal Press.

Eisele, L., D. Hertsgaard, and H. Light. (1986). Factors related to eating disorders in young adolescent girls. *Adolescence,* 21: 283–290.

Ely, R., J. B. Gleason, and A. McCabe. (1996). "Why didn't you talk to your mommy, honey?" Parents and children's talk about talk. *Research on Language and Social Interaction,* 29 (1): 7–25.

Erikson, E. (1950). *Childhood and Society.* New York: W. W. Norton.

Evans, C., and D. Eder. (1993). "No exit": Processes of social isolation in the middle school. *Journal of Contemporary Ethnography*, 22: 139–170.

Fabian, L. J., and J. K. Thompson. (1989). Body image and eating disturbance in young females. *International Journal of Eating Disorders*, 8: 63–74.

Fanon, F. (1967). *Black skin, white masks*. New York: Grove Press.

Findler, B. (ed.). (2001). *Listen up! Voices from the next feminist generation*. Seattle, WA: Seal Press.

Fine, M. (1988). Sexuality, schooling, and adolescent females: The missing discourse of desire. *Harvard Educational Review*, 58: 29–53.

Fine, M., and P. Macpherson. (1992). Over dinner: Feminism and adolescent female bodies. In M. Fine (ed.), *Disruptive voices*. Albany, NY: SUNY Press.

Fisher, J., and E. Silber (1998). Fairy tales, feminist theory, and the lives of women and girls. In J. Fisher and E. Silber (eds.), *Analyzing the different voice: Feminist psychological theory and literary texts*. New York: Rowman and Littlefield.

Ford, R. (May 24, 1998). Razor's edge. *Boston Globe Magazine*.

Fordham, S. (1993). "Those loud black girls": (Black) women, silences, and gender "passing" in the academy. *Anthropology and Education Quarterly*, 24: 3–32.

Fox, K. (1999). Girl-to-girl bullying in early adolescence: Beyond "bully," "victim," "by-stander." Unpublished masters thesis, University of British Columbia.

Fraser, N. (1993). Rethinking the public sphere. In B. Robbins, ed., *The phantom public sphere*. Minneapolis: University of Minnesota Press.

Freitas, K., and M. Chesney-Lind. (August–September 2001). Difference doesn't mean difficult: Workers talk about working with girls. *Women, Girls, and Criminal Justice*, 65–78.

Freire, P. (1970/1993). *Pedagogy of the oppressed*. New York: Continuum Publishing Company.

Furman, W., and D. Buhrmester. (1985). Children's perceptions of the personal relationships in their social networks. *Developmental Psychology*, 21 (6): 1016–1024.

Galamabos, N. L., A. C. Peterson, M. Richards, and I. B. Gitleson. (1985). The attitudes toward women scale for adolescents: A study of reliability and validity. *Sex Roles*, 12: 343–356.

Gilligan, C. (1990). Teaching Shakespeare's sister. In C. Gilligan, N. Lyons, and T. Hanmer (eds.), *Making connections: The relational worlds of adolescent girls at Emma Willard School*. Cambridge, MA: Harvard University Press.

———. (1991). Joining the resistance: Psychology, politics, girls and women. *Michigan Quarterly Review*, 29: 501–536.

———. (1998). Wild voices: Fiction, feminism, and the perennial flowering of truth. In J. Fisher and E. Silber (eds.), *Analyzing the different voice: Feminist psychological theory and literary texts.* New York: Rowman and Littlefield.

Gilligan, C., R. Spencer, M. K. Weinberg, and T. Bertsch. (2003). On the listening guide: A voice-centered relational method. In P. M. Camic, J. E. Rhodes, and L. Yardley (eds.), *Qualitative research in psychology: Expanding perspectives in methodology and design.* Washington, DC: American Psychological Association Press.

Gilligan, C., J. Ward, and J. Taylor (eds.). (1988). *Mapping the moral domain.* Cambridge, MA: Harvard University Press.

Gilligan, J. (1997). *Violence: Reflections on a national epidemic.* New York: Vintage.

Goodwin, M. H. (1985). The serious side of jump rope: Conversational practices and social organization in the frame of play. *Journal of American Folklore,* 98 (389): 316–330.

———. (1995). Co-construction in girls' hopscotch. *Research on Language and Social Interaction,* 28 (3): 261–281.

Greene, M. (1988). *The dialectic of freedom.* New York: Teachers College Press.

Griffin, S. (1981). *Pornography and silence.* New York: Harper and Row.

Grotpeter, J., and N. Crick. (1996). Relational aggression, overt aggression, and friendship. *Child Development,* 67: 2328–2338.

Gurian, M. (2002). *The wonder of girls: Understanding the hidden nature of our daughters.* New York: Pocket Books.

Harris, M. (1988). *Women and teaching.* New York: Paulist Press.

Hey, V. (1997). *The company she keeps: An ethnography of girls' friendship.* Philadelphia: Open University Press.

hooks, b. (1984). *From margin to center.* Boston: South End Press.

———. (1989). *Talking back: Thinking feminist, thinking black.* Boston, MA: South End Press.

———. (1990). Choosing the margin as a space of radical openness. In b. hooks, *Yearning: Race, gender, and cultural politics.* Boston, MA: South End Press.

Horney, K. (1952). Human nature can change: A symposium. *American Journal of Psychoanalysis,* 12: 67–68.

Hughes, L. A. (1988). "But that's not really mean": Competing in a cooperative mode. *Sex Roles,* 19 (11–12): 669–687.

———. (1993). "You have to do it with style": Girls' games and girls gaming. In S. T. Hollis, L. Pershing, and M. J. Young (eds.), *Feminist theory and the study of folklore.* Urbana, IL: University of Illinois Press.

Inness, S. (ed.). (1998). *Millenium girls: Today's girls around the world.* Lanham, MD: Rowman and Littlefield.

———. (1999). *Tough girls.* Philadelphia, PA: University of Pennsylvania Press.

Jack, D. (1991). *Silencing the self: Women and depression.* Cambridge, MA: Harvard University Press.

———. (1999). *Behind the mask: Destruction and creativity in women's aggression.* Cambridge, MA: Harvard University Press.

Jewett, L. (in press). Power beads, body glitter and backseat bad-asses: Girls' power and position on the school bus. In P. Bettis and N. Adams (eds.), *Geographies of girlhood: Identities in-between.* New York: Lawrence Elbaum.

Kelly, J. (2002). *Dads and daughters.* New York: Broadway Books.

Kimmel, M. (1996). *Manhood in America: A cultural history.* New York: Free Press.

———. (February 5, 2002). Adolescent masculinity, homophobia and violence: Some tentative hypotheses about school shootings. Paper presented at the Seminar on Gender and Education, Harvard Graduate School of Education.

Lamb, S. (2002). *The secret lives of girls: What girls really do—Sex aggression, and their guilt.* New York: Free Press.

Lamke, L. K. (1982). The impact of sex-role orientation on self-esteem in early adolescence. *Child Development,* 53: 1530–1535.

Lamott, A. (1994). *Bird by bird: Some instructions on writing and life.* New York: Anchor Books.

Larson, R., and M. H. Richards. (1989). Introduction: The changing life space of early adolescence. *Journal of Youth and Adolescence,* 18 (6): 501–509.

Lorde, A. (1984). *Sister outsider.* Freedom, CA: Crossing Press.

Lyman, P. (1981). The politics of anger. *Socialist Review,* 11: 55–74.

Lynch, M. E. (1991). Gender intensification. In R. M. Lerner, A. C. Peterson, and J. Brooks-Gunn (eds.), *Encyclopedia of adolescence* (vol. 1). New York: Garland.

McLaren, Peter. 1989. *Life in schools.* White Plains, NY: Longman.

McLaughlin, L. (September 11, 2000). Don't clean your plate. *Time.*

McRobbie, A. (1991). *Feminism and youth culture: From Jackie to just seventeen.* Boston: Unwin Hyman.

Magner, C. (October 9, 2002). When they were bad: My daughter is exiled and we suffer a season in hell. Salon.com.

Maguire, G. (1995). *Wicked: The life and times of the wicked witch of the west.* New York: HarperCollins.

Maltz, D., and R. Borker. (1982). A cultural approach to male-female miscommunication. In J. Gumperz (ed.), *Language and social identity.* Cambridge: Cambridge University Press.

Manzano, A. (2000). Charlie's angels: Free market feminism. *Off our backs,* xxx (11): 10.

Meadows, J. (June 3, 2002). Meet the gamma girls. *Newsweek:* 44–51.

Memmi, A. (1967). *The colonizer and the colonized.* New York: Orion Press.

Merten, D. (July 1997). The meaning of meanness: Popularity, competition, and conflict among junior high school girls. *Sociology of Education,* 70: 175–191.

Moretti, M., R. Holland, and S. McKay. (2001). Self-other representations and relational and overt aggression in adolescent girls and boys. *Behavioral Sciences and the Law,* 19: 2, 109–126.

Morgan, R. (ed.) (1970). *Sisterhood is powerful.* New York: Vintage.

Mullis, R. L., and K. McKinley. (1989). Gender-role orientation of adolescent females: Effects of self-esteem and locus of control. *Journal of Adolescent Research,* 4: 504–516.

Muscio, I. (1998). *Cunt: A declaration of independence.* New York: Seal Press.

Mydans, S. (July 22, 2001). Vengeance destroys faces, and souls, in Cambodia. *New York Times:* 3.

Nansel, T. R., M. Overpeck, R. S. Pilla, W. J. Ruan, B. Simons-Morton, and P. Scheidt. 2001. Bullying behaviors among U.S. youth: Prevalence and association with psychosocial adjustment. *Journal of the American Medical Association,* 285: 2094–2100.

Newman, P. R., and B. Newman. (1997). *Childhood and adolescence.* Pacific Grove, CA: Brooks/Cole.

Nichter, M. (2000). *Fat talk: What girls and parents say about dieting.* Cambridge, MA: Harvard University Press.

Okamoto, S., and M. Chesney-Lind. (2002). Girls and aggression: Beyond the "mean girl" hype. *Women, Girls and Criminal Justice,* 6 (6): 81–82, 90.

Okazawa-Rey, M., T. Robinson, and J. Ward. (1987). Black women and the politics of skin color and hair. In M. Braude (ed.), *Women, power and therapy: Issues for women.* New York: Haworth Press.

Olweus, D. (1993). *Bullying at school.* Cambridge, MA: Blackwell.

Orenstein, P. (1994). *Schoolgirls: Young women, self-esteem and the confidence gap.* New York: Doubleday.

Ozick, C. (1983). Notes toward finding the right question. In S. Heschel (ed.), *On being a Jewish feminist.* New York: Schocken Books.

Parker, J., and S. Asher. (1993). Friendship and friendship quality in middle school childhood: Links with peer group acceptance and feelings of loneliness and social dissatisfaction. *Developmental Psychology,* 35 (1): 69–79.

Parker, J., and J. Gottman. (1989). Social and emotional development in a relational context. In T. J. Berndt and G. W. Ladd (eds.), *Peer relationships in child development.* New York: Wiley.

Parker, S., M. Nichter, M. Nichter, N. Vuckovic, C. Simms, and C. Ritenbaugh. (1995). Body image and weight concerns among African American and white adolescent females: Differences that make a difference. *Human organization,* 54 (2): 103–114.

Pastor, J., J. McCormick, and M. Fine. (1996). Makin' homes: An urban girl thing. In B. Leadbeater and N. Way (eds.), *Urban girls: Resisting stereotypes, creating identities.* New York: NYU Press.

Pheterson, G. (1990). Alliances between women: Overcoming internalized oppression and internalized domination. In L. Albrecht and R. M. Brewer (eds.), *Bridges of power: Women's multicultural alliances*. Philadelphia, PA: New Society.

Phillips, L. (2000). *Flirting with danger: Young women's reflections on sexuality and domination*. New York: NYU Press.

Pipher, M. (1995). *Reviving Ophelia*. New York: Ballantine.

Pollack, W. (1998). *Real boys: Rescuing our sons from the myths of boyhood*. New York: Random House.

Pollitt, K. (1994). *Reasonable creatures*. New York: Knopf.

Reagon, B. J. (1983). Coalition politics: Turning the century. In B. Smith (ed.), *Home girls: A black feminist anthology*. New York: Kitchen Table, Women of Color Press.

Reisman, J. (1990). Intimacy in same-sex friendships. *Sex Roles,* 23: 65–82.

Rich, A. (1979). Women and honor: Some notes on lying. In A. Rich, *On lies, secrets, and silence*. New York: W. W. Norton.

Robinson, T., and J. Ward. (1991). "A belief far greater than anyone's disbelief": Cultivating resistance among African-American female adolescents. In C. Gilligan, A. Rogers, and D. Tolman (eds.), *Reframing resistance: Women, girls and psychotherapy*. New York: Haworth Press.

Rogers, A. (1993). Voice, play and the practice of ordinary courage in girls' and women's lives. *Harvard Educational Review,* 63 (3): 265–296.

Rose, A. J., and R. Montemayer. (1994). The relationships between gender role orientation and perceived self-competency in male and female adolescents. *Sex Roles,* 31: 579–595.

Ruby, J. (2000). Embracing hypocrisy: Why I liked Charlie's Angels. *Off Our Backs,* 11: 11, 19.

Rukeyser, M. (1976). *The collected poems of Muriel Rukeyser*. New York: McGraw Hill.

Rys, G., and G. C. Bear. (1997). Relational aggression and peer relations: Gender and developmental issues. *Merrill-Palmer Quarterly,* 431: 87–106.

Savin-Williams, R., and T. Berndt. (1990). Friendship and peer relations. In S. Feldman and G. Eliot (eds.), *At the threshold: The developing adolescent*. Cambridge, MA: Harvard University Press.

Schoefer, C. (March–April 2000). Harry Potter and the magical world of patriarchy. *New Moon Network*: 10–11.

Shandler, S. (1999). *Ophelia speaks*. New York: HarperPerennial.

Sheldon, A. (1992). Conflict talk: Sociolinguistic challenges to self-assertion and how young girls meet them. *Merrill-Palmer Quarterly,* 38: 7–8, 95–117.

———. (1996). You can be the baby brother, but you aren't born yet: Preschool girls' negotiation for power and access in pretend play. *Research on Language and Social Interaction,* 29 (1): 57–80.

————. (1997). Talking power: Girls, gender, enculturation and discourse. In R. Wodak (ed.), *Gender and discourse.* Sage: London.

Siciliano, J. (July–August 2000). Nancy Drew and the case of the disappearing feminist. *New Moon Network:* 10–11.

Simmons, R. (2002). *Odd girl out.* New York: Harcourt.

Simmons, R. G., and D. A. Blyth. (1987). *Moving into adolescence: The impact of pubertal change and school context.* New York: Aldine de Gruyter.

Steiner-Adair, C. (1986). The body politic: Normal female adolescent development and the development of eating disorders. *Journal of the American Academy of Psychoanalysis,* 15: 95–114.

Stoltenberg, J. (1993). *The end of manhood.* New York: Dutton.

Sullivan, H. S. (1953). *The interpersonal theory of psychiatry.* New York: W. W. Norton.

Swearer, S. M., and B. Doll. 2001. Bullying in schools: An ecological framework. *Journal of Emotional Abuse,* 2 (2–3): 7–23.

Talbot, M. (February 24, 2002). Mean girls and the new movement to tame them. *New York Times Magazine:* 24–29, 40, 58, 64–65.

Tanenbaum, L. (2000). *Slut! Growing up female with a bad reputation.* New York: Perennial.

Tappan, M. (unpublished manuscript, November 2002). "Internalized oppression" as mediated action: Implications for critical pedagogy.

Tavris, C. (July 5, 2002). Are girls really as mean as books say they are? *Chronicle Review:* B7, B9.

Taylor, J., C. Gilligan, and A. Sullivan. (1995). *Between voice and silence: Women and girls, race and relationship.* Cambridge, MA: Harvard University Press.

Thoma, P. (unpublished manuscript, 2000). The metaphors and meaning of gossip in public and academic discourse.

Thompson, S. (1994). What friends are for: On girls' misogyny and romantic fusion. In J. Irvine (ed.), *Sexual cultures and the constructions of adolescent identities.* Philadelphia, PA: Temple University Press.

Thorne, B. (1993). *Gender play: Girls and boys in school.* New Brunswick, NJ: Rutgers University Press.

Tolman, D. L. (2002). *Dilemmas of desire.* Cambridge, MA: Harvard University Press.

Tolman, D. L., and T. E. Higgins (1996). How being a good girl can be bad for girls. In N. B. Maglin and D. Perry (eds.), *Bad girls/Good girls: Women, sex, and power in the nineties.* New Brunswick, NJ: Rutgers University Press.

Tolman, D. L., and M. Porche. (2000). The adolescent feminine ideology scale: Development and validation of a new measure for girls. *Psychology of Women Quarterly,* 24 (4): 365–376.

Tolman, D. L., R. Spencer, M. Rosen-Reynoso, and M. Porche. (2003). Sowing the seeds of violence in heterosexual relationships: Early adolescents narrate compulsory heterosexuality. *Journal of Social Issues*, 59 (1): 159–178.

Toth, S. A. (1981). *Blooming: A small-town girlhood.* Boston: Little Brown.

U.S. Department of Justice. (1998). Violence by intimates, NCJ-167237, March 1998. Washington, DC: Bureau of Justice Statistics.

Utne Reader. (July–August 1994). No. 64.

Vivelo, J. (November–December 1992). The mystery of Nancy Drew. *Ms. Magazine*: 76–77.

Walkerdine, V. (1997). *Daddy's girl.* Cambridge, MA: Harvard University Press.

Walstrom, A. G. (November 17, 2002). Why girls read better than boys. *Metro Parent Magazine.*

Ward, J. (1996). Raising resisters: The role of truth-telling in the psychological development of African-American girls. In B. Leadbeater and N. Way (eds.), *Urban girls: Resisting stereotypes, creating identites.* New York: NYU Press.

———. (2000). *The skin we're in: Teaching our children to be emotionally strong, socially smart, spiritually connected.* New York: Free Press.

Way, N. (1995). "Can't you see the courage, the strength that I have?" Listening to urban adolescent girls speak about their relationships. *Psychology of Women Quarterly*, 19: 107–128.

———. (1996). Between experiences of betrayal and desire: Close friendships among urban adolescents. In B. Leadbeater and N. Way (eds.), *Urban girls: Resisting stereotypes, creating identities.* New York: NYU Press.

Weis, L., and D. Carbonell-Medina. (2000). Learning to speak out in an abstinence based sex education group: Gender and race work in an urban magnet school. *Teachers College Record*, 120 (3): 620–650.

Westkott, M. (1986). *The feminist legacy of Karen Horney.* New Haven: Yale University Press.

White, K. (April–May 2000). Ouch! That hurts. *Girls' Life*: 62–63, 68, 86.

Wiseman, R. (2002). *Queen bees and wannabes.* New York: Crown.

Wolf, N. (1997). *Promiscuities: The secret struggle for womanhood.* New York: Random House.

Wong, M., and M. Csikszentmihalyi. (1991). Affiliation motivation and daily experience: Some issues on gender differences. *Journal of Personality and Social Psychology*, 60: 154–164.

Wurtzel, E. (1998). *Bitch: In praise of difficult women.* New York: Doubleday.

Wylie, R. (1979). *The self-concept theory and research: Volume 2.* Lincoln, NE: University of Nebraska Press.

Young, C. M., S. S. Sipin, and D. A. Row. (1968). Density and skinfold measurements: Body composition of pre-adolescent girls. *Journal of American Dietetic Association*, 53: 25–31.

Young, I. M. (September 1979). Is there a woman's world? Some reflections on the struggle for our bodies. Lecture presented to The Second Sex—Thirty Years Later: A Commemorative Conference on Feminist Theory. New York Institute for the Humanities, New York University.

———. (1980). Throwing like a girl: A phenomenology of feminine body comportment motility and spatiality. *Human Studies,* 3: 137–156.

Index

About the Author

LYN MIKEL BROWN, ED.D., is Associate Professor of Education and Women's, Gender, and Sexuality Studies at Colby College in Waterville, Maine. She is the author of *Meeting at the Crossroads: Women's Psychology and Girls' Development* (with Carol Gilligan) and *Raising Their Voices: The Politics of Girls' Anger*. She is also the co-creator of the nonprofit Hardy Girls Healthy Women (www.hardygirlshealthywomen.org). She lives in Waterville, Maine, with her partner and daughter.